A Multidisciplinary Actology

ACTOLOGICAL EXPLORATIONS

A series of books that understand reality as action in changing patterns.

ALSO IN THIS SERIES

Actology: Action, change and diversity in the western philosophical tradition

Two streams run through western philosophy: one characterized by Being, beings, the unchanging, the static, and the unitary, and the other by Action, actions, the changing, the dynamic, and the diverse. This book explores the 'Action' stream as it has wound its way through the Western philosophical tradition, and enables us to see ourselves, the universe and God as action in changing patterns rather than as beings that change.

Mark's Gospel: An actological reading

The second book in the series reads Mark's Gospel in the light of an actological understanding of reality. So it understands God, Jesus, and ourselves, as action, change, and diversity. The result is a unique and somewhat unexpected reading of the text, and a distinctive theology to match.

Actological Readings in Continental Philosophy

The third book in the series continues the journey begun in the first. Understanding reality as action in changing patterns casts new light on the writings of a variety of Continental philosophers and raises and answers some significant new questions.

An Actology of the Given

The fourth book discusses anthropology, continental philosophy, biblical texts, social policy, and a variety of givens, to enable us to explore the concepts of the gift, givenness, giving, and so on, in the light of reality understood as action in changing patterns.

An Actological Metaphysic

The fifth book studies a wide variety of metaphysical concepts, such as causality, time, and space, in the light of reality understood as action in changing patterns

An Actological Theology

The sixth book asks what Christian theology might look like in an actological context.

A Multidisciplinary Actology

MALCOLM TORRY

RESOURCE *Publications* · Eugene, Oregon

A MULTIDISCIPLINARY ACTOLOGY

Actological Explorations

Copyright © 2025 Malcolm Torry. All rights reserved. Except for brief quotations in critical publications or reviews, no part of this book may be reproduced in any manner without prior written permission from the publisher. Write: Permissions, Wipf and Stock Publishers, 199 W. 8th Ave., Suite 3, Eugene, OR 97401.

Resource Publications
An Imprint of Wipf and Stock Publishers
199 W. 8th Ave., Suite 3
Eugene, OR 97401

www.wipfandstock.com

PAPERBACK ISBN: 979-8-3852-4992-3
HARDCOVER ISBN: 979-8-3852-4993-0
EBOOK ISBN: 979-8-3852-4994-7

All Scriptural quotations are taken from the New Revised Standard Version of the Bible (Anglicized Version), copyright 1989, 1995 by the Division of Christian Education of the National Council of the Churches of Christ in the United States of America. Used by permission. All rights reserved.

Contents

Preface and acknowledgments vii

Introduction xiii

1 Actological language 1
2 Actological humanities 13
3 Actological ethics 23
4 Actological mathematics 38
5 Actological natural sciences 55
6 Actological social sciences 78
7 Actological psychology 96
8 Actological politics 107
9 Actological organizational behavior 122
10 Conclusions 141

Epilogue 147

Bibliography 163

Index 185

Preface and acknowledgments

IN 1985 I PREPARED for a theological society convened by the Very Rev'd David Edwards, Provost of Southwark Cathedral, a short paper that suggested that because our society was increasingly characterized by change and diversity, and decreasingly by sameness and the unchanging, the Church's theology needed to be expressed in terms of change and diversity. Life was busy, and further exploration of the idea had to wait until a period of sabbatical leave in 1994. The outcome was an essay, on which both Professor Robin Gill and David Atkinson (then Canon Missioner in the Diocese of Southwark, and subsequently Archdeacon of Lewisham and Bishop of Thetford) offered valuable comment; and that essay subsequently became a series of articles that Bill Jacob, Archdeacon of Charing Cross and Editor of *Theology*, published in the journal. I am most grateful to all of those who contributed in various ways to the writing and publication of those articles.

The first article, "On Completing the Apologetic Spectrum,"[1] suggested that in a context in which the changing and the diverse are becoming more important categories than the unchanging and the unitary, the Church's apologetics, and therefore the metaphysic (in the sense of a "system of metaphysics"[2]) underlying its theology, needed to reflect that trend. The Western philosophical tradition has for two thousand years given priority to the unchanging, to the static, to rest (as opposed to movement), to the unitary, to being, and to Being—being itself—and Christian theology has largely followed suit. Now a different conceptual structure—or perhaps, better, an additional conceptual structure—might be required if we are to express the Christian Faith in today's world: a metaphysic, or foundational conceptual framework, that prioritizes change, the dynamic, movement, diversity, action, and Action: action itself.

1. Torry, "On Completing the Apologetic Spectrum."
2. Oxford English Dictionary.

A further article followed: "Action, Patterns and Religious Pluralism."[3] Just as a Being metaphysic has always needed some way to express the change that we experience, so an Action metaphysic needs to express the continuities that we experience. In this second article I suggested that "patterns of action" or "action in patterns" might be a useful way to do this.

I have always been most grateful to St. John's College, Cambridge, for the hospitality that it has extended to me over many years. Most years for the past forty years I have spent three nights at St. John's to enable me to immerse myself in the Cambridge libraries; and the college has also offered occasional longer periods of residence. On one of my annual visits the Dean of Chapel, the Rev'd Andrew Macintosh, asked whether I might like to visit a former Master of the College who had moved into a care home in South London near to where I was Vicar of St. Catherine's, Hatcham, at New Cross. At the age of ninety John Boys Smith still had a lively mind, and we held an interesting discussion about process theology. He died soon after. On my next visit to Cambridge I discovered that the only theological or philosophical publication listed in the University Library catalogue under his name was a booklet that he had written in 1930, *Christian Doctrine and the Idea of Evolution*.[4] The booklet's contents were in many ways ahead of their time. Further research revealed that Boys Smith's son, Stephen Boys Smith, still possessed a holdall containing many of his father's sermons: so I edited and published the sermons with an introduction, and had the 1930 booklet reprinted as an appendix.[5] The third *Theology* article was an abridged version of the introduction to the edited sermons.[6]

In 2004 Keith Trivasse employed what he called "Torry's model" in a somewhat too adulatory fashion to discuss the relationship between Muhammad and the Christian Faith.[7] This inspired further thought on my part, which led to my next article, "Testing Torry's Model,"[8] which distinguished my "action in patterns" conceptual framework from the conceptual framework underlying process theology, and also related my framework to recent scientific developments. A final article, "'Logic' and 'Action': two new readings of the New Testament,"[9] asked how the conceptual framework might work as a lens through which to interpret passages from the fourth gospel.

---

3. Torry, "Action, Patterns and Religious Pluralism."
4. Boys Smith, *Christian Doctrine and the Idea of Evolution*.
5. Boys Smith, *The Sermons of John Boys Smith*.
6. Torry, "A Neglected Theologian."
7. Trivasse, "May the Prophet Muhammad Be a Prophet to Christianity?"
8. Torry, "Testing Torry's Model."
9. Torry, "'Logic' and 'Action.'"

PREFACE AND ACKNOWLEDGMENTS

That last article was written in 2006 and published in 2008, and for nearly ten years after that I hardly thought about metaphysics. Being Team Rector of the Parish of East Greenwich, Co-ordinator of the Greenwich Peninsula Chaplaincy, Director of the Citizen's Income Trust, and a Visiting Senior Fellow at the London School of Economics, researching and writing on reform options for the benefits system and on the management of religious and faith-based organizations, was quite enough.

For over forty years I have been involved in the debate about Basic Income—an unconditional income for every individual—and in 2014 that debate began to demand rather a lot of my time. I was doing too much, so I retired early from the Church of England's full-time ministry in order to concentrate on the research, writing, and organizing that the Basic Income debate was demanding of me, and also to make time to revisit the subject-matter of the *Theology* articles. Those articles contained the sketchiest of surveys of the western philosophical tradition, so to explore that tradition in more depth seemed like the obvious place to start. I was therefore pleased to be accepted as a candidate for the Archbishop's Examination in Theology. I was initially intending to complete a PhD thesis, but the demands that the Basic Income debate were making on me made it necessary to rein in my ambition and to submit a thesis for the degree of Master of Philosophy. In relation to the thesis I am most grateful to Cambridge University Library, the library of St. John's College, Cambridge, the library of King's College, London, and Gladstone's Library, for hospitality, and to my two supervisors, Professors George Newlands and Simon Oliver.

I eventually found the time to expand the MPhil thesis into a book, *Actology: Action, Change and Diversity in the Western Philosophical Tradition*, that Wipf and Stock kindly published under their "Resource" imprint, and I remain grateful for the interest that Matt Wimer, George and Emily Callihan, Savanah Landerholm, and others at Wipf and Stock have shown in what has become the "Actological Explorations" series.

Following the publication of *Actology*, the pandemic provided some time that could only be used for reading and writing, so I took the opportunity to write *Mark's Gospel: An Actological Reading*: the gospel interpreted through an understanding of reality as action in changing patterns. This became the second book in the "Actological Explorations" series.

Undertaking the Lambeth research degree and writing *Actology* had revealed a significant knowledge gap, which I began to fill by undertaking a master's degree in continental philosophy at Staffordshire University. I subsequently expanded the module essays, dissertation, and my contributions to student-led study groups, into two books, *Actological Readings in Continental*

PREFACE AND ACKNOWLEDGMENTS

Philosophy and *An Actology of the Given*: the third and fourth members of the "Actological Explorations" series. I am most grateful to Professor David Webb and Drs Patrick O'Connor and Bill Ross for helping me to navigate what I experienced as the most significant intellectual challenge that I have ever faced, and am only sorry that Bill died suddenly and too young soon after I completed the degree so that I couldn't send him copies of the books that he had helped to make possible.

For forty years I had fitted whatever philosophical studies I could find time for around the full-time ministry of the Church of England and the research and organizational activity demanded by the Basic Income debate: but by 2022 there were increasing numbers of researchers and activists involved in what is now a global debate about the desirability and feasibility of giving everyone an unconditional income, so it was time for some of us who had been involved since the beginning of the modern Basic Income movement to step aside and allow a new generation the social space that it needed. I returned to voluntary part-time ministry in the Church of England as Priest in Charge of St Mary Abchurch in the City of London, and to some further work on actology: an understanding of reality as Action rather than Being, and as action in changing patterns rather than as beings that change. Three books—*Actology*; *Actological Readings in Continental Philosophy*; and *An Actology of the Given*—had all set out from the writings of a variety of philosophers, both to understand their philosophies on the basis that reality is action in changing patterns, and to enable what they had written to inform the construction of an actology. It was time to take a different approach, so *An Actological Metaphysic* employed both philosophical and scientific texts to study a wide variety of metaphysical and cosmological concepts in the light of reality understood as action in changing patterns in order to construct something like a systematic actology—the "something like" here being a recognition that the change and diversity inherent to any actology means that any particular actology that we might create will be of partial, brief, and local relevance, so that the next moment a new actology will be required. The following book, *An Actological Theology*, employed a similar method to *An Actological Metaphysic*: that is, it understands a variety of theological writings and themes on the basis that reality is action, the dynamic, movement, change, and diversity.

This new book, *A Multidisciplinary Actology*, is designed to fill some gaps. There is plenty of material on philosophy, metaphysics, and theology, in the first six books of the "Actological Explorations" series, and there is occasional mention of what other disciplines might look like in an actological context, but there are no sustained actological treatments of language, the humanities, ethics, mathematics, the natural sciences, the social sciences, psychology, politics, or organizational behavior. This new book is designed to fill those gaps.

As well as those individuals mentioned above, numerous individuals have contributed to the development of the ideas to be found in the "Actological Explorations" series by their willingness to discuss them with me. There are too many to mention, and I cannot remember all of them: but particularly significant contributions have been made at various stages by John Byrom, Stephen Sykes, James Bogle, Renford Bambrough, Jed Davis, chaplains of the South London Industrial Mission, members of the congregations of St. Catherine's, Hatcham, St. George's, Westcombe Park, and Holy Trinity, Greenwich Peninsula, participants in seminars held in relation to the Archbishop's Examination in Theology, and staff and students of Staffordshire University's continental philosophy department. I am more than grateful to those who made possible several periods of study leave of varying lengths: staff members and officers of the parishes that I have served for their willingness to shoulder additional burdens; Bishops of Woolwich for permissions to take sabbaticals; St. John's College for appointing me a Fellow Commoner for a term; and particularly my wife Rebecca and children Christopher, Nicholas, and Jay for their unfailing support.

I am still most grateful to all of the people mentioned above for their encouragement and help along the way.[10]

In relation to this book I am grateful to Edward Elgar Publishing, who have kindly published four of my books on the Basic Income debate, for permission to reuse references previously employed in *A Modern Guide to Citizen's Basic Income: A multidisciplinary approach*, and to include in this new book a certain amount of content similar to that in *A Modern Guide to Citizen's Basic Income*. References are given in the footnotes.

---

10. Torry, *An Actological Theology*, vii–xi.

Introduction to *A Multidisciplinary Actology*

IN THIS INTRODUCTION TO *A Multidisciplinary Actology* I shall define "actology," chart the actological journey so far, define "multidisciplinary," and outline the structure of the book.

"ACTOLOGY"

An actology understands reality as action in changing patterns, as opposed to an ontology that understands reality as beings that change. For an actology, the fundamental category is Action, the source of all action and all actions, whereas for an ontology it is Being, the source of all being and all beings. An actology understands the cosmos and everything else in terms of action, change, movement, and diversity, whereas an ontology understands the cosmos and everything else in terms of being, the unchanging, rest, and the unitary. For an actology, everything is dynamic, and any stabilities and likenesses are a secondary matter, whereas for an ontology reality is essentially static, and change and diversity are secondary factors.

THE ACTOLOGICAL JOURNEY SO FAR

This volume forms the seventh part of the "Actological Explorations" series.

The first book in the series, *Actology: Action, Change and Diversity in the Western Philosophical Tradition*, published in 2020—not actually labelled "Actological Explorations" because there was no series when it was published—sought the thin stream of diversity, Action, action, change, and the dynamic, as it coursed its way through the history of Western philosophy—frequently submerged by the alternative stream about the unitary, Being, beings, the unchanging, and the static—and then asked what the action-based stream might offer to the creation of an actology: an understanding of reality as action in changing patterns rather than as beings that change.

The second book in what was by then a "series" was a somewhat different project, made possible by the acres of time set free for writing by Covid-19: *Mark's Gospel: An Actological Reading*, published in 2022. This was what it said it was: a way of reading Mark's Gospel with reality understood as action in changing patterns rather than as beings that change. Then followed two volumes that trace the "Action" stream through continental philosophy: *Actological Readings in Continental Philosophy* and *An Actology of the Given*, both published in 2023—the former a reading of a variety of philosophers through the lens of reality understood as action in changing patterns, and the latter a more focused volume that understands the "givenness" explored by Husserl, Heidegger, Levinas, Derrida, and Jean-Luc Marion, as a "giving" rather than as a "gift." Again, the journey through the philosophical tradition not only understands the philosophical tradition in a new way but also asks what that tradition might have to contribute to the construction of an actology: a philosophy that understands reality as action in changing patterns.

All of those volumes did philosophy by setting out from a wide diversity of texts written by a variety of philosophers in order to understand their authors' philosophies in a particular way and to seek the resources with which to build an actological tradition. The next two volumes, *An Actological Metaphysic* and *An Actological Theology*, started from a different place: they ask what metaphysics and theology might look like if reality were to be understood as action in changing patterns rather than as beings that change. Here the texts of a wide variety of authors are mined for what they might contribute to an understanding of the particular metaphysical and theological concepts that we discuss, rather than reading them in order to understand what their authors might have to offer to the construction of an actology.

This seventh book in the "Actological Explorations" series fills some gaps. There is plenty of cosmology, philosophy, and theology, in the previous volumes of the series, and other disciplines are sometimes mentioned, but there has been no sustained discussion of what language, the humanities, ethics, mathematics, the natural sciences, the social sciences, psychology, politics, and organizational behavior, might look like in an actological context. This book discusses those disciplines in turn in order to ask what they might look like if reality were to be understood as action in changing patterns.

"MULTIDISCIPLINARY"

The purpose of this book is to understand the potential for an actology from the perspectives of a wide variety of academic disciplines, or fields of study, and to contribute to those disciplines by studying them actologically: that is,

INTRODUCTION TO A MULTIDISCIPLINARY ACTOLOGY

in the context of an understanding of reality as action in changing patterns rather than as beings that change. It is "multidisciplinary," because the different disciplines are employed separately. It does not attempt to be "interdisciplinary": that is, as far as possible it does not employ two or more disciplines at the same time.

There is little more actological than academic disciplines, as they are inherently action in changing patterns: in relation to their subject matter, their methods, their relationships, and so on. In the Mediaeval university, students began their studies with grammar, logic, and rhetoric, and then added arithmetic, music, geometry, and astronomy. Some would go on to study divinity, canon law, civil law, and medicine.[1] Since then disciplines have multiplied. In the seventeenth century, "political economy" meant the study of the financial aspects of government, before its meaning was extended in the nineteenth century to mean the study of what became known as "the economy" as a whole: "the development and regulation of the material resources of a community or state"; and then the term "political economy" was displaced by the term "economics," a word that had previously meant study of the management of the household, but that came to mean "the branch of knowledge (now regarded as one of the social sciences) that deals with the production, distribution, consumption, and transfer of wealth."[2] To take just one example of discipline multiplication from the history of the London School of Economics: What was originally social policy and administration is now the separate disciplines of social policy, criminology, international development, and health policy.

As well as the number of disciplines multiplying, a certain amount of confusion has arisen as to what particular terms might mean. To take the same example of "political economy": since the 1960s the term has seen a somewhat chaotic revival that has led to it having a rather indeterminate meaning, and Groenewegen[3] has concluded that "economics" and "political economy" might best be treated as synonyms, and that their somewhat indeterminate and shifting meanings reflect an important characteristic of the science of economics/political economy. Needless to say, whether to treat "economics" and "political economy" as separate entities will remain a decision for university governing bodies and administrators.

The problem is this: the more disciplines there are, and the more boundaries, the more boundary-crossing we have to do when we find a variety of disciplines useful for studying a particular phenomenon or idea. We cannot separate biology, chemistry, physics, and mathematics, nor can we separate

1. University of Cambridge.
2. Oxford English Dictionary.
3. Groenewegen, "Political economy."

philosophy, ethics, history, literature, and language: and it is not difficult to discover connections between those two lists. All of these disciplines are action in changing patterns, and all of them are entangled with other disciplines across their boundaries.[4]

Academic disciplines are social constructions, they evolve over time, and their boundaries and interrelationships are fluid. Because in this book each discipline has to be understood and then employed in the space of a single chapter, working definitions have had to be provided and adhered to, and the number of sources quoted has had to be limited.

The reader will always need to be aware that different choices might have been made: different disciplines might have been selected; different definitions of those disciplines might have been offered; and different guides to the disciplines might been followed. This, along with space constraints, means that this volume cannot claim to be a comprehensive or definitive reading of the literature of the different disciplines selected, and that what the reader will find here will be a necessarily somewhat arbitrary selection of possible perspectives: but this will at least mean that the reader is being invited to ask how a particular chosen discipline might be understood and practised in an actological context, and so might find themselves asking a similar question about other disciplines.

This book will have served its purpose if experts from a wide variety of academic disciplines contribute their own understandings of how their disciplines might contribute to the debate about actology, and of how that debate might contribute to the development of their disciplines.

THE STRUCTURE OF THE BOOK

Each of the following chapters asks about the contribution that a particular discipline or disciplines might make to the construction of an actology, and what an actological understanding of reality might be able to contribute to those disciplines. First of all, the discipline or disciplines are discussed, generally with the assistance of one or two particular guides; then connections will be sought between actology and the discipline's methods and subject-matter; and finally conclusions will be drawn. A chapter will then draw some overall conclusions.

This is not necessarily the last book in the "Actological Explorations" series—a detailed study of Maurice Blondel's philosophy is in preparation, and a more systematic theology might follow—but there is a sense in which the

---

4. Torry, *An Actological Metaphysics*, 189.

INTRODUCTION TO A MULTIDISCIPLINARY ACTOLOGY

way in which this book fills gaps left by the other volumes in the series brings to completion a survey of actological possibilities. The reader will therefore find an epilogue at the end of the book. The first draft of this more personal text was written twenty years ago, and so at an early stage in the actological project. I hope that this rewritten version will draw the reader into the heart of the actological understanding of the world and of ourselves into which the "Actological Explorations" journey has taken us.

OVERLAPS

A Modern Guide to Citizen's Basic Income: A Multidisciplinary Approach, published in 2020, studies the global debate about the desirability and feasibility of giving to every individual an unconditional income from within a wide variety of different disciplines, and each of its chapters begins with a brief initial summary of the discipline in question. As this new book sets out from a similar set of disciplines, it was going to be inevitable for the initial brief descriptions of the disciplines at the beginning of each chapter to be worded in ways similar to the wording in *A Modern Guide to Citizen's Basic Income*. The publisher of *The Modern Guide*, Edward Elgar Publishing, has kindly given permission for some of the same references to be employed in *A Multidisciplinary Actology*, and for content similar to that in *The Modern Guide* to be included in this book. Such references and similar content are clearly referenced in the footnotes.

In order to create coherent treatments of the different disciplines understood actologically in this new book, some of the material in three previous books in the "Actological Explorations" series—*Actological Readings in Continental Philosophy*; *An Actology of the Given*; and *An Actological* Metaphysic— is summarized here. Again, where this occurs references will be found in the footnotes.

OMISSIONS

A book titled *A Multidisciplinary Actology* might have been expected to contain chapters on philosophy, metaphysics, anthropology, cosmology, and theology. This book does not contain such chapters because previous books in the "Actological Explorations" series already contain substantial treatments of those disciplines. *Actology: Action, Change and Diversity in the Western Philosophical Tradition*; *Actological Readings in Continental Philosophy*; and much of *An Actology of the Given*, are actological philosophy; *An Actological*

Metaphysic explores metaphysics and cosmology from an actological point of view; *An Actology of the Given* contains material on an actological anthropology; and *An Actological Theology* is what it says it is. For a more complete multidisciplinary actology readers might wish to read those previously published books as well as this one.

CONCLUSION

By studying language, the humanities, ethics, mathematics, the natural sciences, the social sciences, psychology, politics, and organizational behavior, in the context of an actology, we hope to contribute to the construction of an actology and to shed new light on the disciplines under discussion. At the end of the book we shall draw some conclusions in relation to those aims.

Chapter 1

Language is actological

Language: The vocabulary or phraseology of a particular sphere, discipline, profession, social group, etc.[1]

INTRODUCTION

THERE IS A SENSE in which what I here call simply "language" is the basis of every discipline discussed in this book, as all them are constituted by spoken and written language. If historians discuss history then they are using language; if ethicists are discussing ethics then they are using language; if scientists write articles and books about their sciences then they are creating texts that we can understand as pure patterns that entangle with the action in changing patterns of the reader to create constantly changing understandings; and the same goes for texts written by historians. The study of language might be divided into a variety of disciplines—linguistics, grammar, English language, English literature, and the language and literature of every other language, both ancient and contemporary—but all of them are the study of language: so in this chapter we shall attempt to understand language, and on that basis we shall ask ourselves how the various disciplines that study language might be understood.

Language will here be discussed as a reality constituted by action in changing patterns. Spoken language is clearly that. Written language is less clearly action in changing patterns, so we shall come to that in the second part

---

1. Oxford English Dictionary.

of the chapter; and in the third part we shall tackle the subject of definitions. In the first part, on spoken language, my guide will be the philosopher Ludwig Wittgenstein, whose understanding of language was driven by how language is used.

THE MEANING OF LANGUAGE IS ITS USE

Wittgenstein envisages a shopkeeper responding to a request for "five red apples": "But what is the meaning of the word 'five'?—No such thing was in question here, only how the word 'five' is used."[2] Language is here action in changing patterns. The customer speaks: that is, they make the air vibrate in a changing pattern. The shopkeeper's brain works on the vibrations, and we then see them pick up five red apples and hand them to the customer. An event has taken place: that is, action in changing patterns around which we have placed a somewhat arbitrary boundary; and as everything within that boundary is action in changing patterns, we have to recognize that there is nothing special about language: so what we call "language" is action in changing patterns around which we have placed a somewhat arbitrary boundary.

As Wittgenstein puts it, we play "language games": "The term 'language-game' is meant to bring into prominence the fact that the *speaking* of language is part of an activity, or of a life-form."[3] A game is action in changing patterns, the rules of the game being a fairly stable but slowing changing patterning of the action: and the same is true of "life-form" or "form of life." Life is action in changing patterns, and a "form of life" is a particular fairly stable but still changing pattern in the action: and it is always within forms of life that language is located. We might understand a "form of life" as an extended event: that is, action in changing patterns around which we have placed a fairly arbitrary boundary; so we can either understand language as boundaried action in changing patterns within a form of life, or we can understand language as itself a form of life: or rather, as many of them.[4]

The meaning of language is its use:[5] but what do we mean by "meaning"? (Reader: beware a dangerous vortex.) Again, we should ask how language is used: that is, what action in changing patterns are we looking at? First of all, we are looking at the precise pattern in the action: that is, how the word is said. Different intonations can mean different things. But most important

2. Wittgenstein, *Philosophische Untersuchungen / Philosophical Investigations*, §1, 2.
3. Wittgenstein, *Philosophische Untersuchungen / Philosophical Investigations*, §23, 10.
4. Grayling, *Wittgenstein*, 97; Torry, *A Modern Guide to Citizen's Basic Income*, 8–9.
5. Grayling, *Wittgenstein*, 90.

will be the context: both the linguistic context and the broader context. If a sentence is spoken, there might have been sentences before it and there will be sentences after it; the sentence might trigger memory of other sentences in other contexts; and there might be explicit or implicit reference to other linguistic events. And then there will be the wider context of location—perhaps a shop—and of objects—maybe apples. All of this constitutes the meaning, an important element of which will be connections with other words. So, for instance, the meaning of "language" is given by "vocabulary" and "phrasing": words with meanings of their own—and so we go on down the vortex, but not before the words and some of the elements of their meanings have embedded themselves in our forms of life: and then the context will change, and the same words will have different meanings.[6]

Within a particular form of life—perhaps in a greengrocer's shop—there will be a particular form of life, and language games that belong to it. There will be sentence structures and vocabulary related to the fruit and vegetables, the customers, the staff, organizational factors, and so on, with each interlocking game played by everyone involved or by subsets of the shop's staff, customers, and suppliers. The shop's language game will have boundaries, but that does not mean that it will be isolated. It will interlock with multiple other language games to form larger and larger games the more we extend the context under investigation.[7] "Our knowledge forms an enormous system. And only within this system has a particular bit the value we give it."[8] Whilst none of those bits will be identical, and all of them will change all the time—for they are always *action* in *changing* patterns—there will be temporary similarities: what Wittgenstein calls *Familienähnlichkeiten*, "family resemblances";[9] and similarly, although the meaning of each word will change as its context changes, each word will have "*eine Familie von Bedeutungen*," "a family of meanings."[10] What we won't be able to identify is a characteristic common to all of the members of the family of meanings of a word. The same is true of games; whilst there are similarities between games, there is no characteristic that is common to all of them. They might all have rules, but all we mean by that is that the action that constitutes each game will be in changing patterns: and all that tells us is that all games belong within an entire reality constituted by action in changing patterns. This is of course a significant result in itself, because it tells us that a

---

6. Sherry, *Religion, Truth and Language Games*, 4.

7. Wittgenstein, *Philosophische Untersuchungen / Philosophical Investigations*, §68, 28;

8. Wittgenstein, *Philosophische Untersuchungen / Philosophical Investigations*, §410.

9. Wittgenstein, *Philosophische Untersuchungen / Philosophical Investigations*, §67, 27.

10. Wittgenstein, *Philosophische Untersuchungen / Philosophical Investigations*, §77, 31; Torry, *A Modern Guide to Citizen's Basic Income*, 8–9.

game is as real as the planet earth, which is not something that an ontology—
an understanding of reality as beings that change—could ever tell us. It also
tells us that any language game, all language games, and the entire language
game, are as real as the planet: in the context of this chapter a particularly
important result. As Wittgenstein puts it:

> We see a complicated network of similarities overlapping and
> criss-crossing; sometimes overall similarities, sometimes similari-
> ties of detail . . . Now I know how to go on . . . *This is how these
> words are used*.[11]

This means that the only way to know "how to go on" and "how . . . words
are used" is by experiencing the action in changing patterns that constitutes
a word in a wide variety of contexts: although here I diverge from Wittgenstein, who goes on to suggest that no non-linguistic foundation will ever be
discovered, that we shall exhaust justifications, and that in the end we can
only say "This is simply what I do . . . *this language-game is played*."[12] We have
recognized that language games relate to broader forms of life, and that all of it
is action in changing patterns: so the language games that we play will always
be influenced by their changing contexts, which means that there will always
be non-linguistic foundations to language games, just as language games will
be foundations to other kinds of changing patterns of action; and we shall usually be able to justify language by reference to other events, and to justify other
events linguistically: so we cannot simply say "This is simply what I do." What
I do linguistically will always be entangled with all of the changing patterns of
action in which I am involved and that to a considerable extent constitute who
I am. I am what I do: and that applies as much to what I say and to what I hear
and understand as it does to my other patterned action.[13]

It is this understanding that J.L. Austin elaborates when he suggests that
to say something is "the doing of an action".[14] To make a promise, name a
ship, or issue a command, constitutes a "performative utterance."[15] Action in
changing patterns is tangling with other action in changing patterns, and we
draw a somewhat arbitrary line around some of it and call it "language." If I
ask directions to somewhere and the person I ask points and says "That way,"

---

11. Wittgenstein, *Philosophische Untersuchungen / Philosophical Investigations*, §66, 27; §180, 62; §179, 62.

12. Wittgenstein, *Philosophische Untersuchungen / Philosophical Investigations*, §217, 72; §654, 141.

13. Torry, *Actology*, 189–99.

14. Austin, *How to Do Things with Words*, 5.

15. Austin, *How to Do Things with Words*, 21; "Performative Utterances," 235.

then what they are doing is giving directions, the whole of what they are doing is required, and only one element of the giving of directions is what we choose to call language. Every discourse is an event: some events might be purely linguistic, some might be an individual speaker engaging with an individual listener, others might be a long oral tradition within which stories evolve,[16] and some might be a mixture of the linguistic and the non-linguistic.[17] We can agree with Ricoeur that language is always an event, but we might disagree with him when he suggests "that discourse is realized temporally and in the present, whereas the system of language is virtual and outside of time."[18] Language is never outside time. It changes constantly. Ricoeur also suggests that meaning is the discourse "codified and regulated according to paradigms."[19] It is we who codify and regulate in relation to a wide variety of factors, all of which are action in changing patterns, so we can only agree with Ricoeur if paradigms are themselves action in changing patterns that encompass the vast diversity of changing patterns of action tangling with the discourse: a meaning compatible with the normal meaning of "paradigm": "a pattern or model, an exemplar; (also) a typical instance of something, an example."[20] [21]

One interesting consequence of this understanding of language is that there is nothing particularly special about what we might call "analogy" or "metaphor." All spoken language is action in changing patterns, and because everything is that, there will never be an exact match between an example of language and some other event: and if ever there was then it would be fleeting as everything would immediately change. We might legitimately understand by "metaphor" a use of a word or phrase different from a dictionary definition but still understood, and by "analogy" a more extended example of language that offers understanding without the words or phrases used conforming to normal definitions: but all of it is language that is action in changing patterns entangling with other action in changing patterns, including the action in changing patterns that constitutes our brains; and our matching of language with dictionary definitions will always be one example among many of the changing patterns of action that constitute our human action. What we can

16. Allejo, *Papyrus*, 73.

17. Ricoeur, *Du Texte à l'Action*, 115; *From Text to Action*, 74.

18. Ricoeur, *Du Texte à l'Action*, 116 : le discours est réalisé temporellement et dans le présent, alors que le systéme de la langue est virtuel et hors du temps; *From Text to Action*, 74.

19. Ricoeur, *Du Texte à l'Action*, 119: codifiés et réglés selon des paradigmes; *From Text to Action*, 76.

20. Oxford English Dictionary.

21. Torry, *An Actological Metaphysic*, 174–76.

say is that by "analogy" and "metaphor" we might mean language of which the changing patterns of action are further from those of the uses to which we normally put the words in the dictionary definitions than are those that constitute what we might call "non-analogical" or "non-metaphorical." Here we are talking about degrees of likeness, and so of closer and less close family likeness. All of this language has meaning, of course, as we can connect all of it with other words and other events, and as we connect those words and other events with other words and other events, and so on.

TEXT

So far we have only tackled spoken language: the action in changing patterns of our brains and vocal chords that vibrate the air into action in changing patterns that then entangle with the action in changing patterns of our ears and brains. Written text is different: it might have been produced by the action in changing patterns of the writer using a pen or hitting the keys of a computer keyboard: but whether on paper or on a screen, it is difficult to interpret the text as action in changing patterns.

The invention of writing, and the subsequent invention of an alphabet, significantly extended the audience of a linguistic event from those who could hear a speaker to those who could read a text:

> An essential characteristic of a literary work, and of a work of art in general, is that it transcends its own psychosociological conditions of production and thereby opens itself to an unlimited series of readings, themselves situated in different sociocultural conditions . . . In contrast to the dialogical situation, where the vis-à-vis is determined by the very situation of discourse, written discourse creates an audience that extends in principle to anyone who can read. The freeing of the written material with respect to the dialogical condition of discourse is the most significant effect of writing.[22]

---

22. Ricoeur, *Du Texte à l'Action*, 124–25: Il est essentiel à une œuvre littéraire, à une oeuvre d'art en général qu'elle transcende ses propres conditions psychosociologiques de production et qu'elle s'ouvre ainsi à une suite illimitée de lectures elles-mêmes situées dans des contextes socioculturels différents. . . . A la différence de la situation dialogale, où le vis-à-vis est déterminé par la situation même de discours, le discours écrit se suscite un public qui s'étend virtuellement à quiconque sait lire. L'écriture trouve ici son effet le plus considérable: l'affranchissement de la chose écrite à l'égard de la condition dialogale du discours; *From Text to Action*, 80.

A text is not action in changing patterns: it is pure pattern; or, as Paul Ricoeur puts it, a "fixation."[23] Action in changing patterns only enters the picture again when the reader reads the text. Initially reading meant speaking the words being read, and then an important transition took place less than two thousand years ago: silent reading.[24] So however significant the abilities to write and read might be, losses have occurred. There is now what we might call an action gap between the writer and the reader, isolating the reader from the writer, and a further loss of action in changing patterns when silent reading isolated the reader from the world around. Such a loss of reality was particularly acute when oral traditions became frozen in a canonical text. "Once transcribed, these stories lost their fluidity, their flexibility, the freedom of improvisation, and, in many cases, their characteristic language."[25] But still there is plenty of reality, constituted by the action in changing patterns of the writer, and the action in changing patterns of readers' eyes and brains entangling with the text as "we breathe life"[26] into it and create the action in changing patterns of our constantly changing understanding.

Whilst the readership of a text might be far more extensive than a participant in a spoken discourse, a certain sense of reality is missing because whilst the process has begun and ended with action in changing patterns, it has passed through a "fixation" that is less real because it is not constituted by action in changing patterns: instead, it is constituted by pure pattern. However, this does not prevent the text from being causal: it can still tangle with the action in changing patterns of its readers; it can communicate to them the action in patterns that constituted the author's writing of the text; it can therefore be for the reader a genuine communication with the past; and the action in changing patterns in the reader's mind will bear a family likeness to the action in changing patterns that constitute the text's writer. "Initially the text had only a sense, that is, internal relations or a structure; now it has a meaning, that is, a realization in the discourse of the reading subject:"[27] and always a unique contribution to the reading subject's discourse because both the reader and their context will be unique action in changing patterns. No reader will know precisely how another reader interprets the same text, although because every reader of the same text will be engaging with the same

23. Ricoeur, *Du Texte à l'Action*, 213: la fixation; *From Text to Action*, 146.
24. Allejo, *Papyrus*, 41.
25. Allejo, *Papyrus*, 84.
26. Allejo, *Papyrus*, 108.
27. Ricoeur, *Du Texte à l'Action*, 172 : Le texte avait seulement un sens, c'est-à-dire des relations internes, une structure ; il a maintenant une signification, c'est-à-dire une effectuation dans le discours propre du sujet lisant; *From Text to Action*, 115.

pattern on the page or the screen we can assume family likeness between different readings, so we might wish to say that a text can generate shared meaning in a community: but there will always be an element of doubt as to the extent and character of family likeness between individuals and therefore across a community.[28]

A text is information that connects the author to the reader, and that connects different readers to each other as the ways in which a text entangles with readers' minds will generate changing patterns of action that bear family resemblances to each other. Texts connect. As Yuval Harari puts it,

> what information does is to create *new* realities by tying together disparate things—whether couples or empires. Its defining feature is connection rather than representation, and information is whatever connects different points into a network. Information doesn't necessarily inform us about things. Rather, it puts things in formation.[29]

DEFINITIONS

The meaning of a word, a phrase, or a sentence, will be its use, and, as we have seen, the context will be an endless variety of events, objects, locations, language, and so on. When we speak of the "definition" of a word, we are referring specifically to other words with which our minds connect it; and the process of definition will be the action in changing patterns that constitutes the changing active connecting of words with other words. It is only within a vast and in principle endless network of interrelated, diverse, and changing language games, and in relation to the shifting meanings in changing contexts of all of the words that we use, that we can explore the meanings of words, which means that we can only explore the meanings of words by referring to a changing diversity of other words.[30] By "definition" we generally mean a set of words that together indicate some of the "meaning" of a word or group of words. Because every word occurs in a changing context, all of the words that we use will constantly change their meanings, so any definition of a word constituted by other words will constantly change its meaning. However, multiple minds might connect a word with a fairly stable set of other words, with change in an appropriate set of words happening fairly slowly: so we might

---

28. Torry, *An Actological Metaphysic*, 177–80.

29. Harari, *Nexus*, 12.

30. Bambrough, *Reason, Truth and God*, 94; Torry, *A Modern Guide to Citizen's Basic Income*, 9.

legitimately claim that settled definitions are possible as long as we recognize that change is ubiquitous and that connections between words can break and new connections might form. Because this process happens slowly in relation to other changes, we might find family resemblances between the different meanings of a word, and it is on that that dictionaries rely when they define a word or group of words. The Oxford English Dictionary lists the uses of words on which it bases its definitions: a strategy that recognizes both the family resemblances between the different meanings of words and the ways in which meanings change across time and space.

But how should we construct the definitions of words? That is: what method should we use to choose the words that we employ to construct a word's definition? There are at least four possibilities: by current usage; by listing characteristics; by comparison with a prototype; and by a legitimate authority.

We have already discussed the first of these options. The strategy is to collect as many uses as possible and then attempt to describe in other words what the word means in all of those different contexts. And so, for instance, "language" means "The vocabulary or phraseology of a particular sphere, discipline, profession, social group, etc." because that is a way of saying what the word means in a wide variety of contexts.

Overlapping with the first method is the second: creating a list of characteristics that determine whether things fit within a category. So, for instance, a square is a four-sided figure with all of its sides equal in length, opposite sides parallel, and all angles right angles. A rectangle is not a square because all of its sides are not equal in length, so it is not a member of the category "square" and cannot be defined as one. The overlap results from the fact that common usage of the word "square" tells us what the characteristics are that determine membership of the category: but once those characteristics are decided they become the definition. However, common usage can subvert the categorization. For instance, "town square" might mean a rectangular patch of land in the middle of a town rather than a square patch; and it might not even be a rectangle if the sides are not parallel. Here we are in the realm of family resemblances: the town square is something like a square. So does it belong in the category "square"? No. Does it conform to common usage of "square"? Yes. A further problematic aspect of definition by characteristics is that not all usage maps onto lists of characteristics in the ways in which "square" does. So, for instance, if being able to fly is decided to be a characteristic of a bird, then an ostrich is not a bird and a bat is one. If having legs and a flat surface is decided to be a characteristic of a table, then a chair is a table, and a folded drop-leaf table is not one. Here we might be in the realm of "more or less": a sparrow is more a bird than an ostrich; and a non-folding table is more a table than a folding one. Nothing is clear-cut, and everything changes.[31]

Perhaps what we are actually doing is comparing things with prototypes in order to decide whether they are in definitional categories. For instance, we might compare things with a robin in order to decide whether they are birds; and we might compare actions with a lie in order to decide whether they are moral.[32] So rather than define a table by its characteristics, we might have a particular table in mind and then compare other tables with it. A chair would then not be a table.

A fourth definitional method would be to trust a legitimate authority in the field. So, for instance, we might expect the Basic Income Earth Network (BIEN)—an organization that facilitates the global debate about unconditional incomes—to define a Basic Income, as in fact it does: "A basic income is a periodic cash payment unconditionally delivered to all on an individual basis, without means-test or work requirement."[33] Again there are overlaps. BIEN has chosen a list of characteristics with which to define "Basic Income," and it has taken account of existing usage. A significant advantage of the "legitimate authority" method is that it enables the community of people interested in Basic Income to understand each other when they use the term "Basic Income": but it might be counted a disadvantage that the process asks individuals entering into the social contract to park their linguistic autonomy.[34] It might be thought that a further advantage of the "legitimate authority" method is that it might prevent constant change in definitions. The previous three methods are all subject to change: the common usage of words changes all the time; the characteristics that we might choose to define a category—possibly in relation to usage—might change; and prototypes might change. It is at least feasible that a legitimate authority might decide on a definition that it then does not permit to change: feasible, but highly unlikely. Whether the legitimate authority is an organization or an individual, change will be ubiquitous: for instance, there has rarely been a time during the past ten years when the definition of Basic Income has not been a matter of often quite vigorous debate. Those working in a field are often loath to trade their autonomy for a social contract.[35]

Agreed definitions to which everyone involved adheres are essential. For instance, scientific research communities require definitions that change little,

---

31. Rosch and Lloyd, *Cognition and Categorization*; Rosch, "Reclaiming concepts,"61–77; Torry, *A Modern Guide to Citizen's Basic Income*, 15.
32. Johnson, *Moral Imagination*; Torry, *A Modern Guide to Citizen's Basic Income*, 17.
33. Basic Income Earth Network, www.basicincome.org.
34. Torry, *A Modern Guide to Citizen's Basic Income*, 19–20.
35. Torry, *An Actological Metaphysic*, 2–18.

and then only very slowly, so that members of the community can understand each other when they share the results of their research, and so that readers outside the community can understand descriptions of research results without having to ask themselves whether definitions of which they have experience are current definitions to which the entire scientific community adheres. Only if all of the individuals and organizations participating in a widespread debate can agree on the meanings of terms and then stick to them will mutual comprehension and useful research collaboration be possible. How we use language matters, and there is nothing more essential to the rationality and comprehensibility of debate than attention to how language is used.[36]

However, none of this changes the fact that language changes all the time. Connections between words are different at different times and in different places; usage changes; the characteristics that constitute categories and therefore definitions can change; prototypes change; and institutions can change their minds. Nothing stays the same. We only have to compare the King James translation of the Hebrew of the Jewish Scriptures and of the Greek of the Christian New Testament with more modern translations to realize just how much written language can change over the centuries, let alone the even more significant changes in the spoken language.

CONCLUSION

Language is actological: it is action in changing patterns, both in relation to the human activity of speaking a language, and in relation to the connections between words. The patterns change all the time: nothing remains the same. On that basis, what shall we say about the various disciplines that study language? Linguistics is "the scientific study of language and its structure,"[37] and so is the development and testing of theory about how languages evolve and how they are structured. As with any other science, it is the practice of the science that is its basic reality because it is that that is action in changing patterns. Any theory proposed on the basis of that practice will be pure pattern, but the testing of it will again be action in changing patterns, as explained in Chapter 5 on the natural sciences. Linguistics is an interestingly spiral science. It uses evolving language to study evolving language, so it will change, and it will change language, so a double process of change will occur. We might therefore say that in terms of its action in changing patterns, linguistics is the most real of all of the sciences.

36. Torry, *A Modern Guide to Citizen's Basic Income*, 23–24.
37. Oxford English Dictionary.

A MULTIDISCIPLINARY ACTOLOGY

As for other language-related disciplines: grammar is the study of the structure of a particular language at a particular time and so is a boundaried aspect of linguistics; "English language" is the study of the structure and vocabulary of English, and so is also a boundaried aspect of linguistics; "English literature" is the study of English texts, and generally of a boundaried set of them—perhaps of "the classics" and of a selection of more modern texts that have come to constitute an evolving canon; and the same is true of the study of the language and literature of every other ancient and contemporary language. All of these disciplines are boundaried aspects of the science of linguistics: they are all action in changing patterns related to spoken and written language.

Chapter 2

Actological humanities

Humanities: The branch of learning concerned with human culture; the academic subjects collectively comprising this branch of learning, as history, literature, ancient and modern languages, law, philosophy, art, and music.

Culture: The distinctive ideas, customs, social behavior, products, or way of life of a particular nation, society, people, or period. Hence: a society or group characterized by such customs, etc.[1]

INTRODUCTION

"The humanities" is a socially constructed category of disciplines as much driven by universities' need to group disciplines into schools or faculties as by any inherent connections between them. The positive dictionary definition above does not quite work because sciences, and particularly social sciences, concern human culture just as much as the fields usually defined as the humanities; and to define the humanities negatively against the sciences does not quite work either because arguably history, literature, languages, law, and so on, are not dissimilar to other sciences as their practitioners frequently propose theories and then seek evidence to corroborate or disprove them.

In Chapter 1 we have already studied language, and whilst we have not explicitly studied literature, we might argue that "literature" is simply socially

---

1. Oxford English Dictionary.

constructed canons of prose, drama, and poetry, deemed worthy of study by tradition, schools, and university departments. Such canons change all the time, and because language spoken and heard is changing patterns of action, so literature canons might best be understood as changing patterns of particular changing patterns of action. Where the literature or poetry are texts rather than spoken, they are pure pattern that influences the changing patterns of action that constitute the reader: and whilst the pure pattern of the text does not change, textual canons change constantly, so even though texts themselves are pure pattern, and so are real in only a secondary manner, literature, being changing patterns of action, is actological in ways in which texts are not.

Among the arts, music is perhaps the most actological, in the sense that it is soundwaves in particular patterns and so is inherently action in changing patterns. Musical scores are to music as text is to language: pure pattern that influences the action in changing patterns that constitutes the music. In the context of an actology, the visual arts are of a secondary reality. The work of art itself, like text, is pure pattern that influences the action in changing patterns that constitutes the person who looks at it. As Rowan Williams puts it,

> Art . . . speaks to intelligence, inviting intelligence to recognize its truth. It demands . . . contemplation, the intellect being shaped by the impress of truth in such a way that the impress of truth on the artistic mind or imagination is continued through the work . . .[2]

The creation of the work of art is actological, as is our looking at it. The picture itself is not. It is as static as its frame and the hooks that fix it to the wall.[3]

Of the disciplines mentioned in the definition of the humanities above, "history, literature, ancient and modern languages, law, philosophy, art, and music," there are two disciplines that we have not explicitly studied in previous volumes in the "Actological Explorations" series: law, and history. Chapter 8 will study politics, and particularly the field of social policy, and so the making of law. It is this aspect of law that is actological: the texts of acts of parliament and the like are not themselves actological until they influence people who make, enforce, obey, or disobey the law. So the one significant discipline that we must address in this chapter is history.

---

2. Williams, *Grace and Necessity*, 22.
3. Torry, *An Actological Metaphysic*, 177–83.

ACTOLOGICAL HISTORY

History: The branch of knowledge that deals with past events; the formal record or study of past events, esp. human affairs.[4]

History itself is clearly actological: it is action in changing patterns. A different question is this: What does the discipline of history look like in an actological context? The history-writing that might have begun with the ancient Greek traveler Herodotus's *"historiai,"* "inquiries,"[5] is also clearly actological, in the sense discussed in the last chapter: history-writing is as much action in changing patterns as is everything else: but what of the history that is written? First of all, it is about the past, and not the present, and there is a sense in which the past is *not* action in changing patterns as well as a sense that it is. The past itself does not change, so from the point of view of the present it is *not* action in changing patterns, and we might understand it as a four-dimensional solid object, with the three dimensions of space and the dimension of time as its four dimensions: a solid object of pure pattern crystallized out of the ubiquitous action in changing patterns that have constituted history. We might say the same about the objectification that occurs in history-writing as Paul Ricoeur suggests happens in the sciences:

> Action itself, action as meaningful, may become an object of science, without losing its character of meaningfulness, through a kind of objectification similar to the fixation that occurs in writing. By this objectification, action is no longer a transaction to which the discourse of action would still belong. It constitutes a delineated pattern that has to be interpreted according to its inner connections.[6]

We can therefore study history as a solid object and understand it as patterns crystallized out of the action in patterns of history. In practical terms, that four-dimensional object is infinitely complex, so history-writing is always a matter of selection; and because the historian choosing what to study and write is action in changing patterns, history-writing is action in changing patterns: and then out of that process comes a text that is again patterns crystallized

---

4. Oxford English Dictionary.
5. Allejo, *Papyrus*, 161.
6. Ricoeur, *Du Texte à l'Action*, II, 213: L'action elle-même, l'action sensée, peut devenir objet de science sans perdre son caractère de signifiance à la faveur d'une sorte d'objectivation semblable à la fixation opérée par l'écriture. Grâce à cette objectivation, l'action n'est plus une transaction à laquelle le discours de l'action continuerait d'appartenir. Elle constitue une configuration qui demande à être interprétée en fonction de ses connexions internes: *From Text to Action*, II, 146.

out of the action in changing patterns of the historian's activity as it encounters the patterns that are the crystallized action in patterns of history. But are those patterns discovered or created by the historian? Any good historian will be seeking evidence in the four-dimensional object for the patterns that they write into their texts: but that does not tell us whether the historian is discovering patterns that are there in the history or is creating patterns as a means to understand the infinite complexity of history.

History-making

It was during the eighteenth and nineteenth centuries, first in Germany and then elsewhere, that historians came to see themselves as a distinct body of writers, and that university departments, libraries, archives, and journals, were established for the study of what became known as "history." Slowly the past came to be understood on its own terms, with evidence being sought in the archives: although lessons were and still are drawn from history in order to inform the present,[7] which requires us to assume family resemblances between the past and the present.[8] As we might expect, historians' writing has always been informed by their own agendas, whether political,[9] philosophical, or theological, so in the absence of any normative structure for history-writing we might expect history-writing to be shaped by historians' own interests at least to some extent, and the search for archive evidence to be similarly shaped so that the evidence collected and reported matches the story told.[10] This is to make the point that Immanuel Kant made when he suggested that our minds shape raw data into experience. But that is not the end of the story. We might discover evidence that causes us to change our minds: so an iterative process might take place in which the historian's agenda determines the history-writing, evidence is sought, evidence causes adjustment to the agenda and therefore the history-writing, more evidence is sought, and so on.[11] This turns history-writing into a science, although because imagination must be employed in order to construct an initial story for which evidence is then sought, and imagination then adapts the story in the light of new evidence, history-writing remains an art. It is not without significance that if we understand history-writing in this way, as an iterative process that spirals around story

7. Harrison et al., "The Institutionalisation and Organisation of History," 11.
8. Harrison et al., "Methodology," 33.
9. Harrison et al., "The Primacy of Political History," 40–41, 51.
10. Harrison et al., "Methodology," 26.
11. von Below, "Über Historische Periodisierungen," 22.

ACTOLOGICAL HUMANITIES

construction and evidence research, then it is ubiquitous action in changing patterns, and art and science coalesce into a single complex process of action in changing patterns.

History-writing has generally been about monarchs and statecraft, simply because those have been more consistently documented and the documents have survived; and it is no surprise that history is often written from the point of view of salaried university teachers:[12] but parish church records, taxation ledgers, workhouse minute books, and so on, have now generated a subdiscipline of social history,[13] and we are now more aware than before that we should interpret archives both on their own terms and against the background of their own times.[14] A further iteration has been the development of economic history,[15] itself an iterative process that constructs models of the economy through time and adjusts them in the light of new evidence; and other histories have followed. Today the historian will always ask what the author of archive material "could in practice have been intending to communicate by the utterance of this given utterance,"[16] but it remains impossible to escape from the multiple pressures on the history-writing that emerge from the author's agenda, other historians and their histories, current interests and debates, and so on. If we have learnt anything so far as we have discussed both language and history, it is that everything is action in changing patterns, that any changing pattern of action is entangled with an in principle infinite number of other changing patterns of action, and that change is ubiquitous. This is particularly true of the study and writing of history, which is always a particular writing of history, and always the writing of a history of change.[17]

A history of social security

As an example of history as history of change, and as a contribution to our study of social policy in Chapter 8, we shall here record a particular history of social security in the United Kingdom as a history of adaptation to new

12. Harrison et al., "The Primacy of Political History," 46, 49.

13. Harrison et al., "The Primacy of Political History"; Welskopp, "Social History," 218; Wrightson and Levine, *Poverty and Piety in an English Village*.

14. Lawrence, "Political History"; Stedman Jones, "Rethinking Chartism," 90, 94; Welskopp, "Social History," 216, 218.

15. Harrison et al., "The Primacy of Political History," 47; Schofield, "The emergence of British Economic History," 65, 69, 71–74.

16. Skinner, "Meaning and Understanding in the History of Ideas," 48–49.

17. *A Modern Guide to Citizen's Basic Income*, 29–32.

circumstances, of evolutionary change relating to multiple factors, and often change that we might characterize as a pendulum moving back and forth between universality and selectivity but never moving far enough from selectivity to prevent it from swinging quickly back again.

The 1601 Poor Law set up local administrations to provide for people unable to provide for themselves, and to provide "houses of correction" for able-bodied men who could not find work. For two hundred years the system worked tolerably well, as people did not travel much, and the economy was basically agricultural: but by the beginning of the nineteenth century the economy was changing and in both the agricultural and the urban worlds wages were not keeping pace with living costs at the same time as unemployment was increasing. The administration of the Poor Law being local, experiment was inevitable, and in 1795 at Speenhamland the Poor Law Guardians began to subsidize low wages as a means of relieving poverty. Amidst fears that this policy would lead to a general reduction in wages and to the loss of the human dignity that was believed then as now to result from a man's inability to earn sufficient to keep himself and his family, a review was ordered. The ensuing debate led to the Poor Law Amendment Act of 1834 and to what has become known as the "New Poor Law" with its concept of "less eligibility": that is, that the unemployed man or woman should not be paid as much as they would get if they were employed. "Out relief" was replaced by the workhouse to which anyone who could not support themselves was admitted and in which they were isolated from the rest of society: a system meant to deter people from voluntary poverty, although in many areas out-relief had to continue because there was not sufficient space in the workhouses.

There was little public pressure for reform, but by the beginning of the twentieth century the poverty in which many elderly people found themselves had become better known through Charles Booth's and Seebohm Rowntree's surveys in London and in York, and in 1908 a flat-rate pension was paid to elderly people who had not received Poor Relief and whose incomes were below £31 per annum. Funding and administration of the pension were undertaken by central government, and throughout the twentieth century there was a constant movement away from local administration of income maintenance and towards centralized administration.

The reasons behind the reforms were far from altruistic. A new Unemployment Benefit in certain industries was paid for out of employee and employer contributions, and the pensions were intended to remove inefficient labor from the labor market. Both provisions reduced pressure on the Public Assistance Committees which administered the Poor Law, and simultaneously reduced pressure for reform of the Poor Law.

Nicholas Barr's assessment of the Liberal Government's reforms is that though they were "one of the earlier examples of nationally organized income support"—Bismarck had instigated social insurance in Germany in 1883 to counter social agitation by giving workers a financial stake in the government's stability—they did not represent "a major discontinuity either with previous arrangements or with developments in other countries."[18]

The 1920s brought high unemployment in some places, but not everywhere, so a return to the New Poor Law's household means test held no threat of civil disorder. By 1934 unemployment was still high, Unemployment Benefit was extended to more industries, and "Unemployment Assistance" was paid to those whose Unemployment Benefit had run out after the prescribed 26 weeks. (In the USA, income maintenance was accepted as a Federal responsibility in 1935).

During the Second World War, the government extended its influence into many areas of people's lives, and the scene was thus set for substantial government intervention in health care, education, and income maintenance: and in 1942 the Beveridge Report proposed a comprehensive system of National Insurance benefits and a centrally administered National Assistance to maintain the incomes of people without sufficient to live on. The 1945 Act led to Family Allowances, the 1946 Act to Retirement Pensions, Unemployment Benefit, and Sickness Benefit, and the 1948 Act to the means-tested National Assistance.

Since then, there have been changes in the names of benefits, and minor changes in regulations, but the only major addition has been a means-tested addition to earnings for families with children from 1971, now extended to everyone without sufficient to live on in the form of so-called "Universal Credit": a return to Speenhamland.

We thus see that during the past four hundred years there has been a trend from local to central administration, an occasional swing of the pendulum towards universality (pensions in 1908, Family Allowances in 1942), evolutionary rather than radical change, and a continuing reliance on means-testing, although with constant tinkering with its regulations. All of it might best be understood as changing patterns of action.[19]

---

18. Barr, *The Economics of the Welfare State*, 19.

19. Barr, *The Economics of the Welfare State*; Berthoud et al., *Poverty and the Development of Anti-poverty Policy in the United Kingdom*; Ermisch, *The Political Economy of Demographic Change*; Jordan, *Paupers: The Making of the New Claiming Class*

A MULTIDISCIPLINARY ACTOLOGY

Patterns in the history

A historian will always be working at a variety of levels: creating or discovering an overall pattern to the history; creating or discovering the detail of history; and everything in between. For instance, a number of texts have been written about the evolution of the now global debate about Basic Income—an unconditional income for every individual[20]—and each of them structures the history in its own way. As Harrison, Jones, and Lambert put it, "history does not have an inner structure, an immanent pattern, other than that imposed by the historian."[21] This means that never will *the* history of a period, place, or institutions, be written: it will always be histories in the plural, so that each history will be *a* history. "Never again shall a single story be told as though it were the only one."[22]

The historian will generally set geographical and chronological limits: for instance, Peter Sloman restricts his study of unconditional and guaranteed incomes to the UK, Walter Van Trier chooses just three episodes from the UK, and Timothée Duverger mainly restricts his study of the Basic Income debate to France;[23] and historians will also construct their histories around chosen structures, whether or not those structures are fully supported by the evidence.

For instance, Peter Sloman constructs an article around "five waves of enthusiasm" for Basic Income,[24] even though some of the waves were of various degrees of enthusiasm for policy instruments that were not Basic Incomes; Karl Widerquist proposes "three waves of support," the second of which, located in the United States and Canada, was of support for a variety of policy ideas and experiments;[25] Walter Van Trier studies three incidents during which enthusiasm for an unconditional income emerged but then evaporated;[26] Van Parijs concentrates on a number of situations in which the idea of a Basic Income or something similar emerged;[27] this author's more

20. Duverger, *L'Invention du Revenu de Ba$€*; Sloman, *Transfer State*; Torry, *Basic Income: A History*; Van Parijs, "A Short History of the Basic Income Idea"; Van Parijs and Vanderborght, *Basic Income*, 51–98; Van Trier, *Every One a King*; Widerquist, "Three Waves of Basic Income Support".

21. Harrison et al., "The Primacy of Political History", 51.

22. Berger, *G*, 133.

23. Duverger, *L'Invention du Revenu de Ba$€*; Sloman, *Transfer State*; Van Trier, *Every One a King*.

24. Sloman "Universal Basic Income in British Politics."

25. Widerquist, "Three Waves of Basic Income Support."

26. Van Trier, *Every One a King*.

27. Van Parijs, "A Short History of the Basic Income Idea."

comprehensive history of Basic Income takes a chronological and geographical approach with an evidenced bias towards the history of the unconditional income idea in the UK;[28] and Timothée Duverger does the same for France.[29]

The authors of these different histories employ the subdisciplines of policy history, economic history, social history, philosophical history, and biography; they bring their own academic, political, philosophical, and social agendas to the task, and particularly their commitment to the Basic Income idea; primary and secondary literature, archive material, interviews, and personal experience are the evidence sought and employed; the different histories vary in relation to the proportions of material on ideas and practice; and they vary in relation to the amount of space that they give to economic and policy context, and in relation to the clarity or otherwise of definitions. A particularly important conclusion that we can draw is that both the history-writing and the search for evidence have been driven by an *imposed* structure, whether of "waves" or some other, with the imposition particularly evident where gaps in the structure have to be filled with material not directly relevant to the stated subject of the history.[30]

Each of our authors has crystallized in a structure of their own choosing the complex action in changing patterns that has constituted and still constitutes the global Basic Income debate. There is so much of that widespread and diverse debate that drastic selection always has to be exercised, which gives to the author of a history plenty of discretion as to how they structure their history, which evidence they look for, and how the evidence is allowed to influence the history-writing. The whole process is action in changing patterns reflecting on action in changing patterns.

Histories' futures

Once a history has been written, or a lecture on a period of history has been delivered and the students have taken notes on what they have heard, or television viewers have consigned to imperfect memory a television program about the Roman Empire, the entirety of the action in changing patterns that has given birth to the text or the memory continues to entangle with the ongoing life of individuals and of society as a whole. However fixed the events might be in the past, the changing patterns of action that constituted the original events—the stone dropped into the pool—continue to send ripples across

28. Torry, *Basic Income: A History*.
29. Duverger, *L'Invention du Revenu de Ba$€*.
30. Torry, *A Modern Guide to Citizen's Basic Income*, 32–47.

time and space, which are themselves constituted by action in changing patterns rather than by fixed grids. This is true of the whole of time past. What might appear to be the least significant event in the past, right down to the spin of an individual electron millennia ago, influences the action in changing patterns that constitute the cosmos today and will influence it until the universe reduces to a singularity and perhaps beyond then as well: and one of the channels of that influence will be the texts that we call "history."

CONCLUSION

The arts are always creative acts: that is, action in changing patterns. The writing of a play, and the performance of a play; the writing of a musical score, and the recital; the painting of the work of art and the gallery visitor contemplating it; the writing of a poem or a novel, and the reading of them; the writing of history, and the reading of history; the writing of philosophy, and the reading of philosophy . . . There might be a static intermediary between the playwright's writing and the actor's performance; between the composer writing the score and the pianist playing the piece; between the sculptor carving the statue and the passer-by being moved by it; and between the academic writing a history and the reader learning from it: but the arts remain intrinsically actological because they always begin and end in action in changing patterns.

Chapter 3

Actological ethics

Ethics: The branch of knowledge or study dealing with moral principles.[1]

INTRODUCTION

Whether we regard moral principles and ethics as the same, or understand moral principles to relate to obligation and ethics to be a somewhat broader concept,[2] the question that we have to tackle in this chapter is "Is ethics actological?" As with the concept of history, the same word, "ethics," indicates particular aspects of individual and societal thought and behavior, and also the study of them: all of this is "ethics." The discipline of ethics encompasses the history of ethics, ethical theories, social policy, such terms as "justice" and "fairness," and multiple issues that face us as individuals and as a society.[3]

ETHICAL THEORIES

The study of ethics will generally begin with discussion of such ethical theories as consequentialism (which asks whether the consequences of an action are good), deontological ethics (which asks whether an action is somehow good in itself), foundationalist ethics (which asks whether actions conform to a given axiom), Aristotelian ethics (which asks whether actions promote

1. Oxford English Dictionary.
2. Williams, *Ethics and the Limits of Philosophy*, 182, 196.
3. Mappes and Zembaty, *Social Ethics*.

wellbeing and happiness, particularly for an ethical person), and virtue ethics (which defines ethics as the action stemming from a virtuous character). In relation to all of these we can ask whether an individual is behaving ethically or whether an institution is. The question that we must tackle in this chapter is whether ethics is actological, which will mean asking that question of a variety of ethical theories.

Deontological ethics: actions good in themselves

According to a deontological ethical theory, my action is ethical if it conforms to a categorical imperative: that is, if I act according to an imperative that I cannot help regarding as a universal law. The classic example is a lie. Because I would not wish someone to lie to me, and both our individual lives and the life of society would descend into chaos if we regarded it as ethical to lie, I have to regard it as a universal law that it is wrong, or unethical, to lie. As Immanuel Kant puts it: "I ought never to act in such a way that I could not also will that my maxim should become a universal law." He gives other examples: I ought not to make a promise that I do not intend to keep, because if the breaking of promises were to become universal then no promise would ever be believed. I would therefore wish the keeping of promises to be a universal law.[4] Similarly, I ought to help those in need, because if I was in need then I would wish to receive the required assistance. I must therefore regard helping those in need as a universal law: or, put differently, it must be a universal law that I must not avoid helping those in need.[5] So the only question to be asked is this: "Can you will that your maxim should become a universal law?"[6] Is this theory actological or non-actological? The concept of a universal law is non-actological because it implies an absence of change. There is no action here, and there are no changing patterns of action. However, the theory is not focused on the concept of a universal law: it simply asks whether I would wish my maxim to become a universal law. This means that we have to ask about the concept of a personal maxim: a maxim that is mine and not somebody else's. Such a maxim will of course change all the time because everything about us does. We are action in changing patterns, so anything that we do and everything that we think will be that as well. A maxim that my mind might formulate in one moment will soon evolve into a different maxim in the context of changing patterns of action that entangle with the action in changing patterns that constitute

---

4. Kant, *Groundwork for the Metaphysics of Morals*, 39 (Ak 4.422)
5. Kant, *Groundwork for the Metaphysics of Morals*, 40 (Ak 4.423)
6. Kant, *Groundwork for the Metaphysics of Morals*, 202–3.

who I am. And so, for instance, we might regard it as ethical for a spy to lie about any accomplices that they might or might not have; and we might also have had experience ourselves of a lie that we could only conclude had done more good than harm.[7] This discussion raises questions about Kant's other examples. Which people poorer than myself am I to help, and how am I to do that? Neither my personal maxim nor a related universal law can tell me that. And just as some lies might be ethical, so the breaking of promises might be ethical in particular circumstances.

Alan Donegan's variant of a deontological ethical theory is that we should "act so that the fundamental human goods, whether in your own person or in that of another, are promoted as may be possible and under no circumstances violated."[8] This is an attempt to take account of those circumstances in which we have to adapt a personal maxim that we might previously have wished to be a universal law.[9] However, it is no more actological than Kant's categorical imperative because it assumes that "fundamental human goods" are somehow fixed and that "under no circumstances" can they be "violated." An actological deontological ethical theory ought not to make such assumptions.

Perhaps we should phrase an actological deontological theory as follows: that we should will that the reasons for our current behavior should be the reasons for everyone else's current behavior if they were in the same situation as ourselves. This might cover both a general presupposition that we ought not to lie, as we would wish everyone else to behave in that way; and it also covers those situations in which we would wish to lie and in which we might wish others to lie as well. It also recognizes the diversity of situations in which we might find ourselves, and the inevitable influence of changing circumstances on our actions. Unfortunately this new formulation, although it looks both actological and like a variant of a deontological ethical theory, is an entirely empty theory, because nobody will ever be in the same circumstances as ourselves.

Deontological ethical theory is also empty, as is Kant's categorical imperative, because neither of them offer anything specific in relation to our behavior. If we experience a decision as one that we might wish to be universalizable, or we wish the reasons for our current actions to be the reasons for the current behavior of everyone in the same situation, then we might be able to state that our decision and its related actions are ethical: but before the act, we could not have known that we would be able to decide that.

---

7. Torry, *A Modern Guide to Citizen's Basic Income*, 49.
8. Donagan, *The Theory of Morality*, 61.
9. Torry, *A Modern Guide to Citizen's Basic Income*, 49.

A MULTIDISCIPLINARY ACTOLOGY

The theory—whether Kant's categorical imperative, Donegan's version, or our formulation—is also empty in a third sense. Ethics are social as well as individual. Deontological ethical theory is framed entirely in relation to an individual's decision-making and actions, and only if we understand society to be a single undifferentiated organism could we ask whether it might wish its maxim to be a universal law, whether it would promote "fundamental human goods,"[10] or whether it would want the reasons for its current behavior to be the reasons for every other society's current behavior if they were in the same situation.

Thomas Scanlon has suggested a formulation that might apply both to an individual and to a society:

> an act is wrong if its performance under the circumstances would be disallowed by any system of rules for the general regulation of behaviour which no-one could reasonably reject as a basis for informed, unforced general agreement.[11]

This allows for maxims that we would not wish to universalize, and it is also intuitive because we do in practice attempt to justify our actions on grounds that others can accept or at least will not reject. But again we have a problem. This formulation is "a device for our mutual protection,"[12] and it neither secures positive benefit nor prescribes actions that we ought to take. As with other deontological ethical formulations, the theory tells us what we might have got wrong, or might be about to get wrong, but it does not tell us what to do nor how to construct the set of rules to which people might not object.[13] A further problem for us is that Scanlon's formulation is as static as the others: its criterion for ethical behavior is a set of rules which no-one could reasonably reject, which assumes either that the rules will not change, or that they will change only slightly and slowly, for only under those circumstances would it be possible to discover whether anyone might wish to reject them.

Perhaps the clue is in the name of this ethical theory: the name is from the Greek words *"deon,"* "duty," and *"logos,"* "reason." These are nouns that assume that duty and reason exist as beings. They are not verbs. We are struggling to discover an actological deontological ethical theory because it would be a contradiction in terms if we found one. We must look elsewhere.

---

10. Donagan, *The Theory of Morality*, 61.
11. Scanlon, "Contractualism and Utilitarianism," 110.
12. Scanlon, "Contractualism and Utilitarianism," 128.
13. Scanlon, "Contractualism and Utilitarianism," 128; Torry, *A Modern Guide to Citizen's Basic Income*, 50.

John Rawls

In his *A Theory of Justice*, John Rawls posits an "original position" in which "all have the same rights in the procedure for choosing principles." He envisages a "veil of ignorance" behind which members of society choose principles while not knowing which position they will hold in society.[14] The two principles that emerge from this argument are, firstly, "equality in the assignment of basic rights and duties," and secondly that

> social and economic inequalities, for example inequalities of wealth and authority, are just only if they result in compensating benefits for everyone, and in particular for the least advantaged members of society.[15]

Among the "basic rights" are "primary goods" such as "rights and liberties, opportunities and powers, income and wealth."[16]

Later in the book we find a different expression of Rawls' two principles:

> First: each person is to have an equal right to the most extensive basic liberty compatible with a similar liberty for others. Second: social and economic inequalities are to be arranged so that they are both (a) reasonably expected to be to everyone's advantage, and (b) attached to positions and offices open to all.[17]

And later still this last proviso is reformulated to require "conditions of fair equality of opportunity" in relation to "positions and offices."[18]

If we look back across all of the terms that Rawls employs, we find complexity everywhere. "Rights and duties" are socially constructed and so are diverse across time and space and across any society; our understanding of inequalities is always open to debate (Who is poorer: someone with a chronic disease but fascinating and fulfilling employment, or someone with no obvious health problems but tedious and meaningless employment?); it is impossible to decide who is the least advantaged member of society; different people might regard different goods as "primary"; liberty in relation to use of time and in relation to choice over the use of resources is incommensurable; it is impossible to compare different people's "advantage"; "positions and offices" are in limited supply and so cannot be open to all; "opportunity" is socially

---

14. Rawls, *A Theory of Justice*, 136–42.
15. Rawls, *A Theory of Justice*, 14–15.
16. Rawls, *A Theory of Justice*, 93–95.
17. Rawls, *A Theory of Justice*, 60.
18. Rawls, *A Theory of Justice*, 302.

constructed and is incommensurable between individuals; and in general each of us has our own preferences, and as our knowledge of each other is limited in the extreme, different people's preferences are incommensurable.[19] We experience a highly dynamic situation in which much is incalculable and uncertain[20] and in which we can only employ Rawls' principles if we understand them to represent dynamic and diverse realities: that is, actologically. If we *do* understand principles, society, the economy, wealth, authority, inequality, justice, benefits, advantage, rights, liberty, positions, offices, fairness, equality, and opportunity, as changing patterns of action, then we can continue to employ Rawls' principles of justice in a diverse and changing society; and because they will be understood as action in changing patterns we shall be able to regard them as as real as anything else.

Actions good in relation to their consequences

Consequentialism regards actions as good if their consequences are beneficial. There is a sense in which this is a particular kind of deontological theory. If we regard the performance of actions that benefit others to be a maxim that we have to wish to universalize because we would wish others' actions to benefit us, then deontological ethics requires us to achieve as much benefit for others as possible. To call the theory "consequentialist" is to focus on the benefit to others rather than on the maxim that we might wish to universalize.

A particular expression of consequentialism is John Stuart Mill's "utilitarianism," which requires us to seek the greatest happiness of the greatest number. "Actions are right in proportion as they tend to promote happiness. By happiness is intended pleasure, and the absence of pain."[21] Jerome Schneewind compares utilitarianism with deontological ethics:

> It cannot be the case that some factual property of acts makes them right, and that this entails that doing them must maximize goodness. It must rather be the case that bringing about the most good is what makes right acts right . . . the utilitarian principle is that the conduct which is objectively right is that which will produce the greater amount of happiness on the whole.[22]

Three main assumptions undergird utilitarian ethics: that we can know what makes other people happy; that we can know how much happiness other

19. Nozick, *The Normative Theory of Individual Choice*, 312.
20. Nozick, *The Normative Theory of Individual Choice*, 322.
21. Mill, *Utilitarianism*, 7.
22. Schneewind, *Sidgwick's Ethics and Victorian Moral Philosophy*, 308, 327.

people experience; and that we can know the consequences of our actions. As for the first and second assumptions: happiness is difficult to define, let alone to measure, so we cannot know what makes other people happy; we cannot know the intensity of the happiness that each source of happiness might offer to someone; and we cannot compare one person's happiness with another's: so there is no way of defining or of knowing the general level of happiness of a society.[23] As Bernard Williams formulates the difficulty: utilitarianism has "too few thoughts and feelings to match the world as it really is."[24] For instance: how could we decide whether a large increase in one individual's happiness in relation to their health could substitute for a smaller increase in another individual's happiness in relation to family relationships?

Just as difficult a problem is the fact that we cannot know the outcome of our actions. This is a problem that we face whenever we take action as an individual or as a society because it is not just our decisions and actions that determine the outcome of our decisions and actions: multiple other factors must be taken into account. To circumvent the impossible task of working out all possible outcome options and evaluating them, we develop heuristics: rules of thumb. We learn "by experience the tendencies of actions"[25] and so can construct "rules of morality."[26] Richard Hare calls by the name "act utilitarianism" a utilitarianism that attempts to operate without rules and so must evaluate separately for every action the societal level of happiness that would be generated and any harm that ought to be taken into account; and he calls "rule utilitarianism" a utilitarianism governed by heuristics or rules that might ensure a consistent approximation to maximum individual and social happiness.[27] Even if we conform our actions to a list of rules based on long experience of ethical and less ethical action—"regulative principles,"[28] and unrealizable ideals necessary as the "final dyke against relativism"[29]—there is no guarantee that our decisions will lead to greater overall happiness. We simply cannot predict the outcome; and we can even less predict the outcome of institutional activity. A former Vice-Chancellor of the University of Cambridge put it like this:

---

23. Hare, *Freedom and Reason*, 119–21.
24. Smart and Williams, *Utilitarianism*, 149.
25. Mill, *Utilitarianism*, 24.
26. Mill, *Utilitarianism*, 25.
27. Hare, *Freedom and Reason*, 130–36; Hare, *Moral Thinking*, 43.
28. Niebuhr, *The Godly and the Ungodly*, 64.
29. Niebuhr, *Christian Realism and Political Problems*, 164.

A MULTIDISCIPLINARY ACTOLOGY

> What we actually achieve is never wholly in our power to determine; it is influenced, in all manner of ways and degrees, by factors beyond our control. But the methods we use in pursuing our purposes are largely within our own power to choose and to determine. For what results from our actions we are only partly responsible; but for the means we decide to employ we carry the responsibility on our own shoulders.
>
> Again, the future . . . we can never clearly or certainly foresee, still less determine; but the methods we choose to use in seeking to mould the future are our own choice. These we can determine. And by these, very largely, we make or mar the world, and ourselves.[30]

What John Boys Smith is arguing for is deontological ethics, which has the distinct advantage that it had no need to calculate anything.[31]

Reinhold Niebuhr was a pastor in Detroit and his first major work was titled *Moral Man and Immoral Society*.[32] It claimed that when people with good intentions get together to carry out by good means a project with good ends, then the result inevitably ends up being tainted with evil. "The higher the aspirations rise the more do sinful pretensions accompany them."[33] Niebuhr quite rightly saw that individual ethics and social ethics have very little to do with each other.

> A sharp distinction must be drawn between the moral and social behavior of individuals and of social groups, national, racial and economic; and . . . this distinction justifies and necessitates political policies which a purely individualistic ethic must always find embarrassing.[34]

We shall know even less of the consequences of society's actions than we shall of the consequences of an individual's actions: and in both cases, given the difficulty of promising and achieving positive outcomes for individual and social ethical actions, we might do better to aim to avoid harmful activity than to pursue activity intended to create greater happiness but without knowing what the whole bundle of actual consequences might be. We might call this latter approach "negative utilitarianism" because it avoids activity that might increase unhappiness, although it still does not decide what decisions and actions might increase the general level of happiness. Similar to the "rule

---

30. Boys Smith, "Do Men Gather Grapes of Thorns, or Figs of Thistles? Matthew 7:6."
31. Torry, *A Modern Guide to Citizen's Basic Income*, 51–52.
32. Niebuhr, *Moral Man and Immoral Society*.
33. Niebuhr, *An Interpretation of Christian Ethics*, 96.
34. Niebuhr, *Moral Man and Immoral Society*, xi.

utilitarianism" that we have already discussed, a "rule negative utilitarianism" of the "strong" kind would understand as unethical any set of rules that reduced the happiness of just one member of society, and a "rule negative utilitarianism" of the "weak" kind would understand as unethical any set of rules that reduced the happiness of the least well off member of society.

"Act utilitarianism" is clearly actological as it deals with real human decisions and actions and real human happiness. However, we have found this basic utilitarianism to be infeasible because of the millions of minute calculations that would be required if anyone were to try to calculate accurately the levels of happiness of both individuals and institutions. More feasible is rule-based utilitarianism of both positive and negative varieties, but even though this might be easier to practice than act-based utilitarianism, it is less actological because it relies on rigid sets of rules.

Aristotle's good life

Aristotle understood that not everyone's happiness was the same, which meant that ethics was about how each individual was to "live well":[35] so "we are not investigating the nature of virtue for the sake of knowing what it is, but in order that we may become good."[36] It is the ethical individual who is in view here, rather than ethical actions, on the basis that an ethical individual's actions will be ethical.[37] The State's task was therefore to develop in citizens the wisdom and prudence required for a life of "action" characterized by

> what is the highest of all the goods that action can achieve . . . both the multitude and persons of refinement speak of it as Happiness, and conceive "the good life" or "doing well" to be the same thing.[38]

It isn't that we understand the virtues and then practice them: "the virtues . . . we acquire by first having actually practised them, just as we do the arts."[39] As Sarah Broadie summarizes Aristotle's purpose in the *Nichomachean Ethics*: "virtue has to be cultivated and happiness depends on that cultivation."[40] This ethical theory is already looking rather actological.

 35. Torry, *A Modern Guide to Citizen's Basic Income*, 54–55.
 36. Aristotle, *Nicomachean Ethics*, II, 1103b, 27–28.
 37. Aristotle, *Nichomachean Ethics*, I, 8; II, 3; II, 6; Broadie, *Ethics with Aristotle*, 3, 7, 50; Hutchinson, *Ethics*, 199–219.
 38. Aristotle, *Nichomachean Ethics*, I, 1095a, 15–19.
 39. Aristotle, *Nichomachean Ethics*, I, 1103a, 31–32.
 40. Broadie, *Ethics with Aristotle*, 50.

Foundationalist ethics

A further ethical theory is foundationalist ethics: the idea that ethics is based on something beyond itself—that is, it has a foundation of some kind: for instance, a single idea treated as an axiom, a set of human rights established by a multinational organization, or a religious tradition. For example, the concept of a gift can function either as an axiom in its own right or as an aspect of a religious tradition.[41] An example of the gift relationship treated as a stand-alone axiom is Richard Titmuss's employment of the idea in social policy. The example that he gives is blood donation.[42] The gift relationship is also an element of religious traditions—for instance, in the Christian Faith, Jesus tells his disciples: "You received without payment; give without payment";[43] and the concept of "grace," understood as unconditional generosity, is at the heart of the Christian understanding of God's relationship with us,[44] who "are now justified by his grace as a gift, through the redemption that is in Christ Jesus."[45]

As Thomas Nagel points out, a gift relationship depends on our recognition of another human being as a person like ourselves, which in turn relies on "the equivalent capacity to regard oneself as merely one individual among many."[46] As Nagel suggests, this looks rather like a categorical imperative,[47] which reveals the porous nature of boundaries between ethical theories and encourages us to look for boundary-crossing. For instance, utilitarianism relies on an obligation to seek the happiness or wellbeing of other people, which again looks like a categorical imperative and could also be an imperative related to a religious tradition, meaning that we are crossing boundaries between utilitarian, deontological, and foundationalist ethics. We only have to read Jean-Luc Marion's *Étant Donné*, "Being Given,"[48] and his other works, to find a philosopher employing the concept of the gift as both an expression of religious conviction and as a philosophical and ethical axiom, and so as both foundationalist and deontological. Now that our global society is best described as multifaith, we shall need to seek relationships between

---

41. Torry, *An Actology of the Given*.
42. Richard Titmuss, *The Gift Relationship*.
43. Matthew 10:8, NRSV.
44. Groves, *Grace*.
45. Romans 3:24, NRSV.
46. Nagel, *The Possibility of Altruism*, 1.
47. Nagel, *The Possibility of Altruism*, 90, 107, 127.
48. Marion, *Being Given*; Marion, *Étant Donné*.

grace—unconditional generosity—in a variety of religious traditions:[49] but whatever its foundationalist roots, it will also be found as an unfounded axiom, so wherever we find unconditionality as the foundation of ethical reasoning, we shall be studying both deontological and foundationalist ethics.[50]

Human beings are incommensurable

A problem that we have come up against in relation to deontological, utilitarian, foundationalist, and Aristotle's "good life" ethical theories, is that human beings are incommensurable. This is particularly a problem for utilitarian ethics, and also for the statesman who in Aristotle's scheme is responsible for ensuring that everyone can live a "good life." We are all different, and no individual can ever know the route to another's welfare or happiness. We might all need food and shelter if we are to survive, and if we are to thrive in society then we shall also need other needs to be met,[51] but beyond the most basic of needs our knowledge of the workings of other people's minds is slim, which is unfortunate, as underlying every ethical theory is an assumption that we can compare different people's desires and motivations. As Emmanuel Levinas puts it, the other person is "other,"[52] in the face of whom we have responsibility, but a responsibility that appears to be impossible to define in relation to our own or other people's motives, needs, and desires.[53] "Every person should be treated as an individual":[54] but in order to live in society at all, we have to assume a level of commonality between ourselves and other individuals, including commonality in relation to such needs as creative work and social interdependence.[55] Take the example of the UK's National Health Service: the way that it is supposed to work is that every individual should receive care in relation to their own unique needs, and everyone should be treated the same both in that sense and in the sense that nobody has to pay for their treatment

---

49. Phillips, *God B.C.*; Woodhead, et al., eds, *Religions in the Modern World*, 85, 187, 207.

50. Torry, *A Modern Guide to Citizen's Basic Income*, 56–59.

51. Dean, *Understanding Human Need*, second edition, 13–26, 47–70; Ferguson et al, *Rethinking Welfare*, 179–82.

52. Levinas, *Entre Nous*.

53. Lévinas, *Entre Nous*, 9–11, 111–12, 184–87.

54. Spicker, *Social Policy*, 25–26.

55. Dean, *Understanding Human Need*, 26; Torry, *A Modern Guide to Citizen's Basic Income*, 55–56.

in a hospital or for visits to a General Practitioner.[56] Thus both unconditionality and our incommensurability are satisfied.

ACTOLOGICAL ETHICAL THEORY

If reality is action in changing patterns, then not only is every person unique, but every person is different in every moment, the relationships between different people are different in every moment, and the relationship between every individual, the community in which they live, the society to which they belong, their environment, and the rest of the world, is different in every moment. Not only is the person "other," but they are a constantly changing other, and the responsibility of one person for another changes constantly. This poses some interesting problems for the ethical theories that we have discussed.

Any maxim that we might wish to be a universal law will first of all change all the time, because we do, and secondly the concept of a universal law becomes difficult to apply because any form of words in which we express it will relate differently to every individual, and every individual and every society will experience a different range of variants of the law: and so, for instance, the concept of a lie is problematized by the shifting boundary between truth and untruth (and where do we locate economy with the truth?), and every individual will have experienced a different set of situations and so will have different ideas as to what might count as valid exceptions to any law claiming to be universal.

In relation to consequentialism, our experienced utilities will change all the time, and the extent to which we can evaluate other individuals' utilities will also change constantly, so even though in a static context we might have felt able to compare one person's utilities with another's, in an actological context that becomes entirely impossible.

The foundations on which foundationalist ethical theories are founded are shifting foundations, so any ethical principles that we might derive from a religious or other tradition will change all the time. And so, for instance, the concept of a gift changes, both within cultures and between them, so to base an ethical theory on such a concept—or on any concept—becomes seriously problematic.

Aristotle's concept of a good life has always been difficult to apply, but it becomes impossible in an actological context. Such an idea changes constantly for any individual, so any hope that we might be able to understand what a good life might mean for someone else becomes forlorn in the extreme. I might be able to shape what I feel to be a good life at this particular time, but

---

56. Torry, "Primary care, the basic necessity," 377–84.

then myself, my circumstances, and my relationships will change, and that good life will be gone.

So is an actological ethics possible? It would appear that any validity that an ethical theory might possess will be fleeting: but that is not necessarily the case if we recognize that the theories might be truly actological: that is, we might be able to understand them as changing patterns of action. Interestingly, this would make them real in a way in which ethical theories in the context of an ontology cannot be.

If I espouse a foundationalist ethics, then I am setting out from my current understanding of a religious or ideological tradition to which I am committed and working out what that might imply for a particular decision with which I am faced at this time and in my current situation. The entire process is action in changing patterns: the religious or ideological tradition, my grasping of it, my entanglement with my context, and my connecting of my understanding of the religious or ideological tradition with the decisions that demand to be taken and then the actions that I perform. I might then connect back from my actions to my understanding of the religious or ideological tradition in order to justify the decisions that I have made and the actions that I have taken. All of this is action in changing patterns, and it is ethics, suggesting that an actological foundationalist ethics is entirely feasible.

Much the same will be true of deontological ethics. A maxim will be a changing pattern of action in my brain and either spoken or written. It will therefore change constantly: that is, every moment there will be a new maxim, and every maxim will be influenced by the changing patterns of action that constitute my context. At any moment I might experience multiple actual or potential maxims, and I might wish one or more of them to be a universal law: that is, I might wish the changing patterns of everyone's action to conform to one or more of my maxims. The probability that that could ever occur would be vanishingly small: but I might still wish that it could be so, and it is that that matters. Because deontological ethics is a process among the changing patterns of action that constitute my brain, and because my wishing that a particular maxim at a particular time might become a universal law does not require that it should do so, we can legitimately decide that an actological deontological ethics, like an actological foundationalist ethics, is entirely feasible.

Equally feasible is an actological ethics of the good life. What I might regard as a good life will change, as it will for everyone else, so in each moment I shall be able to decide what is a good life, and, as far as possible, aim to achieve it. As we change, and as our circumstances change, what we regard as a good life, and the extent to which we can achieve it, will evolve: but the decision to achieve a good life, for ourselves and for others, and the attempt to achieve it, will remain feasible, so such a "good life" ethics will be feasible.

Aristotle offered an additional formulation of the ethical life in terms of the development of virtues understood as means between extremes (for instance, courage, between cowardice and foolhardiness).

> The virtues . . . we acquire by first having actually practised them, just as we do the arts. We learn an art or craft by doing the things that we shall have to do when we have learnt it: for instance, men become builders by building houses, harpers by playing on the harp. Similarly we become just by doing just acts, temperate by doing temperate acts, brave by doing brave acts.[57]

Virtues are what we do, so they are inherently actological. How we understand virtues will change as both we and our circumstances change, but that does not need to prevent us from pursuing changing virtues—indeed, to pursue changing virtues is itself actological; and the fact that each of us will understand the virtues differently need not prevent us from pursuing them either, because it is our own understandings of the virtues that we would be attempting to develop. There is a sense in which Aristotle's virtues ethic is highly suited to an actological interpretation. He is encouraging his readers to develop their personalities in a virtuous direction: a process in which the changing patterns of action that constitute our minds evolve virtuous concepts and in which we then change the patterns of action that constitute who we are to conform to those concepts: and in which we continue to do that as the virtuous concepts continue to change.

We have found that foundationalist, deontological, and "good life" ethics can all be interpreted actologically. This is at least partly because these ethical theories set out from the individual's understanding of what is demanded of them: by a religious or ideological tradition, by a categorical imperative, or by an understanding of a good virtuous life. However, if I espouse a utilitarian ethics then I am attempting something rather different: the entanglement of the action in changing patterns that constitute my needs and desires with the action in changing patterns that constitute everyone else's, or at least with those of everyone relevant to the particular maximization in view: for instance, the maximization of the happiness of everyone in a particular community. Here we really are in the realm of the impossible. It is difficult enough to envisage how we might both know and evaluate the happiness, wellbeing, needs, and desires of everyone in a community if those are static variables: that is, if nothing changes. Given sufficient time, we might be able to test sets of individual and societal behaviors for their effects on every individual's wellbeing and happiness, and by that means to decide that a particular set of behaviors

---

57. Aristotle, *Nicomachean Ethics*, II, 1, 4: 1103b.

maximizes happiness and wellbeing across the whole community and is therefore to be counted as ethical. But that is not how things are. We change all the time, and so does everyone else, which means that the process needs to be run repeatedly, moment by moment, each time in a new context, and that on each occasion we might reach a new decision, and different actions might be ethical. This is simply infeasible. Admittedly utilitarianism is only one version of consequentialism, but the same will apply to other varieties: any consequences of our decisions and actions will entangle with the action in changing patterns of the rest of the cosmos; our decisions and actions will change all the time, so consequences will change all the time; any attempt at maximization of anything will require all of the consequences of our decisions and actions to be known from moment to moment, and to be evaluated from moment to moment, and for the desired factor to be maximized from moment to moment. Again we are in the realm of the impossible.

CONCLUSION

We began this chapter with a definition of ethics from the Oxford English Dictionary: "The branch of knowledge or study dealing with moral principles."[58] In the light of this chapter, and in pursuit of actological ethical theory, we might choose to amend it: "The branch of knowledge or study dealing with moral action": for ethics is what we do, and not simply what we think.

As we have also discovered in this chapter, all of the ethical theories that we have studied, apart from consequentialism, and particularly its utilitarian version, can be understood actologically. As Michael Stocker suggests,

> plurality and conflict are absolutely commonplace and generally unproblematic features of our everyday choice and action. They had thus better not be a bar to sound judgement, resolute informed action, and a sound and rational ethics.[59]

Life is made up of "disparate and incommensurable values and emotions,"[60] and we have no need to commit ourselves to a single ethical theory to the exclusion of others.[61] An actological ethical theory will be necessarily diverse, will change constantly, and will include changing elements of the theories that we have discussed, and of other theories besides. This is all as we would expect.

58. Oxford English Dictionary.
59. Stocker, *Plural and Conflicting Values*, 2.
60. Stocker, *Plural and Conflicting Values*, 3.
61. Brandt, *A Theory of the Good and the Right*, 286.

Chapter 4

Actological mathematics

Mathematics: the science of space, number, quantity, and arrangement, whose methods involve logical reasoning and usually the use of symbolic notation, and which includes geometry, arithmetic, algebra, and analysis; mathematical operations or calculations.[1]

INTRODUCTION

Any science requires clear and agreed definitions consistently applied, as only then will all of its practitioners be researching the same things, and only then will they be able to communicate with each other. So this chapter will begin by attempting to define numbers. We shall then go on to study how a number of philosophers have understood the role of mathematics before discussing what an actological mathematics might look like.

DEFINITIONS

In their *Principia Mathematica* Alfred North Whitehead and Bertrand Russell attempted to define numbers as members of classes. "We define 1 as the class of all unit classes . . . In like manner, we . . . define 2 as the class of all couples,"[2] with ordered couples generating the ordinal number 2 and unordered couples

---

1. Oxford English Dictionary.
2. Whitehead and Russell, *Principia Mathematica*, volume I, 345.

the cardinal number 2.[3] As "1" is the name of the class of all classes with one member, and that class has multiple members, it is clearly not a member of itself; the same is true of the class denoted "2"; and so on. This is intuitive, but it leaves us with ambiguities. Take a carrot that divides in two: a common phenomenon. It has two roots, but one head. Is it one carrot or two? Does it belong in the class "1" or the class "2"? In a definition that relies on the concept of a class, this matters. And there is also something problematic about a class of which we cannot know every member, which is clearly the case with the classes "1," "2," and so on.

In the section of Chapter 1 that discusses definitions, we recognized that we can create definitions—sets of words that give what we call the meaning of a word—by studying usage, by listing characteristics, by relying on some recognized authority, or by choosing a prototype and comparing things with it. So where should we now look for a definition of numbers? In Chapter 1 we encountered Wittgenstein's discussion of how language works in which he envisages a shopkeeper responding to a request for "five red apples": "But what is the meaning of the word 'five'?—No such thing was in question here, only how the word 'five' is used."[4] Language is here action in changing patterns. The customer speaks: that is, they make the air vibrate in a changing pattern. The shopkeeper's brain works on the vibrations, and we then see them pick up five red apples and hand them to the customer. In this context the word "five" means an aspect of an event: a shopkeeper counting out five apples. Let us suppose that someone else in the shop is asked to count out five oranges. They might watch the shopkeeper and match the actions of their hand to the actions of the shopkeeper's hand. They are treating the shopkeeper's counting of five apples as a prototype: and once we have more than one usage of a word we can ask about family resemblances—for instance, between the counting of the apples, the counting of the oranges, and the counting of the fingers on the shopkeeper's hand—and we can then compare other countings of things with the developing prototype and ascribe the number "five" to those as well. The separate countings that we compare with the prototype are events, and so are action in patterns with a family resemblance that we might designate "five": but that is all it is, a resemblance. There must then be some doubt as to whether we can legitimately locate these countings into a class that we label "five," as first of all the class would be of events unlike each other in many ways, and secondly the class would not be action in changing patterns and so would not be real in any sense. All the family resemblance would be would be pure pattern that we might represent by a diagram:

3. Whitehead and Russell, *Principia Mathematica*, volume I, 376.
4. Wittgenstein, *Philosophische Untersuchungen / Philosophical Investigations*, §1, 2.

A MULTIDISCIPLINARY ACTOLOGY

FIGURE 1

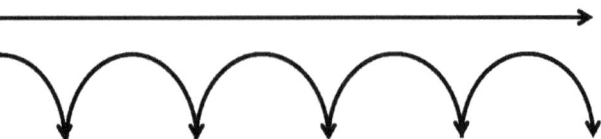

Diagrammatic representation of counting five apples.

Like any other text, such pure pattern would be unreal in actological terms, and would only affect reality when a reader read the text "five" and the pure pattern of the text impacted the action in changing patterns that constituted the reader: for instance, if they then counted out five bananas and added another example to the disparate collection of fivesomes.

Let us suppose that we now do define a class as the collection of changing patterns of action for which we have used the word "five" in relation to their family resemblance to the prototype "counting out of five apples." And now let us label "four" a class in which we place changing patterns of action that bear a family resemblance to a prototype changing pattern of action that we might label "counting four apples" and that we might represent by another diagram:

FIGURE 2

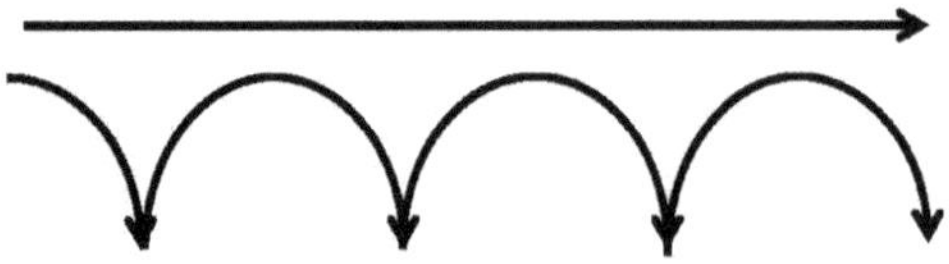

Diagrammatic representation of counting four apples.

We might similarly establish classes labelled "one," "two," "three," "six," and so on. We might then notice that "counting one apple" and immediately "counting four apples" looks remarkably like "counting five apples": so we write "1 + 4 = 5": and we go on to create an entire science of numbers using these symbols. There is no reality here, as all we have is pure pattern without any action: but as soon as our minds engage with the text "1 + 4 = 5" we can envisage the three different countings of apples and the relationship between them and we can ascribe a subsidiary reality to the mathematical symbols and to equations constructed with them.[5] We have not defined numbers logically, as Russell and Whitehead had: we have defined them in relation to changing

5. Torry, *An Actological Metaphysic*, 91–92.

patterns of action that bear family resemblances to a prototype and to each other. A divided carrot is no longer a problem. If we count the divided part with two roots, there are two carrots; and if we count the head there is one carrot. Of we decide to touch the head and then each of the two divided parts, we might decide that there are three carrots.

Of course, most mathematics is conducted entirely in the realm of symbols, many of which do not bear an obvious family resemblance to the counting of apples. A particularly clear example is a number that we represent by the symbol i, which means the square root of -1, which cannot represent the real counting of real apples. It is an "imaginary number." However, if we were to employ analogy, then we could label an apple i and write "$i + 4i = 5i$": again pure pattern, but with a new family resemblance to "$1 + 4 = 5$." And so by working with symbols that represent pure pattern, and by employing analogy, we can go on building the superstructure that we call mathematics.

PATTERNS OF ACTION

Numbers might look like universals—that is, having some reality apart from the particular instances in which counting occurs—but they are not: they are always patterns abstracted from the action in patterns that constitute the cosmos, including ourselves. They are abstracted phenomena that rely on actual phenomena for any reality that we might ascribe to them. And once we are creating relationships between numbers, we are in the realm of pure pattern, and so in the field of phenomena abstracted from abstracted phenomena, and two degrees away from actual phenomena. But it is that tenuous connection to actual phenomena that invites and enables the use of mathematics as a predictor. The equation "$4 + 1 = 5$" is abstracted from the abstracted numbers 4, 1, and 5, and it predicts that if I count four apples and then 1 apple then I shall have counted five apples. Every such counting will be different, but they will share family resemblances, and it is on those that depend our ability to relate "$4 + 1 = 5$" to more than one pattern of action—to more than one combination of countings—and so to regard it as a natural law: always with the recognition, of course, that natural laws are always of only local and temporary application.[6]

Because it is actual phenomena that are at the root of our entire discussion of numbers, we must be ready for complexities. For instance, if the shopkeeper counts four apples, puts one back, and then counts two apples, how many apples have been counted? Five? Six? Because we are discussing action in changing patterns we are not discussing unchanging universals, so the

---

6. Cartwright, *The Dappled World*.

meanings of the symbol-represented patterns can change. Does "five" mean the number of counting actions or the number of apples that the customer carries out of the shop? In actological terms, probably the former.

To take another example of abstracted phenomena: If we draw three non-parallel lines on a piece of paper then we call the area surrounded by all three of them a triangle. We might draw several of these. On another sheet of paper we might draw a straight line and then use a pair of compasses to draw a line perpendicular to it. We define the angle between the line and the perpendicular a right angle, and if we use a protractor then we might find that the right angle is approximately ninety degrees and that the triangle's angles add up to approximately one hundred and eighty degrees: two right angles. By drawing additional lines we can develop a proof that the angles of the triangle must add up to two right angles, and we can then generalize and suggest a rule that the angles of any triangle will always add up to two right angles: until we find that the angles of a triangle drawn on a curved surface don't, and we have to invent new rules.

Once we have abstracted ideas from phenomena, and have left the phenomena behind, we are playing games: not language games, but symbol games. When I play with abstracted patterns in this way I might represent them by drawing shapes, or by writing equations, or by using words: but any reality that all of this possesses continues to rely on the phenomena from which the ideas were abstracted.[7] For instance, we might prove Pythagoras's theorem that if the three sides of a right-angled triangle are a, b, and c, with c the longest side, then $a^2 + b^2 = c^2$. We might test the result on actual triangles: but neither the proof nor the test will be able to assure us that the result would hold universally. All we can say is that as far as we know, if the three sides of a right-angled triangle on a flat surface are a, b, and c, with c the longest side, then $a^2 + b^2 = c^2$: at least here and now.

All of mathematics, like numbers, is the crystallization of patterns of action: that is, patterns of action stripped of their action. So, for instance, in a version of the Chinese *Nine Chapters on the Mathematical Art*, written by Liu Hui during the third century CE, we find a method for approximating the value of π: the ratio of the circumference of a circle to its diameter. As we increase the number of sides of a polygon it increasingly resembles a circle. We can measure the circumference of a polygon (it is made up of identical isosceles triangles). The number of sides of the polygon multiplied by the length of the short side of the triangle and divided by the length of the long side gives an approximation of the value of π:[8] so increasing the number of sides

---

7. Torry, *An Actological Metaphysic*, 92.
8. Kitagawa and Revell, *The Secret Lives of Numbers*, 31–33.

ACTOLOGICAL MATHEMATICS

of the polygon enables us to approach the true value of π from below. We'll never reach it, but we shall get closer and closer to it. Such a calculation is a process of potentially infinite length as we increase the number of sides of the polygon: it is a changing pattern of action that delivers a changing value. There is genuine pattern, genuine change, and genuine action. It is actological. And once we have ceased the process, a number has been discovered: pure pattern that we have abstracted from a process of action in changing patterns.

We can discern the same process when we study the differential calculus. As two points on a curve approach each other, the straight line between them, if extended, increasingly approximates to a tangent to the curve, and the slope of the line to the slope of the curve. In terms of a graph with y on the vertical axis, and x on the horizontal axis, we represent the slope of the line, and therefore of the curve, by dy/dx, and by calculating that from the equation for the curve we can determine the slope of the curve for any value of x. Once we have left behind the process and are employing the resulting equation, we are in the realm of pure pattern without action. The same is true of the integral calculus which calculates the area under a curve by adding together rectangles the width of each of which approaches zero, and the number of which approaches infinity. Again the calculation might be pure pattern without action, but it is based on a process whereby the widths of rectangles approach zero, and the quantity of them approaches infinity.[9]

Only within an actology can all of this be understood, because the concept of the "limit" that calculus requires—that is, that the difference between two values tends towards zero, but never reaches it—means that no understanding of mathematics in terms of states and beings can provide a basis for calculus. Only changing patterns of action will suffice.[10] But once we are speaking what we might call the calculus language, or playing the calculus game, we find that the mathematical equations, the patterns that we call mathematics, might bear family resemblances to real-world action in changing patterns: for instance, to events such as the acceleration of an object dropped from a tower. Similarly, a set of symbols constructed by Paul Dirac exhibits a family likeness to the action in patterns that we call electrons.[11] Both the relationship between calculus equations and an accelerating object, and the relationship between Dirac's equations and the behavior of electrons, are examples of a more general relationship proposed by Dirac when he looked forward to "every branch of pure mathematics having its physical application."[12] Mathematics is always

9. Kitagawa and Revell, *The Secret Lives of Numbers*, 118–38.

10. Torry, *An Actological Metaphysic*, 92–93.

11. Farmelo, *The Strangest Man*, 142.

12. Dirac, "The Relation Between Mathematics and Physics," part II, 122–29; Farmelo, *The Strangest Man*, 301; Torry, *An Actological Metaphysic*, 93.

patterns abstracted from action in changing patterns, and potentially returns to that when the pure patterns by which it is constituted meet the action in patterns of the cosmos.

CONTINENTAL PHILOSOPHERS ON MATHEMATICS

We have already discussed Alfred North Whitehead's and Bertrand Russell's contribution to our understanding of numbers, and we have also found in Ludwig Wittgenstein's philosophy a means of understanding them. Whether the Austrian Wittgenstein counts as a continental philosopher is a matter for debate, but here we shall be engaging with a few philosophers who were indubitably continental.

Edmund Husserl

It is from Edmund Husserl that we have abstracted the concept of "abstracted" phenomena. According to Husserl, we abstract from actual phenomena such givens as space, time, logic, and mathematics, and because they exist in the mind as phenomena they are as much phenomena as the phenomena from which they are abstracted: for instance, a shopkeeper counting five apples.

> Phenomenology ... lays bare the "sources" from which the basic concepts and ideal laws of *pure* logic "flow," and back to which they must once more be traced, so as to give them all the "clearness and distinctness" needed for an understanding, and for an epistemological critique, of pure logic.[13]

We experience logic and mathematics: they appear to us, so they are phenomena given birth by phenomena.[14]

> We are concerned with a *phenomenological origin* ... we are concerned with *insight into the essence* of the concepts involved, looking methodologically to the fixation of unambiguous, sharply distinct verbal meanings.[15]

The first part of this passage recognizes that numbers and other mathematical concepts are phenomena in the mind that are abstracted from other phenomena, but the second part veers into a more Platonic and universalist

13. Husserl, *Logical Investigations*, I, §1, 166.
14. Torry, *An Actology of the Given*, 23.
15. Husserl, *Logical Investigations*, §67, 153–54.

understanding of mathematics of which Husserl spends much of his *Philosophical Investigations* attempting to convince us. In that context number is an

> ideal form-series, which is absolutely one in the sense of arithmetic, in whatever mental act it may be individuated for us in an intuitively constituted collective, a species which is accordingly untouched by the contingency, temporality and transience of our mental acts. Acts of counting arise and pass away and cannot be meaningfully mentioned in the same breath as numbers.[16]

This is to treat numbers as universals: as Platonic Forms that exist in some realm of reality in which they are beings that never change. They are "abstractly apprehended universals."[17] However, what we actually experience as phenomena are not universals, but changing patterns of action in our brains, and it is difficult to see how we might travel conceptually from an individual's contingent mind-constructed insights to objective exterior mathematics and logic.[18] Phenomena abstracted from actual phenomena is as far as we can get along that road, and any sense of objective universality has to be based on each of us making similar abstractions from actual phenomena and then learning to employ mathematical symbols as members of mathematical communities.

To understand mathematical concepts as action in changing patterns in the brain that relate to action in changing patterns in the world around us is to understand mathematics actologically rather than ontologically. Perhaps what we might be able to say about numbers as universals is that any ideal and objective-seeming mathematics is a bit like a mathematical limit: it is a theoretical limit that is pure pattern and that we might choose to read in much the same way as we read a text. It is the action in changing patterns that constitute our minds that access the pure pattern of such a mathematical text and enable it to influence the changing patterns of action that constitute ourselves and the world around us. Husserl's phenomenology, consistently practiced, would recommend an actology, and an actology would provide a useful basis for a consistent Husserlian phenomenology.[19] Any understanding of numbers as universals would then be an extrapolation of our experience of numbers as counting into the limit case of abstracted phenomena that we might understand as the names of classes of different countings. As Husserl himself

---

16. Husserl, *Logical Investigations*, 8, §46, 110.
17. Husserl, *Logical Investigations*, I, §2, 167.
18. Torry, *An Actology of the Given*, 174–75.
19. Torry, *An Actological Metaphysic*, 27.

suggests, there really is "an unbridgeable difference between sciences of the ideal and sciences of the real."[20]

Do we have to choose between treating logic, mathematics, theories and so on as contingent mind-dependent entities accessed via phenomena and not significantly different from other phenomena, and regarding mathematics and logic as floating free from the real world? Perhaps not if what is "given" is both phenomena that appear to be ordered mathematically and a universalist objective mathematics.[21] Perhaps numbers and mathematical concepts and equations can be given adequately as indubitable,[22] and might at the same time be understood as real-world phenomena via objects and other phenomena.[23] And perhaps we do experience the phenomenon of mathematics as a given universal: as a text with which the action in changing patterns that constitutes our minds engages. Our minds are where the gulf between the ideal and the real is bridged. And all of it is given: ideal mathematics, ideal logic, and the action in changing patterns of the real universe.[24]

Husserl's argument has led to diverse kinds of givenness: a "given world";[25] givenness of the *cogitatio* (what is thought); "the *cogitatio re-lived in a fresh memory*"; "the *unity of appearances* persisting in the phenomenal stream"; "the *change* in such a unity"; "the *thing* in 'outer' perception"; "the different forms of imagination and recollection"; "manifold *perceptions* and other kinds of *representations* that are synthetically unified in corresponding connections"; the "experienced Other, given to me in straightforward consciousness";[26] "*universality*"; logic; and mathematics.[27] But there remains a question as to whether the logic and mathematics are in any sense real unless immediately abstracted from real-world action in changing patterns.

Jean-Luc Marion

In his book *Étant Donné* (*Being Given*) Jean-Luc Marion introduces the concept of a "saturated phenomenon": an idea that he develops in detail in *Du*

---

20. Husserl, *Logical Investigations*, 8, §48, 113.
21. Torry, *An Actology of the Given*, 175.
22. Berghofer, "Husserl's Conception of Experiential Justification," 168.
23. Husserl, *Philosophy of Arithmetic*, 493; Torry, *An Actology of the Given*, 24.
24. Torry, *An Actology of the Given*, 175–76.
25. Husserl, *Cartesian Meditations*, 82.
26. Husserl, *Cartesian Meditations*, 90.
27. Husserl, *The Idea of Phenomenology*, 54. Italics in the original; Torry, *An Actology of the Given*, 26.

ACTOLOGICAL MATHEMATICS

Surcroit (In Excess). Immanuel Kant believed that phenomena conform to categories in the human mind, but in Marion's view this restricts "phenomenal autonomy."[28] If phenomena are "given," then some of them will be "in excess" of what the categories might construct,[29] and Marion defines them as "saturated." A consequence is that "the saturated phenomenon contradicts the subjective conditions of experience precisely in that it does not admit constitution as an object":[30] so "this phenomenological extremity" that "exceeds what comes forward" is a "paradox" in which the self is constituted by the phenomenon rather than vice versa.[31] Not only does the saturated phenomenon exceed what Kant's categories might construct and therefore control: it cannot be intended or constituted by our consciousness,[32] nor can it be conditioned by any horizon. We are here well beyond Husserl's understanding of a phenomenon.[33] In the saturated phenomenon

> intuition always submerges the expectation of the intention, in which givenness not only entirely invests manifestation but, surpassing it, modifies its common characteristics.[34]

Marion suggests that time is "given" and so is a saturated phenomenon, which means that some saturated phenomena are not only autonomous of our mind's categories: they are also autonomous of our intuition.[35] In relation to the subject of this chapter: In *Being Given* Marion suggests that mathematics is a "poor" phenomenon because it implies certainty and is therefore characterized by a "deficit of givenness":[36] that is, it is not an autonomous phenomenon but is to be found in the mind's categories, in consciousness, and in intuition. However, there would be another way of looking at it. In the phenomenon of the shopkeeper's counting of apples, if the number five is given to us, then it is *given*. In an actological context in which the number five is pure pattern abstracted from a number of counting events, five is given through those events. We might then internalize it in our minds, but that is not where it started, so it is neither a Kantian category nor the result of consciousness, because

---

28. Marion, *Being Given*, 213.
29. Marion, *Being Given*, 199.
30. Marion, *Being Given*, 214.
31. Marion, *Being Given*, 216.
32. Marion, *Being Given*, 218.
33. Husserl, *Ideas pertaining to a pure phenomenology*, 44 (§24); Torry, *An Actology of the Given*, 80–81.
34. Marion, *Being Given*, 225.
35. Marion, *Being Given*, 245.
36. Marion, *Being Given*, 225.

although our minds might have abstracted it from phenomena, it was given to be abstracted. It would be as legitimate to understand five as a saturated phenomenon as to call it a "poor" one.[37]

All is given: time, space, action, action in changing patterns, logic, and mathematics. They are saturated phenomena, are abstracted from phenomena, and characterize phenomena, and although we might treat them as somehow ideal—as universals, Platonic Forms, objects in which we participate, and so on—we can never decide that question. What we can say is that they are given as abstracted phenomena that become phenomena in our brains that then become the means by which we appropriate other phenomena. And all of it is action in changing patterns, which suggests that all of it can and should be understood in terms of an actology.[38]

Gaston Bachelard

A very different perspective is offered by Gaston Bachelard on the basis of a study of the role of mathematics in scientific advances. Because it is the relationship between mathematics and science that interested Bachelard, this section could have been in the next chapter: but because of the priority that he gave to mathematics, the reader will find it here.

Because "nothing is given. Everything is constructed,"[39] we must discard "everyday" thinking about "substance," particles, and so on, and develop a "total reorganization of the system of knowledge" characterized by "dynamic ways of thinking that escape from certainty and unity" and directed towards "specifying, rectifying, diversifying."[40] The process is always the same: "epistemological obstacles" such as unexpected experimental results, changes in the context, and so on, lead to a search for new mathematics; new mathematics is discovered; on that basis "epistemological acts" generate new theories; on the same basis new experimental methods test the theories; and then the process starts again as new epistemological obstacles lead to "better questions," a search for new mathematics, and so on.[41]

> Through technical progress, the reality studied by the scholar changes appearance, thus losing that character of permanence

37. Torry, *An Actology of the Given*, 186.
38. Torry, *An Actological Metaphysic*, 36–37.
39. Bachelard, "The Idea of the Epistemological Obstacle," 25.
40. Bachelard, "The Idea of the Epistemological Obstacle," 26.
41. Bachelard, "The Idea of the Epistemological Obstacle," 26, 30; Kotowicz, *Gaston Bachelard*, 47.

ACTOLOGICAL MATHEMATICS

which forms the basis of philosophical realism. For example "the reality of electricity" of the nineteenth century is very different from "the reality of electricity" of the eighteenth.[42]

Scientific change always has the same structure: the same pattern of action. "Rectification,"[43] which means "critique," is not a particular event but a continuous process in which error "gives rise to more precise tasks and drives knowledge on . . . to make a whole:"[44] a "whole" that remains "a limit that is never reached."[45] Bachelard gives the example of the "rectifications" that led to scientists understanding substance as structured energy, and so to the development of the periodic table and the discovery of the new elements needed to fill the theoretical gaps.[46] Here everything is action in an "open . . . field of action":[47] "As thinking has no means to stop its own minimal becoming, it can no longer measure the vertiginous and multiple becoming of atoms."[48]

Bachelard is clear that new mathematics is always at the heart of scientific change, and it sometimes looks as if physics is simply applied mathematics.[49] For instance, Albert Einstein found new geometries useful as he developed his theory of General Relativity: but it is not always clear whether such new mathematics is invented or discovered, nor whether it is understood before the scientific change takes place or during the process of change. Once new mathematics has generated new theories, they are then tested by experiments that are again generated by the new mathematics as well as by processes of scientific change, so the experiments are "materialized theories":[50] and the priority that Bachelard gives to mathematics in the whole process means that science is of a "wholly mathematical constructivist nature."[51] In such a context, the mathematics is the originator and so is "noumenal":[52] a somewhat

---

42. Bachelard, "Le Philosophie Dialoguée," 18: Par les progrès techniques, la réalité étudiée par le savant change d'aspect, perdant ainsi ce caractère de permanence qui fond le réalisme philosophique. Par exemple «la réalité électrique» au dix-neuvième siècle est bien différente de «la réalité électrique» au dix-huitième.
43. Bachelard, "Objectivity and Rectification," 243.
44. Bachelard, "Objectivity and Rectification," 249.
45. Bachelard, "Objectivity and Rectification," 252.
46. Bachelard, *The Formation of the Scientific Mind*, 61–65; Kotowicz, *Gaston Bachelard*, 61–65.
47. Bachelard, "Objectivity and Rectification," 254.
48. Bachelard, "Objectivity and Rectification," 257.
49. Tiles, "Technology, Science, and Inexact Knowledge," 24.
50. Castelao-Lawless, "Phenomenotechnique in Historical Perspective," 44, 50, 57.
51. McArthur, "Why Bachelard is not a Scientific Realist," 172.
52. Bachelard, "Noumenon and Microphysics," 79, 83.

different use of the word "noumenon" from Immanuel Kant's, for whom a "noumenon" was the inaccessible reality of which we only experience accessible "phenomena." For Bachelard, "new phenomena" are "made up . . . from scratch. . . . In the beginning was the Relation, and that is why mathematics governs reality";[53] and because it is mathematics that determines both theory and experiment, and therefore reality, there is no need for a prior ontology.[54] "Complementary realities"[55] can emerge in multiple domains and with multiple possibilities for explanation in relation to the "essentially mathematical . . . hidden world which modern physics describes."[56] It is no longer a problem that we can discover no overall theory to explain the behavior of both gravity and electromagnetic waves; and neither is it a problem that multiple inconsistent theories can describe the same aspects of reality.

> In the unknown world of the atom, could there be a kind of fusion between the act and the being, or between the wave and the corpuscle?[57]

Just as science evolves and delivers no universal, eternal, or necessary laws, but only local and contingent ones, mathematics evolves—for instance, Riemannian geometry can relate to curved surfaces, whereas Euclidean geometry can only relate to flat planes. Once any particular mathematics is discovered or invented it becomes necessary, at least in relation to the time and place in which it was invented or discovered: but the "structure of the noumenon" can change,[58] and

> a mathematician can be led—through experiments as well as through reason—to start new constructions based on both a novel axiomatic and a new noumenal intuition. . . . it is through similar steps that the mathematician will change his axioms of mathematics and the physicist will change his operational definitions.[59]

Just as there are no universal or eternal natural laws, so there is no universal or eternal mathematics:[60] change and diversity are ubiquitous.[61] It is no

53. Bachelard, "Noumenon and Microphysics," 80–81.
54. Kotowicz, *Gaston Bachelard*, 71–72; Privitera, *Problems of Style*, 11–13.
55. Bachelard, "Noumenon and Microphysics," 76.
56. Bachelard, "Noumenon and Microphysics," 80.
57. Bachelard, "Noumenon and Microphysics," 76.
58. Bachelard, "Noumenon and Microphysics," 83.
59. Bachelard, "Noumenon and Microphysics," 81–82.
60. Cartwright, *The Dappled World*.
61. Privitera, *Problems of Style*, 13–14.

surprise to find that Thomas Kuhn's theory of the paradigm shift[62] was influenced by Bachelard.[63] The difference is that for Kuhn the entire process is contingent, whereas for Bachelard it is always mathematics that precedes new theory, so within the process of scientific change there is a non-contingency, even if the process by which the new mathematics is discovered or invented is contingent. In practice, scientific change can begin anywhere in the process: in new mathematics, in an unexpected experimental result, in the discovery of a logical problem with a theory, or in a new understanding of the origin of the universe. To argue that mathematics fulfils a privileged role is itself a contingent choice. As Lee Smolin points out:

> Mathematics is one language of science, and it is a powerful and important method. But its application to science is based on an identification between results of mathematical calculations and experimental results, and since the experiments take place outside mathematics, in the real world, the link between the two must be stated in ordinary language. Mathematics is a great tool, but the ultimate governing language of science is language.[64]

There might be a certain stability about a scientific process normally comprised of mathematics, theory, and experiment, and that constantly "rectifies" knowledge, but that stability will itself constantly change, and it might not always include mathematics. Science is a "working phenomenology,"[65] and is never access to noumena existing independently of our discovery of them, so presumably the same has to be said of mathematics: and because Bachelard does in fact understand the importance of the imagination, he has to recognize that mathematics is not the only place that scientific change can begin:

> Contrary to a universe where masses are stable, where the events are lazy and chained up, imagine a world that is multiple, discontinuous and of a perfect mobility, without friction and kinetic wear. Just make sure that all this is rationally possible, that is that no intimate contradiction slips into your first suppositions. Make also sure that nothing superfluous is added, in other words, that the system of postulates is complete and close[d]. Once these preliminaries are established, close your eyes on the real and entrust

---

62. Kuhn, "A Function for Thought Experiments," 6, 26; Kuhn, *The Structure of Scientific Revolutions*.
63. Simons, "The Many Encounters of Thomas Kuhn and French Epistemology."
64. Smolin, *Time Reborn*, 247.
65. Bachelard, "Noumenon and Microphysics," 77.

yourself to intellectual intuitions. That way you will construct a rational world and you will produce unknown phenomena.[66]

Whilst having relevant mathematics available might always assist scientists to develop and consolidate new understandings of how things work, it is often imaginative leaps that have inspired new paradigms and theories and that have then inspired a search for appropriate mathematics. Whether mathematics is contingent or eternal and unchanging is not here in question, as what matters is the role of mathematics in the dynamic process of scientific change.[67]

Mary Tiles describes science as "something dynamic, something in process, not finalized," so any description of it must be "a multidimensional portrayal of the dynamics of scientific progress."[68] Knowledge is always "incomplete" and "approximate," rather than an approximation to knowledge,[69] so everything about the scientific method and its discoveries is characterized by change, and often radical change, and that change must surely include the role of mathematics in the scientific process.[70] It might be a paradox that what does not change is the ubiquity of change, but what Bachelard has helped us to understand is that however much we might wish the process of change to have some kind of still center, whether mathematics or something else, there is not one. Everything is contingent, including both mathematics itself and its role in the process of scientific change.

MATHEMATICAL LAWS

In the next chapter we shall be asking questions about the natural laws that we deduce from correlations between phenomena. We might be tempted to treat them as universal and eternal laws whereas in reality they are local and contingent temporary stabilities.[71] Because of the complexity of the cosmos we create models to enable us to relate to it, and those models evolve as new discoveries force them to change. Given our actological understanding of reality, any models that we develop today will have to have action, change, and diversity at their heart rather than beings, the unchanging, and the unitary.

---

66. Bachelard, *Les Intuitions Atomistiques*, 150–51, quoted in Kotowicz, *Gaston Bachelard*, 173–74.
67. Kotowicz, *Gaston Bachelard*, 181.
68. Tiles, "Technology, Science, and Inexact Knowledge," 158, 160.
69. Tiles, "Technology, Science, and Inexact Knowledge," 171, 161–63.
70. Tiles, "Technology, Science, and Inexact Knowledge," 160; Torry, *An Actology of the Given*, 176–81.
71. Cartwright, *The Dappled World*.

However, the world exhibits stabilities as well as change—relatively stable patterns as well as changing patterns: so even though our models might only apply in particular localities and particular periods of time, we can still develop and employ models that represent relatively stable situations. For instance, $E = mc^2$—where E is energy, m is mass, and c is the speed of light—is a useful statement of a stability for which we have evidence: but it is only a local approximation that might cease to hold and that might not hold in a different universe or in a different area of this one. Space changes, time changes, energy changes, and mass changes, so $E = mc^2$ might represent a particular case, with the more general case being represented by equations waiting to be discovered, just as Newton's equations for motion represented a particular case and Einstein's a more general one. Change might be slow, and laws of nature might remain stable over long periods of time, and during those periods we might be able to express them mathematically:[72] the pure pattern of mathematics expressing the temporary and local pattern into which action has fallen.[73] And because patterns of action can be fairly stable for long periods of time we can sometimes predict future phenomena with a fair degree of accuracy: but that accuracy will never be complete, because any laws will always be approximate, local, and contingent.[74]

Is there any reason to think that mathematics and logic are any different? Might mathematics and logic be different elsewhere and at different times? After all, mathematics is pure pattern abstracted or crystallized from action in changing patterns,[75] so if the changing patterns of action were to be different then the pure patterns represented by mathematical symbols and equations would also be different. As Leemon McHenry puts it,

> Our cosmic epoch emerged from the disintegration of its predecessor epoch, and another epoch will emerge from the disintegration of our epoch, perhaps at the moment cosmologists call "the omega point" at the conclusion of "the big crunch" or at the rebounding initiating cycle of expansion. A new cosmic epoch emerges, like the phoenix from the ashes, from the collapse of its predecessor.[76]

---

72. Penrose, *The Road to Reality*.
73. Penrose, *The Road to Reality*.
74. Torry, *An Actological Metaphysic*, 69–70.
75. Torry, *An Actological Metaphysic*, 86.
76. McHenry, *The Event University*, 73.

CONCLUSIONS

It would appear likely that logical and mathematical laws would be consistent across our social system, across our galaxy, and across our universe, but there is no reason to think that mathematics and logic would work in the same way in different universes or at the extreme points of our own: that is, at its origin and at its future collapse.[77] As James Miller tells us, "the world is not a thing which has a history: it is history":[78] and that history is never complete. Similarly, Gödel's theorem tells us that no mathematics is ever complete, again suggesting that mathematics might be local and contingent:[79] and if we are to ascribe any kind of reality to mathematics then we shall have to understand it as action in changing patterns and as as dynamic as the cosmos that it attempts to express.[80]

In relation to the midrange distances and time intervals that we usually experience, time and space will change little, but in relation to the macro- and micro-levels of the cosmos we might expect rather more change. The same might be true of mathematics. Mathematics, time, and space might be givens, but they are not given once and for all: they are constantly given, and constantly change, and so contribute to the entangled changing patterns of action that constitute the universe and beyond.[81] As Bergson put it, "There are changes, but there are underneath the change no things which change."[82]

---

77. Davis, "Whiteheadian Cosmotheology," 426; Torry, *An Actological Metaphysic*, 67–68.
78. Miller, "The Emerging Postmodern World," 9.
79. Torry, *An Actological Metaphysic*, 82.
80. Torry, *An Actological Metaphysic*, 95.
81. Torry, *An Actology of the Given*, 196–97.
82. Bergson, *The Creative Mind*, 173.

Chapter 5

Actological natural sciences

Natural science: The branch of knowledge that deals with the natural or physical world; a life science or physical science, such as biology, chemistry, physics, or geology; (in *plural*) these sciences collectively, in contrast to the social sciences and human sciences.[1]

INTRODUCTION

Much of what we call the natural sciences—physics, chemistry, and by extension biology—is expressed mathematically, so we have encountered a fair amount of science in Chapter 4. Here we shall continue that discussion, both by asking what the sciences might look like when understood through an actological lens, and by asking what some additional philosophers have had to say, and particularly Georges Canguilhem, Michel Foucault, and Michel Serres.

Friedrich Schelling suggested that each science is based on an axiom that cannot be conditioned by the science, and went on to argue that as philosophy conditions science, it cannot be conditioned by a science, so its own axiom must be "absolutely unconditional"[2] and can only be "the originally self-posited I."[3] But what of the other sciences? Here we shall set out from the axiom that reality is action in changing patterns and see where that takes the

---

1. Oxford English Dictionary.
2. Schelling, *The Unconditional in Human Knowledge*, 41.
3. Schelling, *The Unconditional in Human Knowledge*, 45.

natural sciences. Such an axiom clearly fulfils Schelling's condition that the axiom cannot be conditioned by the science. Later in the book we shall take the same approach in relation to psychology and to the social sciences sociology and economics.

By positing the axiom "reality is action in changing patterns," we are saying that this is where scientific reasoning begins. However, Paul Ricoeur asks us to understand that

> action itself, action as meaningful, may become an object of science, without losing its character of meaningfulness, through a kind of objectification similar to the fixation that occurs in writing. By this objectification, action is no longer a transaction to which the discourse of action would still belong. It constitutes a delineated pattern that has to be interpreted according to its inner connections.[4]

Whether the sciences can legitimately study action in changing patterns if action in changing patterns is now an axiom is an interesting question to which the answer might be that in the context of an actology a circular argument might be entirely legitimate.

The sciences that we shall study in this chapter will be the natural sciences, generally understood to be physics, chemistry, and biology. These can be subdivided (for instance, biology into zoology and botany), and other sciences, such as geology, might sometimes be included in the category. Elsewhere in this book we study the social sciences sociology and economics, we might also count politics and social policy as social sciences, and the social psychological aspects of psychology might count as well. In one sense there is no difference between the natural and social sciences as they all develop scientific methods appropriate to their subject matter and scientific communities, and they all seek evidence with which to support or disprove hypotheses: but in another sense the complexity of the social sciences—which study society, the economy, and the network of human beings that constitute society—means that experimental results might not always so clearly support or disprove hypotheses. A further complexity is that boundaries between the social sciences are generally less clear than those between such natural sciences as physics,

---

4. Ricoeur, *Du Texte à l'Action*, 213: L'action elle-même, l'action sensée, peut devenir objet de science sans perdre son caractère de signifiance à la faveur d'une sorte d'objectivation semblable à la fixation opérée par l'écriture. Grâce à cette objectivation, l'action n'est plus une transaction à laquelle le discours de l'action continuerait d'appartenir. Elle constitue une configuration qui demande à être interprétée en fonction de ses connexions internes; *From Text to Action*, 146.

chemistry, and biology, although there is of course some degree of overlap between those as well.

What connects all of the sciences together is that they are all constituted by complex changing patterns of action with multiple connections with the changing patterns of action that constitute other disciplines, other subject matter, and ultimately the cosmos as a whole, and that they all study action in changing patterns. The same is true of what are generally called the humanities: philosophy, literature, history, theology, languages, and geography, although the last two might legitimately be regarded as both sciences and humanities. This does not mean that we can identify some characteristic pattern of action contributing to the constitution of all of these different disciplines. Any likeness is of the family resemblance kind: so although we can recognize similarities between one discipline and another, we cannot identify a commonality relating to all of them.[5]

KARL POPPER AND THOMAS KUHN

As Karl Popper suggests, a system is

> empirical or scientific only if it is capable of being *tested* by experience. These considerations suggest that not the *verifiability* but the *falsifiability* of a system is to be taken as a criterion of demarcation. In other words, I shall not require of a scientific system that it shall be capable of being singled out, once and for all, in a positive sense; but I shall require that its logical form shall be such that it can be singled out, by means of empirical tests, in a negative sense: *it must be possible for an empirical scientific system to be refuted by experience.*[6]

Because just one piece of evidence might falsify a theory, no theory can ever be conclusively proved to be universally true. This means that there is a fundamental asymmetry at the heart of the natural sciences: whereas no amount of corroborating evidence can prove a theory to be true, just one piece of evidence against it can destroy it.[7]

But where do theories come from in the first place? Experimental results can test existing theory, but on their own they cannot deliver theoretical propositions that then need to be tested. The search for a theory will

5. Torry, *An Actological Metaphysic*, 188–89.
6. Popper, *The Logic of Scientific Discovery*, 40–41.
7. Keuth, *The Philosophy of Karl Popper*, 31; Popper, *The Logic of Scientific Discovery*, 41.

generally begin when a problem emerges:[8] perhaps an experimental result that problematizes an existing theory. Ideas might then emerge from the scientist's imagination, and generally from what we might call the metaphysical imagination, perhaps fertilized by some mathematics (on which see the section on Bachelard in the previous chapter).[9] Sometimes it takes a long time for what began as metaphysics to be tested and found to be theories that still await refutation. A clear example is the ancient Greek proposal that reality is constituted by atoms: a theory only tested in modern times, and although our understanding of atoms continues to evolve, the fundamentals of the Greek theory remain intact.[10]

As Popper recognized, "the most important source of our knowledge—apart from inborn knowledge—is tradition":[11] so in response to the emergence of new problems scientists will look back at the tradition preserved by the scientific community in search of ideas to adapt and reapply as new theories, each of which

> should proceed from some simple, new, and powerful, unifying idea about some connection or relation (such as gravitational attraction) between hitherto unconnected things . . . or facts . . . or new "theoretical entities."[12]

Popper goes on to insist that "the new theory should be *independently testable*"; that it "should pass some new and severe tests";[13] that it must "make assertions about structural or relational properties of the world; and that the properties described by an explanatory theory must be, in some sense or other, deeper than those to be explained,"[14] with "deeper" left without further definition; and that it should be bold:

> Our main concern in science and in philosophy is, or ought to be, the search for truth, by way of bold conjectures and the critical search for what is false in our various competing theories.[15]

---

8. Popper, *Conjectures and Refutations*, 155.
9. Gattei, *Karl Popper's Philosophy of Science*, 33–34, 52–53.
10. Gattei, *Karl Popper's Philosophy of Science*, 33–34; Keuth, *The Philosophy of Karl Popper*, 34.
11. Popper, *Conjectures and Refutations*, 27.
12. Popper, *Conjectures and Refutations*, 241.
13. Popper, *Conjectures and Refutations*, 241–42.
14. Popper, *Objective Knowledge*, 197.
15. Popper, *Objective Knowledge*, 319.

Popper also suggested that theories should be universal: "that is to say, must make assertions about the world—about all spatio-temporal regions of the world":[16] although we now know that at extreme spatial and temporal limits theories found to be explanatory in less extreme spatio-temporal fields might no longer hold.[17]

We might understand a scientific paradigm as a collection of theories that cohere with each other and that together provide a general understanding of how the universe works. Clear examples are the Newtonian, relativity, and quantum paradigms, that respectively understand reality as held within spacetime as a rigid grid; as matter, space, and time as relative to each other; and as matter understood as probabilistic energy levels. We might understand a paradigm as a tradition that determines the assumptions that a scientific community makes, the theories that it formulates and tests, the questions that it asks, the experiments that it holds, and so on. As Thomas Kuhn suggests, if evidence builds up against theories related to the paradigm, then the paradigm itself will be brought into question, a period of turbulence will ensue, thought experiments might lead to new paradigms being suggested,[18] along with related theories, experiments, and so on, and eventually a new paradigm might emerge that is corroborated by experimental results[19] and is not immediately contradicted by any of them. This might then become the accepted tradition of the scientific community: a paradigm that determines assumptions, theories, experiments, and so on, until evidence builds up against it, new turbulence emerges, and a new search begins for another new paradigm.[20] (In our previous chapter we noted the fact that Thomas Kuhn's theory of paradigm shift was influenced by Bachelard.[21])

Popper draws an important conclusion from the scientific method that he describes:

> The task of science, which I have suggested is to find satisfactory explanations, can hardly be understood if we are not realists. For a satisfactory explanation is one which is not *ad hoc*; and this idea—the *idea of independent evidence*—can hardly be understood without the idea of discovery, of progressing to deeper layers of

---

16. Popper, *Objective Knowledge*, 197.
17. Cartwright, *The Dappled World*.
18. Kuhn, "A Function for Thought Experiments."
19. Gattei, *Karl Popper's Philosophy of Science*, 41.
20. Kuhn, *The Structure of Scientific Revolutions*.
21. Simons, "The Many Encounters of Thomas Kuhn and French Epistemology."

explanation: without the idea that there is something for us to discover, and something to discuss critically.[22]

Which of course raises the question as to how reality is to be understood. Our proposal is that reality might best be understood as action in changing patterns: and it is interestingly consistent with this that not only is the process by which paradigms and theories change best understood actologically as action in changing patterns, and therefore as much an element of reality as anything else, but also that an action in changing patterns paradigm represents precisely the kind of paradigm shifting that Thomas Kuhn might have envisaged. In the previous chapter and in this one we are beginning to see the kinds of theory that might emerge from such a paradigm shift—theories that will themselves be changing patterns of action that represent changing patterns of action and that will be tested by changing patterns of action. If realism might be "the only sensible hypothesis,"[23] it now needs to be a realism understood as action in changing patterns until we prove otherwise.

CONTINENTAL PHILOSOPHERS ON THE SCIENCES

In Chapter 4 we have explored what Edmund Husserl called the "unbridgeable difference between sciences of the ideal and sciences of the real."[24] On the "ideal" side lies mathematics, and on the "real" side the natural sciences: although we have recognized that both the ideal and the real are phenomena that are given, and that mathematics might be understood as having its roots in the act of counting, thus providing us with at least two bridges across the divide between the ideal and the real. But what of the phenomena constituted by the sciences? Their purpose is to bring order into the phenomena that we experience as given: and so, for instance, the phenomenon of perception is "a phenomenon in keeping with the sense of the positive science we call psychology,"[25] but what matters to Husserl is that

> *to every psychological experience there corresponds, by way of the phenomenological reduction, a pure phenomenon that exhibits its immanent essence* (taken individually) *as an absolute givenness.*[26]

---

22. Popper, *Objective Knowledge*, 203.
23. Popper, *Objective Knowledge*, 198; Gattei, *Karl Popper's Philosophy of Science*, 54.
24. Husserl, *Logical Investigations*, 8, §48, 113.
25. Husserl, *The Idea of Phenomenology*, 33.
26. Husserl, *The Idea of Phenomenology*, 34. Italics in the original.

The problem with phenomenological *reduction*, whether just once to phenomena, or twice to phenomena and then to givenness, is that it is the "psychological experience" that grounds the phenomena in a science and enables us to evaluate it. Scientific method is required: and Karl Popper suggests that within a scientific community theories are "conjectural," we seek evidence to corroborate them, and we abandon them when we discover evidence against them,[27] whereas for J.L. Austin justification and reliability come in degrees rather than absolutely one way or the other, as hypotheses are more or less undermined by new experimental results. "Reliabilism" depends on a "process," so knowledge is something that we do, not something that we have.[28] This is an actological understanding of science in which scientific knowledge is diverse and dynamic: diverse hypotheses that change evidence-gathering and that are regularly changed by new evidence; diverse and changing experiments; and knowledge that changes all the time and that changes its environment. Nothing is static, unchanging, or unitary.

We could have included a discussion of Gaston Bachelard's philosophy of science here, and particularly a discussion of his understanding that changing science constantly "rectifies"[29] knowledge and so creates new realities: for instance, as when James Clark Maxwell predicted radio waves on the basis of his equations. However, we included a section on Gaston Bachelard's philosophy of science in Chapter 4 about mathematics because he regarded mathematics as the main driver of scientific change. Here we shall include sections on Georges Canguilhem's philosophy of medical sciences, Teilhard de Chardin's evolutionary philosophy, and Michel Serres' philosophy.

Georges Canguilhem

For Canguilhem, there are no laws, but rather an "order of properties."

> By "order of properties" we mean an organization of forces and a hierarchy of functions whose stability is necessarily precarious, for it is the solution to a problem of equilibrium, compensation, and compromise between different and competing powers. From such a perspective, irregularity and anomaly are conceived not as accidents affecting an individual but as its very existence.[30]

---

27. Popper, *The Philosophy of Karl Popper*, 31; Popper, *Conjectures and Refutations*, 36–37, 117, 241–42; Popper, *The Logic of Scientific Discovery*, 41.

28. Austin, "Performative Utterances," 235; Torry, *An Actological Metaphysic*, 111.

29. Bachelard, "The Idea of the Epistemological Obstacle," 26.

30. Canguilhem, *Knowledge of Life*, 125.

Canguilhem questions whether seeking any kind of order is appropriate in the biological and medical sciences. In physics and chemistry we can experiment on identical examples of elements and replicate the experimental methods and usually the results; but "the obstacle to biology and experimental medicine resides in individuality: one does not encounter this sort of difficulty when experimenting on purely physical entities."[31] In biology and medicine there are no identical samples, which makes ordering and replication problematic. In biology and medicine, nothing is commensurable: but the same might in fact be true of physics and chemistry. We might discover some regularities, but we now know that laws are local and contingent approximations,[32] that divergence is not an anomaly and is essential to life, and that "individual singularity" is "an adventure."[33]

Because each human being is a unique person, "normal" can only mean the mean of some quantifiable characteristic: which again is problematic because, apart from such basic measurements as height and weight, in relation to any meaningful characteristic of a human being or other organism quantities are difficult or impossible to compare between individuals. [34] So, for instance, "health" will be different for each individual, and the only person who can evaluate someone's health is themselves; and conversely, pathology can only be evaluated by the person who experiences it. We might be able to guess that an organ failure, such as heart failure, might be experienced by someone as a pathology, but it is perfectly possible that the person whom we had evaluated as an unhealthy sufferer might understand themselves as in good health and as not suffering from a pathology; and that the person who is about to die might regard that as a healthful outcome. This suggests to Canguilhem that health can have no scientific status.[35] "Health, the body's truth, does not arise out of an explanation of theorems. There is no health for a mechanism."[36]

Health and pathology are not only diverse between persons; they also change in relation to an individual as their norms, contexts, and experiences change over time.[37] Health,

> as the expression of the *produced* body, the body as product, is lived assurance . . . it is the feeling of a capacity to surpass initial

31. Canguilhem, *Knowledge of Life*, 124.
32. Cartwright, *The Dappled World*.
33. Canguilhem, *Knowledge of Life*, 125.
34. Canguilhem, *Knowledge of Life*, 127, 129.
35. Canguilhem, *Writings on Medicine*, 46.
36. Canguilhem, *Writings on Medicine*, 47.
37. Canguilhem, *Knowledge of Life*, 130–31.

capacities, a capacity to make the body do what initially seemed beyond its means. . . . Let us call this health free, unconditioned, unaccountable. This health is not an object for those who believe themselves to be specialists in it.[38]

Each of us is action in changing patterns, and the changing patterns of action that constitute one person will not constitute another: theirs will be radically different; and both of them will change, will diverge and converge, and will entangle with each other, either intimately or from a distance; and the same will be true of every individual: this is what makes a society within which norms evolve that both affect every individual and are influenced by every individual. So social norms relating to health will evolve and will continue to change, each individual's experience of health will affect everyone else's, and so on. Perhaps the only thing that does not change is the ubiquity of change and diversity. However, we experience stabilities as well as change. Those stabilities might be local and contingent, and there might be change within them, but we might still be able to identify social norms that change only slowly. These Canguilhem calls "regulative ideals that guide the life sciences."[39] This might suggest that there is something consistent about the sciences when there is not. The sciences are themselves action in changing patterns, and they entangle with the world of galaxies, stars, planets, forests, persons, animals, and so on, so there is no firm boundary between a science and its subject matter: which is why we can study sciences in the same way as we study the subject matter of the sciences.[40] Anything that is real is action in changing patterns, and that goes for both life and the life sciences.

Michel Foucault

For Michel Foucault, sciences are "discourses that rectify and correct themselves, and that carry out a whole labor of self-development governed by the task of 'truth-telling.'"[41] New ways of truth-telling change the sciences so that "science is always making and remaking its own history,"[42] and any normativity relates to particular sciences in the particular ways in which they are

---

38. Canguilhem, *Writings on Medicine*, 49.
39. Chimisso, "The Tribunal of Philosophy and its Norms," 321.
40. Chimisso, "The Tribunal of Philosophy and its Norms," 322.
41. Foucault, "Life: Experience and Science," 471.
42. Foucault, "Life: Experience and Science," 472.

carried out at a particular time and place.[43] There is nothing unchanging: there is only diversity and change.[44]

> The history of the sciences is not the history of the true, of its slow epiphany; it cannot hope to recount the gradual discovery of a truth that has always been inscribed in things or in the intellect, except by imagining that today's knowledge finally possesses it in such a complete and definitive way that it can use that truth as a standard for measuring the past . . . In the history of the sciences one cannot grant oneself the truth as an assumption, but neither can one dispense with a relation to truth and to the opposition of the true and the untrue.[45]

The fundamental problem is that science

> aspires to the universal while developing within contingency, that asserts its unity and yet proceeds only through partial modifications, that validates itself by its own supremacy but that cannot be dissociated in its history, from the inertias, the dullnesses, or the coercions that subjugate it.[46]

Because everything is contingent,[47] including the power relations that determine the theories that scientists develop and the experiments that they conduct, science has to be self-critical as well as critical: and because science will always operate in a particular context, as will critique, what is required is a "practical critique" that studies discourses and practices and the social power relations underlying them and that remains entirely among the singular rather than the universal.[48] Foucault understands critique as "archaeology" that studies particular effects, and that is followed by "genealogy" that seeks out relationships between power and knowledge, and then by "analysis" of what genealogy uncovers. If structured like this, critique will find that "power and knowledge operate in a dimension that is full, structured, and dynamic, a network of relationships,"[49] and so actologically and entirely in relation to the particular phenomenon under discussion and to related contingencies. There

---

43. Foucault, "Life: Experience and Science," 473.
44. Torry, *An Actology of the Given*, 181–85.
45. Foucault, "Life: Experience and Science," 471.
46. Foucault, "Life: Experience and Science," 469. See also Braunstein, "Historical Contingency," 39.
47. Lemke, "Critique and Experience," 39; Webb, *Foucault's Archaeology*, 52.
48. Foucault, "What is Critique?" 64.
49. Webb, "Microphysics," 124.

will be no "principle of closure,"⁵⁰ and critique will always be "strategic," because choices will always have to be made as to which science-affecting social sources are to be studied.⁵¹ Occasionally a science might experience stability for a period, but any such stability will be contingent upon future change and so will be short-lived.⁵²

Critique is a pattern of action that constantly changes, but with family resemblances⁵³ between the different critical methods that emerge from time to time. Critique reveals the sciences to be dynamic, diverse, and contingent, their data, theories, experiments, and results, to be likewise dynamic, diverse, and contingent, and critique itself to be dynamic, diverse, and contingent. For both Canguilhem and Foucault, science is contingent and actological, as is everything that it studies.

Pierre Teilhard de Chardin

Whether Pierre Teilhard de Chardin's writings should be regarded as science, cosmology, philosophy, or theology, is a question to which the answer should probably be "yes." Particularly in *Le Phénomène Humaine* (*The Human Phenomenon*),⁵⁴ but also in more theological language in other books, Teilhard de Chardin expounded an evolutionary vision that envisaged increasing degrees of complexity in which step changes occurred, giving us matter, then life (the biosphere), then the mind (the noosphere), and then on to the "Omega Point": a final destination of the evolutionary process sometimes expressed theologically and sometimes not.⁵⁵ Teilhard de Chardin proposes consciousness as the single driving force from the creation of matter (which possesses as its "within" a kind of consciousness),⁵⁶ through the biosphere and the noosphere to the Omega Point; and in *L'Avenir de L'Homme* (*The Future of Humanity*), following the evolution of the noosphere, a new more

---

50. Foucault, "What is Critique?" 64.

51. Koopman, *Genealogy as Critique*, 44, 142–43; Lemke, "Critique and Experience," 32–33; Torry, *Actological Readings in Continental Philosophy*, 223–33.

52. Koopman, *Genealogy as Critique*, 144.

53. Wittgenstein, Ludwig. *Philosophische Untersuchungen / Philosophical Investigations*, 32, 36.

54. Teilhard de Chardin, *Le Phénomène Humain*; Teilhard de Chardin, *The Phenomenon of Man*. Subsequent editions of the English translation were published under the title *The Human Phenomenon*.

55. Wildiers, *An Introduction to Teilhard de Chardin*, 14.

56. Teilhard de Chardin, *Le Phénomène Humain*, 42; Teilhard de Chardin, *The Phenomenon of Man*, 59.

social stage is inserted,[57] apparently between the noosphere and the Omega Point. A connecting filament throughout the evolutionary process is energy, because matter, life, and the mind, can all be understood as "a kind of homogeneous, primordial flux in which all that has shape in the world is but a series of fleeting vortices":[58] or, as we might put it, as action in changing patterns.[59] The cosmos is a whole as well as being composed of matter, examples of life, minds, and a trajectory to beyond the noosphere.[60]

To what extent is all of this science? Teilhard de Chardin's considerable theological output is clearly not science, and neither is the Omega Point, but although it is difficult to see how Karl Popper's criterion for a scientific theory—that it should be falsifiable[61]—could be met by much of Teilhard de Chardin's scheme, we know that some previously metaphysical ideas—such as ancient Greek speculation about the existence of atoms—have subsequently become corroborated scientific theories:[62] so perhaps we shall find that one day the "within" of matter[63] and other Teilhardian proposals will become testable and corroborated theories.

Michel Serres

We must

> make peace by a new contract between the sciences, which deal relevantly with the things of the world and their relations, and judgment, which decides on men and their relations. It is better to make peace between the two types of reason in conflict today, because their fates are henceforth crossed and blended, and because our own fate depends on their alliance.[64]

---

57. *rebondit*

58. Teilhard de Chardin, *Le Phénomène Humain*, 29–30: une sorte de flux homogène, primordial, dont tout ce qui existe de figure au Monde ne serait que de fugitifs "tourbillons"; Teilhard de Chardin, *The Phenomenon of Man*, 45–47. And see below on Lucretius.

59. *pouvoir de liaison*

60. Teilhard de Chardin, *Le Phénomène Humain*, 30; Teilhard de Chardin, *The Phenomenon of Man*, 49; Torry, *Actology: Action, change and diversity in the Western philosophical tradition*, 131–49.

61. Popper, *Conjectures and Refutations*, 36–37.

62. Gattei, *Karl Popper's Philosophy of Science*, 33–34; Keuth, *The Philosophy of Karl Popper*, 34.

63. Teilhard de Chardin, *L'Avenir de L'Homme*, 268; Teilhard de Chardin, *The Future of Man*, 218.

64. Serres, *Natural Contract*, 93.

For Michel Serres "law" or "judgment" is human decision-making, the sciences study the world and relationships with it, and law and science need each other. Today human decision-making controls science and enables it to pollute nature. The answer is for law to establish a "natural contract" to reshape the relationship between nature and humanity[65] and for "a single reason"[66] to emerge within which both science and law can belong.

Leibniz's principle of sufficient reason requires everything to have a reason, a *principium reddendae rationis*, where the *reddendae* requires that a reason should be given back or rendered.[67] A reciprocity is thus established on the basis of the envisaged natural contract. Nature is given to us, and we must give back reason in return. "The principle of reason thus consists in the establishment of a fair contract... This rational contract... balances the given with reason."[68] However,

> the given itself is disappearing under the weight and power of reason's productions.... Today, we ourselves, reasonable men, are brought to plead on the side of the given, which, for some time, has been laying down its arms.[69]

We might say that law and science are two changing patterns of action that need to tangle with each other and with the changing patterns of action that constitute nature so that a single complex changing pattern of action emerges that incorporates nature, law, science, and ourselves.

NATURE: ACTION IN CHANGING PATTERNS

Serres references a suggestion originally made by Lucretius and revived by Leibniz that the universe that we know emerged from a laminar flow within which particles always moved in the same direction and within which a single particle veered off course just slightly—the *clinamen*—and cannoned into other particles, creating a cascade of angled trajectories. The laminar flow is itself a kind of chaos because it has no pattern; and so is what emerges from the *clinamen*; and so is a third kind that emerges from that chaos: turbulence, which Michel Serres calls the "passage from fundamental physics to the

---

65. Serres, *Natural Contract*, 86, 93.
66. Serres, *Natural Contract*, 89.
67. Serres, *Natural Contract*, 89.
68. Serres, *Natural Contract*, 90.
69. Serres, *Natural Contract*, 91.

science of phenomena, from ontology to phenomenology."[70] He recognizes that the *clinamen*

> is an absurdity. A logical absurdity ... the cause of itself before being the cause of all things ... a differential and, properly, a fluxion ... the lightning path obliquely crossing the rainfall ... the *clinamen* is the smallest imaginable condition for the original formation of turbulence ... It is the minimum angle for the formation of a vortex, appearing by chance in a laminar flow.[71]

As all of laminar flow, the *clinamen*, turbulence, and the resulting temporary vortices, constitute a single process,[72] and all of it is action in changing patterns, we can understand it as the origin of the universe, as the birth of physics,[73] and as both "science and myth."[74] All of it is action in changing patterns, with varying degrees of change at each stage. The laminar flow can be interpreted both as chaos, because unpatterned, and as radically patterned, because the direction of flow does not change; the *clinamen* can be interpreted as either minor change or radical change; turbulence is ubiquitous change; and vortices change both less and more slowly and might be relatively stable for periods of time.

This reflects the reality that we experience. Within our own universe we experience substantial degrees of stability as well as ubiquitous change, so it makes sense to speak of laws of physics. It is only at the extremities of time and space that those laws break down. But we cannot assume that the same laws would apply in a different universe; and neither can we assume that the same laws will always apply in our own universe. Any fairly stable order can experience turbulence and then change in such a way that any laws that we might have proposed and tested might no longer hold, and—if we are still here—we might have to formulate new laws that describe how the new relatively stable changing patterns of action behave—until yet more change occurs. Laws evolve as the things and events that they are supposed to govern evolve.[75]

---

70. Serres, *Birth of Physics*, 66.
71. Serres, *Birth of Physics*, 21–25.
72. Torry, *An Actological Metaphysic*, 60, 62–63; Torry, *Actological Readings in Continental Philosophy*, 237–45.
73. Serres, *Birth of Physics*, 22.
74. Serres, *Incandescent*, 14.
75. Torry, *An Actological Metaphysic*, 67–68.

The assumption that no modification of these laws is to be looked for in environments, which have any striking difference for which the laws have been observed to hold, is very unsafe.[76]

Alfred North Whitehead terms the current epoch "electromagnetic," which implies that other epochs might not function by way of electromagnetism; and Leemon McHenry comments:

> Physical laws are grounded in the periodicity of nature that is exhibited within each cosmic epoch. Other laws, such as those of geometry and mathematics, hold not only for our cosmic epoch but for all others contained in the geometrical society. In the most general society of pure extension, extremely general mereological laws apply, such as the relation of whole to part and extensive connection; these will likewise hold in any possible cosmic epoch, but even here Whitehead is hesitant to claim this as a necessary conclusion.[77]

In order to understand the world, we create heuristics: models, often called natural laws or laws of nature, that describe and predict events. Because reality is action in changing patterns, all such models or laws can only be approximations, and the degrees to which they approximate to reality will constantly change. What we do know is that no longer can we employ models that leave no room for constant, ubiquitous, and radical change. And so the equation $E = mc^2$ that we encountered in Chapter 4 is a useful statement of a temporary stability for which we have evidence. Events—temporary relatively stable bundles of changing patterns of action—impinge on the changing patterns of action that constitute ourselves and our experiments, and we can match the experience to the equation. However, future experience might find that $E = mc^2$ represents a special case that holds under certain conditions, and that a different equation is required for the generality of reality.[78]

Everywhere we look—across the universe, or into what we call fundamental particles—we find action, change, movement, and diversity; and we find the same when we study the sciences, institutions, or our own minds.[79] The sciences are composed of traditions that exhibit both continuity and change: which means action in changing patterns. No ontology of Being, beings, the unitary, and the unchanging, will ever be adequate as a basis for

---

76. Whitehead, *Science and the Modern World*, 133–34.
77. McHenry, *The Event Universe*, 74.
78. Torry, *An Actological Metaphysic*, 69–70.
79. Kuhn, *The Structure of Scientific Revolutions*; Moscovici, "Social Influence and Conformity"; Sargant, *Battle for the Mind*.

understanding our universe or our sciences, institutions, or language. Only an actology structured around Action, action, diversity, change, and the generally dynamic, would possibly be adequate to any kind of realistic understanding of all of that.[80]

SCIENCE AS ACTION IN CHANGING PATTERNS

If everything is action in changing patterns, then what can we now mean by scientific traditions: the relatively settled conclusions on which scientific communities base their further research? After all, we have to start from somewhere. In response to Jean-François Lyotard's description of postmodernity as an inability to give credence to metanarratives,[81] including scientific metanarratives, is it sufficient to say with Robert Bellah that we now have to become "multilingual,"[82] and with Wittgenstein that we play different language games?[83] But Wittgenstein's language games were not necessarily disconnected from each other:

> Our mistake is to look for an explanation—we ought to look at what happens as a "protophenomenon"... That is, where we ought to have said: *"this language-game is played."* ... grammatical substantives do not necessarily denote a single thing or essence.[84]

In Wittgenstein's own words, we might suggest that different scientific narratives bear family resemblances to each other.[85] This reflects the reality, because we do move between different language games all the time; we experience connections, however fleeting; and we can compare different language games with each other. As Renford Bambrough points out, dictionaries define words in relation to other words,[86] so first of all there is no single point from which definition evolves, and secondly the connections from one word to

---

80. Torry, *An Actological Metaphysic*, 30.

81. Lyotard, *La Condition Postmoderne*, 7: On tient pour «postmoderne» l'incrédulité à l'égard des métarécits ... A la désuétude du dispositive métanarratif de légitimation correspond notamment la crise de la philosophie métaphysique, et celle de l'institution universitaire qui depend d'elle."

82. Bellah, "Christian Faithfulness in a Pluralist World.

83. Lyotard, *La Condition Postmoderne*, 8: Il y a beaucoup de jeux de langage différants, c'est l'hétérogénéité des elements.

84. Wittgenstein, *Philosophische Untersuchungen / Philosophical Investigations*, part I, §654; §§66, 67.

85. Wittgenstein, *Philosophische Untersuchungen / Philosophical Investigations*, §67, 27.

86. Bambrough, *Reason, Truth and God*, 94.

another and then to another and so on can take us along paths throughout the entire extent of a language. There might be language games, but in principle they belong to a single flexible game, and we can therefore understand science as a single complex changing pattern of action that we might describe as a metanarrative, as long as we recognize that it is infinitely revisable.[87] Every science lives with approximation, uncertainty, and fluid language, but as long as definitions are as clear as possible and are widely shared, researchers can work together to generate and communicate scientific results. These will always be revisable, but they will still be results. And equally important is the ability to cross the boundaries between scientific and other language games, because only then can science be informed by ethics and related disciplines, and can ethics and other disciplines be informed by scientific results.[88] It is such boundary-crossing that reveals each of language, science, the cosmos, and the natural world, to be single complex changing patterns of action, and together to constitute a single complex changing pattern of action. There are no boundaries that cannot be crossed.

Nancy Cartwright has found that

> the laws of physics apply only where its models fit, and that, apparently, includes only a very limited range of circumstances

and that

> our most wide-ranging scientific knowledge is not knowledge of laws but knowledge of the nature of things, knowledge that allows us to build new [methods] never before seen giving rise to new laws never before dreamt of.[89]

Writing in 1903, James Clark Maxwell made the reasonable assumption that

> none of the processes of Nature, since the time when Nature began, have produced the slightest difference in the properties of any molecule,[90]

and because no evolution of the molecule appeared to have occurred, he concluded that molecules had not been made by natural processes but by God. The underlying assumption was wrong. Molecules had evolved. Natural laws that appear to apply across today's cosmos seem not to have applied at its

---

87. Torry, *An Actological Metaphysic*, 49–50.
88. Huyssen, "The Search for Tradition," 40; Habermas, "Modernity versus Postmodernity," 5.
89. Cartwright, *The Dappled World*, 4.
90. Maxwell, "God and Molecules," 167.

beginning, as then the patterns of action appear to have been changing faster than we can imagine. As Smolin and Unger put it:

> The trouble is that [our present] laws and other regularities of nature fail to explain change beyond or before nucleosynthesis. Beyond or before that time, the composition and organization of nature, and even the extent to which causal connections displayed law-like regularity, may have been radically different from what they became in the cooled-down universe.[91]

Science has to be able to reflect that reality, so in relation to the origin of the cosmos science has to be rapidly changing patterns of action. But in principle there is nothing special about the origin of the cosmos. The whole of reality is action in changing patterns, and what changes is the speed of change. As Michel Serres suggests, time is multiple: "different rhythms of a flowing . . . lightning-fast or with an infinite slowness."[92] The time of a mountain forming and the time of an atomic vibration are different "chronic rhythms . . . so vastly diverse times."[93]

The question for us is whether this understanding of ubiquitous change and diversity presages a new scientific paradigm or simply the emphasis of an aspect of the current one. Given that we still regularly speak of particles, substances, and so on, it might be time for the kind of "thought experiment" that Thomas Kuhn recommended as a way of recognizing a sense of unease about accepted theories and of moving science on.[94] Kuhn suggests that we should turn unease into contradiction in the cause of seeking potential new paradigms, and similarly Lee Smolin suggests that we should treat time as real as a means of abandoning presuppositions about timeless substrates[95] and of recognizing that natural laws are within the universe and therefore subject to change by the changing patterns of action that constitute the universe.[96] As Thomas Hertog puts it: "it is not the laws as such but their capacity to change that is fundamental."[97] Both the cosmos and science are diverse and dynamic, so we should expect the cosmos to behave differently at different times and in different places—and particularly at its origin, its demise, and its boundaries, whatever they are—and we should expect science to be different in different

---

91. Unger and Smolin, *The Singular Universe and the Reality of Time*, 210.
92. Serres, *Incandescent*, 5.
93. Serres, *Incandescent*, 5, 8.
94. Kuhn, "A Function for Thought Experiments," 6, 26.
95. Smolin, *Time Reborn*.
96. Smolin, *Time Reborn*, 121.
97. Hertog, *On the Origin of Time*, 256.

places and at different times, but always reflecting changing patterns of action that constitute the cosmos.[98] Laws are local and temporary generalities that we derive from particular local and temporary correlations. That is what science is about. It is not an exercise in deciding how the universe should behave on the basis of a priori laws of nature.[99]

We can look back and see where paradigm shifting has occurred. For instance, Copernicus, Galileo, and Newton, explored the universe on the basis of an ontology based on the concept that reality is things that change: an ontology reinforced by their experience of an orderly universe. Later on, Newton's theories proved inadequate to new experimental results that appeared to reinforce Albert Einstein's rather different theories.[100] Since then we have seen quantum mechanics, quantum field theory, string theory, and so on, that tend to understand the universe in terms of energy and probability; and Einstein's theories understand space, time, mass, energy, and gravity, as relative to each other: and these theories might turn out to be approximations that apply within certain parameters and represent special cases of a broader new theory. As Peacocke and Pederson suggest:

> Physical reality, especially as revealed by quantum mechanics and relativity theory, is . . . characterized by its incompleteness of becoming and its pulsational character; the compatibility of the emergence of novelty with past causal influences; the individuality of events within the continuity of flux; the impossibility of instantaneous space and of simultaneous time and their replacement by that of "co-becoming."[101]

And we are now beginning to understand reality as self-organizing complex systems.[102] Reality is

> complex dynamical systems . . . [that] exhibit a delicate sensitivity to circumstance which makes them intrinsically unpredictable. The future is no longer contained in the past; there is scope for real becoming.[103]

It is not difficult to identify in this historical process an evolution from science understood within an ontological conceptual structure to science understood

---

98. Unger and Smolin, *The Singular Universe and the Reality of Time*, 19.

99. Torry, *An Actological Metaphysic*, 71–72; Unger and Smolin, *The Singular Universe and the Reality of Time*, 281.

100. Hodges, *Alan Turing*, 44.

101. Peacocke and Pederson, *The Music of Creation*, 14.

102. Davies, *The New Physics*, 4.

103. Polkinghorne, *Science and Providence*, 2

actologically: science understood as action in changing patterns relating to reality understood as action in changing patterns. And not just science and the universe: we might now understand ourselves more actologically than ontologically. We "co-become" with the universe: something understood by quantum theory that recognizes that observer and phenomenon influence each other.[104] As James Miller puts it: "At its most fundamental level, the universe does not seem to be composed of stuff or things at all, but rather of dynamic relations":[105] interactions exemplified by the instantaneous action at a distance experienced by electrons that were once adjacent but are now at opposite ends of the universe. We live in an informational universe.[106] Similarly, as Karen Barad suggests, we become who we are through our interactions with other people[107] and with the world around us: so "we need to meet the universe halfway, to take responsibility for the role that we play in the world's differential becoming."[108] All of this is of course far easier to understand within an actological framework of change, diversity, and the generally dynamic, than in an ontological framework of the unchanging, the unitary, and the generally static.

However, things might be even more complex than that. If diversity is a fundamental category, then perhaps we should recognize that both ontological and actological frameworks have something to be said for them. This would cohere with how we now understand the micro-level of the universe as both particles and wave motions. But even if we do recognize that such diversity might cohere with an actological view of the world, we must also recognize that to understand subatomic particles as action in changing patterns enables us to understand a particle as a changing pattern of action and a wave motion likewise. The particle and wave motion understandings of reality therefore converge, and an electron is a changing pattern of action, with the change occurring within certain parameters: at least at this time and in this universe. Equally interesting, and coherent with an understanding of the universe as action in changing patterns, is the way in which complexity can generate order as new changing patterns break out in differently patterned action.

> Positive feedback loops among particles can result in self-organizing processes that, despite their superficially chaotic appearance, in fact embody very sophisticated degrees of order. . . . as a result of neural feedback loops . . . globally coherent wave patterns entrain

104. Bub, "The Entangled World," 15–18; Polkinghorne, *Science and Theology*, 34, 46.
105. Miller, "The Emerging Postmodern World," 9.
106. Bub, "The Entangled World," 30.
107. Barad, *Meeting the Universe Halfway*, 352.
108. Barad, *Meeting the Universe Halfway*, 396.

ACTOLOGICAL NATURAL SCIENCES

and self-organize into high-dimensional dynamic structures in the brain possessing emergent mental properties such as consciousness, intentionality . . . and so on . . . Brain states can have causal efficacy in virtue of being (embodying, being entrained into) complex neural states with emergent mental properties:[109]

except that "brain processes" and "neural processes" might be more relevant expressions than "brain states" and "neural states," because living systems are

open, dynamic, complex . . . every aspect of human development and capacities was shaped by environment and culture from the moment of conception if not before. . . . the brain is the most open, complex and dynamic organ in the human body . . .[110]

Within such a context our "free will" is the way in which the changing patterns of action that constitute our brains influence the changing patterns of action that we call consciousness, will, human action, and so on:[111] and just as our own action is open to novelty, so the cosmos as a whole is open to wholly new changing patterns of action emerging.[112] The universe is "endowed with becoming":[113] so the sciences too are "endowed with becoming," and are influenced by all manner of other changing patterns of action: political, social, ethical, psychological, economic, and so on. What research is undertaken, and how results are communicated, are extremely sensitive to non-scientific changing patterns of action.[114] And the concepts that sciences use, and that we use in other contexts, will constantly cross boundaries: so "relativity," "evolution," and so on, can just as easily represent ethical realities as they can scientific theories.[115]

An interesting possibility is that to shift to an actological conceptual framework might make available to us resolutions of longstanding problems that an ontological framework might have prevented us from seeing. So, for instance, a significant long term problem is that it has so far proved impossible to relate Einstein's General Theory of Relativity relating to gravity to our understanding of electromagnetic and atomic forces. Within an actological

109. Juarrero, "Intentions as Complex Dynamical Attractors," 262, 264, 266.
110. Rose, "Brains Matter," 10–11.
111. Juarrero, "Intentions as Complex Dynamical Attractors," 275.
112. Polkinghorne, *Science and Providence*, 13; Torry, *An Actological Metaphysic*, 80–85.
113. Polkinghorne, *Science and Providence*, 2.
114. On the way in which science has become "research traditions" see Bellah, "Christian Faithfulness in a Pluralist World."
115. Torry, *An Actological Metaphysic*, 80–81.

framework we might decide that gravity and electromagnetism are diverse changing patterns of action that relate differently to time and space, both of which we understand in terms of action in changing patterns, and that no direct relationship between gravity and electromagnetism is required. They function effectively in each other's company, without the one being a function of the other. This might be all that we need to know.[116]

CONCLUSIONS

By studying the natural sciences through an actological lens we have been able to comprehend them more coherently than would have been possible through an ontological lens. Take Einstein's Special Theory of Relativity's $E = mc^2$, where E is energy, m is mass, and c is the speed of light. Energy is action in changing patterns; space can be interpreted as changing patterns of action, and in this context it is the space within which energy becomes mass and mass becomes energy; and the speed of light is also changing patterns of action—changing because if two bodies move towards each other, each travelling at the speed of light, their relative speed is the speed of light and not double that, so the speed of light is a pattern of action that changes in relation to other changing patterns of action. Similarly, Einstein's General Theory of Relativity treats space and time as changing patterns of action, and gravity is likewise changing patterns of action that entangle with the changing patterns of action that constitute space.

But as we have discovered, phenomena can sometimes be understood as waves, particles, or both, and such diversity of explanation is more easily understood within an actology than within an ontology; and as we have also discovered, the diversity at the heart of an actology suggests that narratives need to be as diverse as what they are about, so we should expect ontology to still be useful, which it is in relation to medium-sized objects. And we should also expect further frameworks, that we cannot now imagine, to add to the diversity: for instance, reality understood within a "momentum space" in which we have to add energy and three dimensions of momentum to the existing now far from rigid four dimensions of space and time.[117] If we went down this road then the eight-dimension framework would work for a while until further experimental results forced yet another rethink, and we might find that momentum space was an approximation that worked as a model of reality within certain conditions and that we were then able to replace it with

---

116. Torry, *An Actological Metaphysic*, 87.
117. Gefter, "Beyond Space-time."

yet another model. Wholly new changing patterns of action might appear, or alternatively we might be left with unpatterned action and the universe will dissolve.[118]

118. Torry, *An Actological Metaphysic*, 159–60.

Chapter 6

Actological social sciences

Social sciences: The study of human society and social relationships; a subject within this field, as economics, politics, sociology, etc.[1]

INTRODUCTION

SCIENCES PROPOSE HYPOTHESES OF how things work (that is, they propose statements that might describe the mechanisms underlying our experience of the world), and from these they build theories (more general hypotheses), models (proposals that describe complex systems), and paradigms (overall explanations as to how entire fields of interest work). Scientists then conduct experiments to test the hypotheses, models, and paradigms; and if they discover evidence that does not fit a hypothesis, model, or paradigm, then revision occurs. This can happen rapidly in relation to a hypothesis, but inevitably more slowly in relation to a model or a paradigm, because although revising a single hypothesis might not be too difficult a task, a model or paradigm might still offer accurate predictions most of the time, so a substantial amount of new evidence that does not fit has to build before there will be sufficient motive to seek for new models and paradigms, and, crucially, new models and paradigms will have to be found that fit both old and new experimental results. This is why paradigm shift can be slow, and can then occur suddenly as a new paradigm emerges, is tested, and is found to be more coherent with

1. Oxford English Dictionary.

existing evidence, and more predictive of new experimental results, than a previous one.[2]

Social sciences are precisely that: sciences that study society. In this chapter we shall study two of those: sociology, which is the study of society; and economics, which is the study of how goods, services, and money behave. Both of these are sciences in the sense that they create theory that they then test empirically. Psychology is sometimes included among the social sciences because the ways in which our minds behave are social realities as much as they are realities related to the individual person: but it can also be counted among the natural sciences as an aspect of biology, so in this book we shall give to psychology a chapter of its own, in which both individual and social aspects of psychology will be found. And although politics is clearly a social science, we give it a chapter of its own simply because there is quite enough material on actological politics and social policy for a chapter, and this chapter already has quite enough in it as well.

We might sometimes wonder whether a section ought to have been in another chapter. For instance, the section on behavioral economics in the psychology chapter could easily have been located in this chapter. As we might expect, many of the aspects of our society and of our economy do not sit neatly within a single discipline, but instead any study of them requires methods from a variety of disciplines. Readers might legitimately have made different decisions from those made by the author as to what should have been located in which chapter.

ACTOLOGICAL SOCIOLOGY

Sociology: The study of the development, structure, and functioning of human society.[3]

In this section of the chapter we shall study the work of thinkers who gave birth to sociology and then tackle aspects of our society sociologically.[4]

As we have discovered in previous chapters, society is action in changing patterns and so is intrinsically actological. We shall therefore expect sociology to treat it in that way, as the definition at the head of this section suggests that it should. That we are to study the "development" and "functioning" of society immediately suggests that; and to study the "structure" of society does as well as long as we understand structure actologically as the changing patterns in

2. Thomas Kuhn, *The Structure of Scientific Revolutions*.
3. Oxford English Dictionary.
4. Hamilton, "The Enlightenment and the Birth of Social Science."

which we encounter action. To study society actologically requires us to concentrate on societal change, which is what we shall be doing in this chapter.

Sociologists understood actologically

The early sociologists Karl Marx, Emile Durkheim, and Max Weber, were all students of societal change, as were the more recent sociologists George Herbert Mead and Herbert Blumer, and all of them can be understood actologically.

For Karl Marx, although some concepts, such as class and capital, seem to function as unchanging universals, society itself experiences ubiquitous change via a dialectic: thesis, generating antithesis, with resolution into a synthesis that becomes a new thesis. And of course class and capital do change, with class and capital in one period and one place bearing family resemblances to class and capital at other times and in other places. The alienation from the product of our labor of which Marx wrote is still a reality for many, and capitalists still extract surplus value from their workers, but those experiences change as well, with the changing patterns of action that those terms represent being different in different places and at different times; and, as always, any similarities are of the family resemblance variety. Whereas Marx believed the deeper structures of society to control the superstructure that we experience, in an actological context we have to recognize that change is in every conceivable direction, and that as all of it is action in changing patterns, any boundary between structure and superstructure is socially constructed and itself experiences constant change. Every changing pattern of action affects every other: and if we interpret Marx's work with that in mind then it will continue to inform our study of society.[5]

Emile Durkheim was a true scientist in the sense that he set out from social facts, and in particular from the fact of suicide, in relation to which he concluded that a region's prevalent religious tradition influenced its suicide rate.[6] But those religious traditions were not stable societal structures: they were changing patterns of action; and still society in all of its aspects is action in changing patterns that influence every member of society, and that are influenced in their turn by the action in changing patterns that constitute every one of those members. To take an example from economics: money is one of society's structures, it changes all the time, it changes us, we change it, and it is only money because we constantly create it and we say that it is money. Durkheim wrote that "When I fulfil my obligations as brother, husband, or

5. Giddens, *Sociology*, 11–13, 283–85.
6. Durkheim, *Suicide*.

citizen, when I execute my contracts, I perform duties which are defined externally to myself and my acts, in law and in custom."[7] Every aspect of that sentence can be understood actologically. Our family and civic relationships change, our obligations change, the meanings of the words of any contract change over time, law and custom change from time to time and from place to place, and all of that changes the action in changing patterns that I am, and the changing patterns of action that constitute who I am change everything around me. We change social facts, and they change us.[8]

For Max Weber, there were no universal laws, society was action rather than structures, we change society, society changes us, and the ascription of meaning is an active process. On the basis of his research, he concluded that Protestantism, and particularly Puritanism, had created the conditions for the capitalism of his time. If God chooses some for salvation and some not, and if an ascetic and virtuous lifestyle are taken to be signs of God's favor, then we are incentivized to live ascetic and virtuous lives: precisely the kind of lifestyle amenable to the accumulation of income that is then available for investment in capital, and to customers trusting our promises and advertised prices.

Another of Weber's interests was authority types, which he researched in a variety of societies. He concluded that there were three main types: 1. traditional (with authority residing in hierarchically appointed and often hereditary leaders); 2. charismatic (with authority residing in the charismatic leader); and 3. the bureaucratic or rational (with authority residing in a bureaucratic structure in which postholders conform to rules, posts relate to tasks, and postholders are appointed on merit). It is this last authority type that made possible the large-scale capitalist industry of Weber's time. Weber was aware of the organizational changes driven by religious and technological change of his own time, and we are just as aware that in every period and in every place technology, authority types, organizational structures, ideologies, religions, and everything else, change each other. And so, for instance, today we find hereditary leadership in capitalist enterprises (think the Murdoch empire and current Murdoch family battles over its control), charismatic leadership in capitalist enterprises (Elon Musk), and religion driving political change and politics driving religious change (the United States, the Balkans, Afghanistan, Iraq, Iran . . .). It would appear that everything changes everything, all of the time. Weber suggested that religious change had caused organizational and economic change, and could equally well have suggested that technological change had driven organizational and economic change,

---

7. Durkheim, *The Rules of Sociological Method*, 1.

8. Durkheim, *The Rules of Sociological Method*; Durkheim, *Moral Education*; Durkheim, *The Division of Labour in Society*; Giddens, *Sociology*, 8–11, 382; Taylor, *Durkheim and the Study of Suicide*.

which in turn had influenced religious change; and if he had understood that capitalist industry was to be found in Italy as well as in Germany then he might also have understood that religion could not have been the only source of economic change.[9] Change begets change, and the sociologist's task is to seek as many causes of particular change as possible. This will reveal that any changing pattern of action will entangle with vast numbers of other changing patterns of action, that the relationships between them will change constantly, and that causal chains will always be in principle endless and will be subject to ubiquitous change.

Two sociologists who might be of particular interest to us are George Herbert Mead and Herbert Blumer. For Mead, individuals evolve through their symbolic interactions with their environment and with each other, and Blumer extended this insight into an understanding of society as its members' symbolic interactions with each other.[10] We might be able to discern patterns in these interactions, but reliable evidence can only relate to the small scale: to the interactions that we might be able to study within groups within society.[11] "It is the social process in group life that creates and upholds the rules, not the rules that create and uphold group life."[12] It was Blumer's work that inspired Erving Goffman's work on individual and group behaviors in institutions, particularly in relation to stigma as a set of behaviors.[13]

We have discovered significant differences between the ways in which our five sociologists have understood society. For Karl Marx, capitalism, class, and alienation function as universals, as does the dialectical method; for Max Weber, a religious explanation of capitalism is fundamental, and the three authority types function as universals; and Emile Durkheim is clear that social facts are where our study of society should begin. In an actological context none of this is static: class, capitalism, alienation, religion, authority types, and everything else, change constantly, we change them, they change us, they change each other, and multiple other factors change them and are changed by them.[14]

---

9. Giddens, *Sociology*, 11–13, 348–49; Weber, *The Sociology of Religion*; Max Weber, *The Protestant Ethic and the Spirit of Capitalism*.

10. Cuff et al., *Perspectives in Sociology*, 123–26; Giddens, *Sociology*, 17–18; Gosling and Taylor, eds, *Principles of Sociology*, 130–32.

11. Cuff et al., *Perspectives in Sociology*, 125–33; Gosling and Taylor, *Principles of Sociology*, 132–34.

12. Blumer, *Symbolic Interactionism*, 18.

13. Goffman, *Asylums*; Goffman, *The Presentation of the Self in Everyday Life*; Goffman, *Stigma*; Torry, *A Modern Guide to Citizen's Basic Income*, 113–17, 138–39.

14. Benedict, *Patterns of Culture*; Peter Berger, *Invitation to Sociology*; Blumer, *Symbolic Interactionism*.

For all five of our sociologists, society is a reality, it is constituted by relationships between individuals, it is structured, and it changes constantly. Within an ontology it is difficult to encapsulate this complex meaning because the only beings are individual human beings and society can only be a reality in a secondary manner because it is not a single being. Within an actology, which understands reality as action in changing patterns, we can understand each individual human being as action in changing patterns and so as real, the interactions between human beings as action in changing patterns, and so as real, and society as action in changing patterns, and so as real. Society can be envisaged either as multiple changing patterns of action entangling with each other, or as a single complex changing pattern of action, or as both at once. There is such a thing as society, and it is as real as the unique individuals who constitute it.[15]

Societal change

The Institute for Social and Economic Research at the University of Essex summarizes their recent research on families and households in the UK:

> Family life in the UK is changing. One in four children under 15 no longer live with both biological parents, cohabitation is growing and children are leaving the parental home later. Families also contribute to the growing number of informal carers in the UK and there is increasing evidence of a "sandwich generation" looking after both their children and their parents.[16]

By 2011 "there had been a meltdown in the traditional nuclear family."[17]

The Institute for Social and Economic Research has also documented the rise of temporary and zero hour contracts, and of precarious self-employment:

> The quality of work has major implications for long-term career progression and for a wide range of wellbeing outcomes for people and their families. With the rise of non-standard work and self-employment, the nature and quality of employment has become a key policy debate.[18]

---

15. Torry, *A Modern Guide to Citizen's Basic Income*, 129–33.
16. Understanding Society, "Family and Households."
17. Centre for the Modern Family, *Family*, 4; Torry, *A Modern Guide to Citizen's Basic Income*, 133–39.
18. Understanding Society, "Employment."

Social attitudes have changed rapidly, too: for instance, civil partnerships for same sex couples in 2004, and same sex marriage in 2014.

A major factor driving all of this societal change is globalization, which has been a major topic for discussion among sociologists.

Globalization

Globalization is

> the social process in which the constraints of geography on economic, political, social and cultural arrangements recede, in which people become increasingly aware that they are receding, and in which people act accordingly.[19]

Social media platforms now enable us to contact someone on the other side of the world regularly and for free; the same company logos appear throughout the world; and in a news broadcast about an anti-globalization march the young man kicking in a shop window was wearing Nike trainers. We have generally trusted the local shopkeeper, we have learnt to trust supermarkets, and we now trust retailers elsewhere in the world. The internet and global supply chains mean that what happens thousands of miles away can affect all of us.[20]

But globalization is not a consistent phenomenon, and it is not static. It functions differently in different fields, and it is dynamic. In 2001 Malcolm Waters suggested that "material exchanges localize; political exchanges internationalize; and symbolic exchanges globalize,"[21] which means that economic exchange tends to remain local, politics is international, and cultures globalize. A quarter of a century later things are looking somewhat different. The rise of massive transnational companies, global supply chains, and increasing global transport of finished goods, mean that the economy is increasingly global; politics is now global and not only about national governments; cultures are globally accessible; and similar social policies are found throughout the world. The outcome is local, national, regional, international, and global aspects of all three of the economy, politics, and culture. It is no wonder that national governments now have little control over events, that manifesto commitments are so often derailed by events elsewhere in the world, and that protectionist governments are increasingly elected.

---

19. Waters, *Globalization* (London: Routledge, 2001), 5.
20. Giddens, *Sociology*, 50–76; Gosling and Taylor, *Principles of Sociology*, 159–77.
21. Waters, *Globalization*, 20.

For every action there is a reaction: and in relation to globalization this means resistance by the local. For instance, the globalization of the English language has contributed to a resurgence of Welsh and Scottish language and culture; and although Brexit was to some extent a result of lies being told, and a lack of understanding of the European Union, it was also a reassertion of national identity.[22]

The reality of globalization is that it is a complex network of changing local, national, regional, international, and global patterns of action. It is utterly real, constantly changing, constantly changing every other changing pattern of action, and constantly changed by them. Economics will continue to be local, national, regional, international, and global, with every level constantly interacting with every other; politics will continue to be local, national, regional, international, and global, with every level constantly interacting with every other; and culture will continue to be local, national, regional, international, and global, with every level constantly interacting with every other.[23] Because of the global, diverse, and constantly changing nature of globalization we shall never be able to predict its trajectory. New changing patterns of action will emerge and will change every other changing pattern of action.

ACTOLOGICAL ECONOMICS

> Economics: The branch of knowledge (now regarded as one of the social sciences) that deals with the production, distribution, consumption, and transfer of wealth; the application of this discipline to a particular sphere; (also) the condition of a state, etc., as regards material prosperity; the financial considerations attaching to a particular activity, commodity, etc.[24]

In this section of the chapter we shall study the "classical" model of economics and its traditional methods; how money is created and how it behaves; how values might relate to economics; and what economics looks like in an actological context.

---

22. Torry, *A Modern Guide to Citizen's Basic Income*, 140–43.
23. Waters, *Globalization*.
24. Oxford English Dictionary.

Classical economic models: Indifference curves, consumption, and employment choices

Because hours not spent in paid employment ("leisure") are useful to us, we say that they have utility; the goods that we buy with income that we earn also have utility; and so does each combination of leisure and earned income. If there is a number of combinations of leisure and earned income that an individual regards as offering equal utility then we say that they are indifferent as to which of the combinations they experience. We might picture this situation on a graph. In order to do that we have to simplify somewhat by employing earned income as a proxy for the various different goods that we might purchase with it. The vertical y axis of the graph represents earned income, and the horizontal x axis leisure hours (the total number of hours in a week minus the number of hours for which we are employed earning an income). We then plot on the graph the points where the combinations of earned income and leisure hours have equal utility, and then draw a curve through those points. This is an "indifference curve," because we are indifferent as to which of the different combinations of leisure and income we might experience. We might be able to draw a number of such curves, on each of which utility is equal and we are indifferent as to which combination of leisure and income we experience. The higher up the graph the curve lies, the higher the overall utility: so for maximum utility we shall wish to find ourselves on the highest curve possible.[25]

FIGURE 3

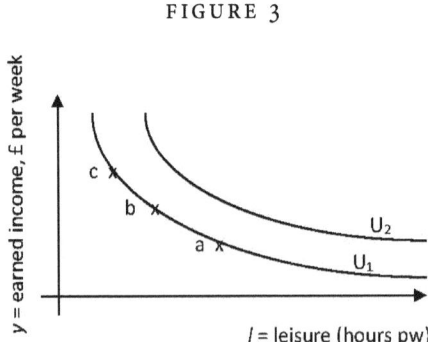

Indifference curves. At every point on each of the curves the combinations of the levels of leisure and income provide the individual with equal levels of utility. The level of utility along curve U_2 is higher than the level of utility along curve U_1.

25. Lipsey and Chrystal, *Economics*, 108–15; Torry, "Research Note: The Utility—or Otherwise—of Being Employed for a Few Hours a Week," 14–16; Torry, *A Modern Guide to Citizen's Basic Income*, 70–71.

We can draw utility curves as high as we wish, but that does not mean that infinite utility is available to us. The more hours we spend earning money, the less leisure we have, and vice versa, so we can draw a straight line on the graph: the "budget line," or "budget constraint." w represents the wage rate.

FIGURE 4

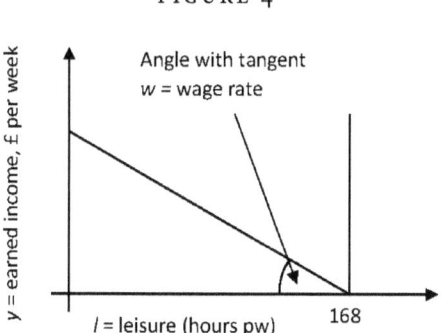

Budget line, showing the relationship between the number of hours of leisure and the earned income. Points above the line are not feasible.

Below the budget constraint utility levels are available to us, but above it they are unobtainable. This means that maximum utility is available to us where the budget restraint is at a tangent to a utility curve. The higher the wage, the higher the utility curve to which the budget restraint is a tangent.[26]

FIGURE 5

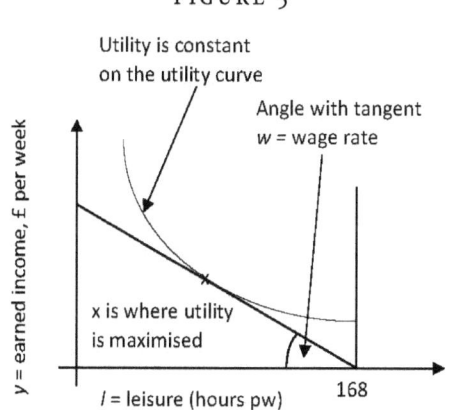

Utility is maximized where the budget constraint is at a tangent to an indifference curve.

26. Torry, "Research Note"; Torry, *A Modern Guide to Citizen's Basic Income*, 71–72.

A MULTIDISCIPLINARY ACTOLOGY

By employing the theory represented by these graphs, social scientists can make testable predictions: for instance, that a means-tested benefits system with specified characteristics is likely to incentivize an individual to seek employment for fewer hours per week than would a benefits system differently specified.[27] In relation to this example, and in relation to others, there is evidence that in some cases and under some circumstances lived experience matches classical economic theory's predictions, but there are plenty of cases in which this is not the case. There are several reasons for this. One is that the theory makes assumptions that might not be accurate. For instance, if only employment at forty hours per week is available, then the only point on a utility curve that will be available will be lower than the one that forms a tangent to the budget constraint.

FIGURE 6

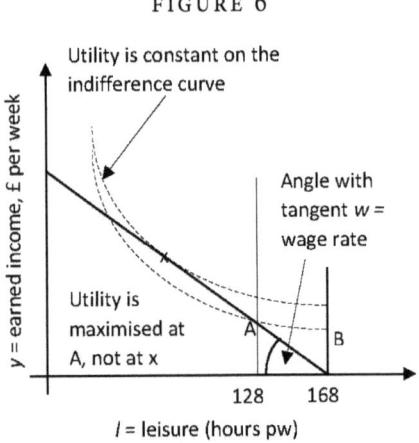

If only full-time jobs at 40 hours per week are available, then utility is maximized at point A, and not at x.

It is easy enough to incorporate such an employment hours constraint into the theory and its predictions: but there are other factors that are not so easy to incorporate. So far the factors that we have taken into account are wage rate, time spent in paid employment, the individual's utility levels in relation to disposable income and leisure (hours not spent in paid employment), and the employment hours available. None of these complicate the model. However,

27. Atkinson and Flemming, "Unemployment, Social Security and Incentives," 6–16; Brown and Levin, "The Effects of Income Taxation on Overtime; Deaton and Muellbauer, *Economics and Consumer Behavior*, 282; Deaton, *Understanding Consumption*, 193; Shone, *Applications in Intermediate Microeconomics*, 1–24; Torry, "Research Note"; Torry, *A Modern Guide to Citizen's Basic Income*, 73–74.

there might be other factors that do.[28] For instance, we have assumed that the whole of the individual's earned income is available for purchasing goods that generate utility: that is, that earned income is equal to disposable income. This might not be the case. For instance, the higher the number of hours of employment, the less the individual might need to spend on heating their home. Under such circumstances, the budget constraint becomes a curve concave to the origin and no longer a straight line.

So far we have found additional factors that might complicate the model, but they leave it intact. The more serious challenge comes from questions posed by the foundational presuppositions on which the entire model is based. For instance, the very idea of an indifference curve on which utility is equal at every point is seriously open to question. The concept relies on an individual being able to ascribe a single utility value to a combination of a specific number of paid work hours and a specific level of disposable income and then being able to compare that with the value of the utility related to a different combination of paid work hours and a different amount of disposable income. Given the complexity of our personalities, needs, and desires; of the circumstances in which we might find ourselves; and of the bundle of factors that would affect differently every combination of income and paid work hours, it is difficult to see how we might be able to ascribe the same value to two situations that would be better described as incommensurable, and even more difficult once we recognize that our needs, desires, and circumstances change all the time: so even if we might be able to say that one combination of income and paid work hours had the same value as another, the next moment it would not. The same would be true of another complicating factor: each of us is enmeshed in a complex set of personal relationships, and each of those relationships' participants will have their own preferences relating to our income and paid work hours. This will be particularly true of spouses and children. Those preferences will only add to the unpredictability of any value that we might ascribe to combinations of disposable income and paid work hours; and those preferences, like ours, will change over time, making the ascribing of comparable values even more problematic. All of this suggests that the situation that each of us faces is extremely diverse and dynamic, so the concept of a stable indifference curve is beginning to look extremely dubious. Because indifference curves are at the heart of classical economics, the entire edifice is beginning to look like a work of fiction, which in turn suggests that practical policy that relies on the assumptions and predictions of classical economic theory should start to look elsewhere for a theoretical basis, and

---

28. Mideros and O'Donoghue, "The Effect of Unconditional Cash Transfers on Adult Labour Supply."

preferably for one that makes no assumptions. The most likely candidate in relation to social policy would appear to be unconditionality of provision and access, as no questions of economics or human behavior would then arise, and no assumptions would need to be made.[29]

So what should we now be looking for in terms of economic theory? As Nancy Cartwright has suggested, economic theories might work to some extent in particular circumstances, but we cannot assume that any of them would work in every set of circumstances.[30] There are no economic laws. So first of all we should not regard the kind of economic theory that we have discussed so far in this chapter as in any way normative, and neither should we be looking for a single theory that would accurately describe and explain the highly diverse and dynamic reality that we call the economy. As we have seen, it is difficult if not impossible to operationalize such a central economic concept as utility as the basis of economic theory. We now turn to a concept even more central to the economy and ask whether we can construct usable theory around it.

Money

There is nothing inevitable or natural about money. Economies have operated without it: but it is difficult to see how the kinds of modern complex economies within which we live could function if money had not been invented and if it had not evolved to become a means of exchange, a store of value, and a unit of account.[31] Money is a classic example of a social construct: it is constantly constructed by billions of daily transactions in which participants ascribe value to it; and as long as it is created in that way it acts as a player in the economy. Money has value because we say that it has; it can be exchanged for goods because we say that it can be; and we can construct accounts with it because that is what we do and we have found it to be useful. And because money can do all of these things because we say that it can do them, it now ascribes value, controls the exchange of goods, and determines the way in which accounts are kept. As Michel Serres has pointed out, money is to the economy rather like a rugby ball is to a game of rugby. It is the focus of attention and the most important player in the game, because together we decide that it is

---

29. Peters, *Policy Problems and Policy Design*; Torry, *Unconditional*.
30. Cartwright, *The Dappled World*.
31. Galbraith, *Money*, 15; Lipsey and Chrystal, *Economics*, 480–92; Mason, *PostCapitalism*, 10–15.

those, and because it is those things it controls the other players in the game. A rugby ball is therefore more subject than object, and so is a "quasi-object."

> In most games, the man with the ball is on offense; the whole defense is going to organize itself relative to him and his position. The ball is the center of the referential system for the moving game ... Participation is ... the abandoning of my individuality or my being into a quasi-object that is there only to be circulated. Strictly, it is the transubstantiation of being into relation. Being is abolished for relation.[32]

Money is like the rugby ball:

> It circulates like a ball—money—a quasi-object. It marks the subject; it marks it effectively: ... I am rich, therefore I am. Money is integrally my very being.[33]

As Serres suggests, money has no being: it is simply relation, controlling and controlled by relationships around it. Whenever I make a transaction that involves money I influence the way in which money behaves and so change what it is; and at the same time money controls the ways in which I make transactions. Money is quintessential action in changing patterns entangling with the action in changing patterns that constitute the cosmos and all of the changing patterns of action that constitute it; and because money can only be described in terms of action in changing patterns, and not in terms of being, in an actological context it is more real than anything else—which of course it is.

Money creation

The dynamic diversity begins with the creation of money. If a bank lends money to someone then it writes money to their account, and by that means it creates money that the loan's recipient can spend on goods and services. When the debtor pays back the money, the electronic entry falls to zero and the money no longer exists. The same occurs when we use a credit card. We create money when we buy something with our credit card; and when we pay off the debt we destroy the money. In neither case is the bank lending only money that depositors have deposited with it. It is always lending more than that, on the usually reasonable assumption that all of its depositors will not demand the return of their deposits at the same time. If that happens then the

32. Serres, *The Incandescent*, 167, 169.
33. Serres, *The Parasite*, 169.

bank collapses, so governments establish bank lending limits related to the level of deposits, and also guarantee bank deposits up to a certain level.

Another source of money is governments, which through their central banks can create as much money as they wish in order to pay for public services. What they must not do is create too much money, because as soon as the value of money in circulation is greater than the value of goods and services available for purchase, money starts to lose its value and inflation occurs. This is why governments levy taxes: to withdraw money from the economy. So there are two ways to think of tax revenue: either as a means of paying for public services, or as a means of keeping control of the amount of money in circulation once the government has created money to spend on public services. Either way, the government has to ensure that it can collect taxes and that it can pay for public services. Theoretically anyone can create money by creating and distributing tokens: but if that were to happen to any significant extent then it would displace the sovereign currency, and the government's ability to withdraw money from the economy through taxation would be reduced. This is why alternative currencies are restricted to such local projects as babysitting circle tokens, small-scale local currencies that can only be spent in local businesses, and the global cryptocurrencies that governments can do nothing about.[34]

The problem with this description of how money is created is that it treats money as an object rather than as relational. A rather more dynamic discussion of how money begins is represented by the demand equation $PQ = MV$, where P is price, Q the quantity of production, V the velocity of money—the number of times that the same money is spent each year; and M the quantity of money. PQ is the Gross Domestic Product (GDP): so the equation tells us that if the velocity of money remains constant, then the rate of change of GDP is equal to the rate of change of the money supply, whereas if the velocity of money rises—that is, the same money changes hands more often—then GDP can increase even if the amount of money in the economy remains constant.[35] The question that the demand equation does not answer is that of causality. Does an increase in the money supply, or an increase in the velocity of money, increase GDP, or does an increase in the value of the economy's production (PQ) drive an increase in the money supply and/or the velocity of money? Evidence from US government spending during the Great Depression suggests the latter.[36] Demand will grow until the economy has reached the limits of material and human resources available to it as long as there is enough

34. Mellor, *Money*.
35. Galbraith, *Money*, 221; Lipsey and Chrystal, *Economics*, 499.
36. Miller, "Demand Side Economics and its Consequence."

money, and the money moves fast enough, to enable the goods and services produced to be purchased.[37]

One important question to ask now is this: *Should* GDP grow? Might such economic growth put at risk the climate and our environment and therefore the human race?[38] Not necessarily. It all depends on what is produced. If we create wind turbines that then displace coalmines then we might be reducing carbon emissions and thus ameliorating climate change. Another important question to ask is this: Will increasing automation increase unemployment, reduce labor income, reduce consumption, and thus both increase inequality and shrink the economy? Quite possibly: hence the suggestion that the corporations to which increasing proportions of the proceeds of production are flowing should be taxed and the proceeds used to pay unconditional incomes to every individual to enable them to pay for the goods and services produced.[39] A few individuals amassing large fortunes does little for the velocity of money, whereas circulating money through individuals' incomes and into consumption would increase its velocity. The economy would grow without additional money having to be created. One complexity is that because poorer people's propensity to consume is greater than that of wealthier people, redistribution from rich to poor might cause an increase in consumption, and much of that consumption might cause additional carbon emissions and thus additional climate change.[40] A relevant response would be to charge a carbon tax and to circulate the proceeds to households via an unconditional income. This policy package would not only reduce inequality further, but it would also ameliorate and potentially cancel out any increase in carbon emissions due to economic growth.[41] Something similar to this approach is already operating in Canada.[42]

Rather than saying that money *is*, it would be more accurate to say that money *happens*. It happens when a bank employee, an account-holder, or anyone else, accesses a banking website or a card transaction website page and types letters and figures on their keyboard; it happens when I hand over a banknote and I am provided with a product or a service; and it happens when

---

37. Torry, *A Modern Guide to Citizen's Basic Income*, 242–44.

38. Gough, *Heat, Greed and Human Need*.

39. Clifford, "What Billionaires and Business Titans Say about Cash Handouts in 2017"; Huczynski and Buchanan, *Organizational Behavior*, 424; Piketty, *Capital in the Twenty-First Century*, 281; Wilkinson and Pickett, *The Spirit Level*.

40. Sager, "Income Inequality and Carbon Consumption.".

41. Howard et al., "Ecological effects of Basic Income."

42. Government of Canada, "Government of Canada Fighting Climate Change with Price on Pollution."

an employer completes a monthly tax return. Money has velocity. And all we have discussed so far is how money behaves within a single country. Add the global economy to our discussion, and money is multiple layers of activity: it is highly complex action in changing patterns. It is actological, and it is as real as anything else.

CONCLUSIONS

In this chapter we have studied two social sciences: sociology, and economics; and in subsequent chapters we shall study psychology and politics, the latter of which will include discussion of the arguably separate discipline of social policy. All of these are sciences in the sense that theories are constructed, empirical evidence is sought, and theories are either corroborated or defeated. All of them—and particularly the sociology and economics discussed in this chapter—are actological in the sense that society and the economy are action in changing patterns, and study of them is likewise action in changing patterns.

Society is changing patterns of action, globally, internationally, regionally, nationally, and locally, and every aspect of it, such as those that we have discussed in this chapter, is action in changing patterns around which we have placed a socially constructed boundary. In order to match the society that it studies, sociology, and the theories that it develops and tests against the evidence, must be changing patterns of action as well.

We have studied classical economic theory and found it somewhat wanting, which has led us to ask about the possibility of a more actological economic theory more attuned to the diversity and dynamism of the actual economy; and we have studied the creation and behavior of money, and have found that money is already actological: it is action in changing patterns. We can extrapolate that finding to the discovery that the entire economy is action in changing patterns: the performance of services, the production of goods, financial transactions, money creation, the behavior of money, and so on. The only elements of the economy that we could possibly treat as beings that change are objects that are bought and sold, and individual human beings who buy and sell. Every other aspect of the economy is clearly action in changing patterns. It is "relating" rather than "relationships," and it is multiply entangled action in changing patterns. For instance: increasing automation, and resultant increasing monopoly in technology, retail, and so on, are causing a higher proportion of the proceeds of production to go to capital and a lower proportion to labor. This is having a knock-on effect on people's ability to purchase the goods and services produced, which in turn has an effect on demand, and therefore on investment and supply. This suggests that a social policy priority might be to recycle at least some of the proceeds of production to the population as a whole so that they can afford the goods and services produced and maintain an active economy.[43] There is no boundary to action in changing patterns: every changing pattern of action changes every other, at least to some extent: and any proposed policy change has to take into account a seriously complex network of relatings.

So what we need now is theory to match this understanding of the economy as actological. The problem with the graphical and mathematical expressions of economic theory with which we are familiar in the context of classical economic theory is that they represent an essentially static economy, and not one understood as action in changing patterns with all of the dynamism and diversity that an actological understanding of the economy implies. One approach is to abandon graphical and mathematical expressions and to employ narrative techniques in the way in which we have done in our discussion of sociology and in the latter sections of this chapter. We shall then need to take lessons from complexity theory's understanding of institutions, for money clearly is an institution: an organized system of activity. Göktuğ Morçöl asks us to treat institutions as complex networks of activity that might be self-organizing to some extent,[44] which means treating them as emergent, self-organizing, and dynamic complex systems. The relationships among the actors of this complex system are nonlinear, and the system's relationships with its elements and with other systems are co-evolutionary.[45]

Quite what graphical and mathematical expressions of an actological economics might look like is a task for another day, and probably for someone else: but one thing that we know already is that at its heart money will have velocity and will not be an object.

---

43. Clifford, "What Billionaires and Business Titans Say about Cash Handouts in 2017"; Huczynski and Buchanan, *Organizational Behavior*, 424; Piketty, *Capital in the Twenty-First Century*, 281; Torry, "Review Article; Wilkinson and Pickett, *The Spirit Level.*"
44. Morçöl, *A Complexity Theory for Public Policy*, 158–59.
45. Morçöl, *A Complexity Theory for Public Policy*, 266.

Chapter 7

Actological psychology

> Psychology: The scientific study of the nature, functioning, and development of the human mind . . . the branch of science that deals with the (human or animal) mind as an entity and in its relationship to the body and to the environmental or social context, based on observation of the behaviour of individuals or groups of individuals in particular (ordinary or experimentally controlled) circumstances . . . The psychological aspects *of* an event, activity, phenomenon, etc., esp. considered as a subject for study.[1]

INTRODUCTION

THE RELATIONSHIP BETWEEN THE mind and the body is far from simple. The brain is part of the body, but what of the mind? Is it somehow separate from the brain? And what do we make of research that shows that we make decisions before we are conscious of them, and further research that shows that consciousness of a decision emerges during a complex decision-making process?[2] There is nothing that we do, say, or think, that does not relate somehow to our minds, so psychology—study of the mind—relates to all of that. And once we include social psychology—the study of minds working

---

1. Oxford English Dictionary
2. Guggisberg and Mottaz, "Timing and Awareness of Movement Decisions"; Koenig-Robert and Pearson, "Decoding the Contents and Strength of Imagery before Volitional Engagement."

together—we find ourselves studying social activity and everything to which it connects. Here we shall only be able to touch on a few aspects of psychology, but it will be enough to reveal that it is an inherently actological discipline.

PSYCHOLOGY

The contents page of Ronald Smith's 1993 textbook *Psychology*[3] reveals the breadth of the discipline: psychology as the science of behavior; research methods; the roots of behavior in biology and in the influences encountered during infancy, childhood, adolescence, and adulthood; sensation; perception; states of consciousness; learning; memory; reasoning; problem-solving; intelligence; motivation; emotion; personality; stress; coping; wellbeing; psychological disorders and their treatment; social influences on behavior; social interaction; and applications of the discipline of psychology.

Psychological indicators of a healthy society

A briefing paper from Psychologists for Social Change lists "five evidence based psychological indicators of a healthy society": agency, security, connection, meaning, and trust.

> A sense of agency and mastery over one's life is crucial for positive mental health and well-being . . . Employment insecurity is associated with a range of individual and family psychological difficulties, including distress . . . depression . . . strained relationships, and overall poorer life satisfaction . . . Similarly, insecure housing resulting in frequent house moves impairs academic performance and probably other aspects of child well-being, particularly for low-income families. Financial insecurity worries often form a basis for family stress, which can contribute to poorer outcomes for children, including their mental health . . . Positive mental health and well-being is deeply connected to our relationships with others and is a core psychological need. One of the greatest protective factors for positive mental health is social support, and indeed its opposite, loneliness, is very bad for our health . . . [we need] more time to spend on activities that connect to values, potentially creating more meaningful lives that are more psychologically fulfilling . . . social policies that improve social cohesion and trust are likely to reduce mental health problems.[4]

3. Smith, *Psychology*.
4. Psychologists for Social Change, *Universal Basic Income*.

On the basis of their five psychological requirements for a healthy society, Psychologists for Social Change argue for a Basic Income—an unconditional income for every individual—on the basis that it would improve agency, security, connection, meaning, and trust. For our purposes their paper is useful because it shows how connected our minds are to every aspect of our lives and of the life of the society in which we live, and that it is activity that makes those connections. Our minds are constituted by changing patterns of action that entangle with the changing patterns of action that constitute the people to whom we relate, the communities and societies in which we live, and the institutions with which we engage.[5]

Stress

If in situations full of uncertainty and complexity the demands made on us overwhelm the cognitive and other resources available to us, then we experience stress.[6] Stress was useful when it prepared the prehistoric hunter to prepare for fight or flight, but the kind of longer term stress that we suffer from today, whether generated by poor job quality, overwhelming caring responsibilities, poverty, or inequality, can damage both mental and physical health.[7] The World Health Organization has found that "the greater the inequality, the higher the inequality in risk":[8] and in relation to social inequality, poor job quality, and more generally in complex and risky circumstances, it is failure to meet psychological needs that is at the root of long-term stress.[9] Simply the possibility of impending insecurity can create stress, and when stress increases, the cognitive capacity required to manage the situation is reduced, so

---

5. Torry, *A Modern Guide to Citizen's Basic Income*, 91–95.

6. Bekker et al., "Combining Care and Work," 28–43; Smith, *Psychology*, 466.

7. Dekker and Schaufeli, "The Effects of Job Insecurity on Psychological Health and Withdrawal," 57–63; Jones et al, *Family Stressors and Children's Outcomes*; Murali and Oyebode, "Poverty, Social Inequality and Mental Health"; Paterson and Neufeld, "The Stress Response and Parameters of Stressful Situations."

8. World Health Organization and Calouste Gulbenkian Foundation, *Social Determinants of Mental Health*, 9.

9. Butterworth, et al., "The Psychosocial Quality of Work Determines whether Employment has Benefits for Mental Health"; Di Domenico and Fournier, "Socioeconomic Status, Income Inequality, and Health Complaints"; Dooley, "Unemployment, Underemployment, and Mental Health"; Fryers, et al., "Social Inequalities and the Common Mental Disorders," 236; Murphy and Athanasou, "The Effect of Unemployment on Mental Health"; Paterson and Neufeld, "The Stress Response and Parameters of Stressful Situations," 8; Sverke et al., "No Security."

stress can become overwhelming:[10] and as soon as a stressed person becomes embroiled in the daily "microstressors" of government bureaucracy, normal functioning can be reduced to almost zero.[11] Climbing out of the situation can become impossible, and the result is "alarm, resistance, and exhaustion"[12] and "persistent psychological distress, reduced task performance, and over time, declines in cognitive capabilities."[13] The ability to employ normal coping strategies evaporates,[14] and the effects can be permanent.[15] The only way to reduce the problem of today's high levels of stress is to reduce social risk.[16]

This discussion of stress offers yet another recognition that there are no boundaries to action in changing patterns. Every changing pattern of action tangles with every other to some extent. This is why our circumstances affect our mental and physical health, our physical and mental health affects our circumstances, and all of it is affected by large-scale societal changing patterns of action, and we together affect those. There is no escape: so if we want to see change in any aspect of this tangled bundle of action in changing patterns then we have to seek change beyond ourselves.

Motivation

Motivation is "an internal process that influences the direction, persistence, and vigor of goal-directed behavior":[17] so we study motivation in order to discover "why human . . . organisms think and behave as they do."[18] There are two kinds of motivation: "Intrinsic motivation" "is the energy source that is central to the active nature of the organism."[19] When our psychological

---

10. Carr and Chung, "Employment Insecurity and Life Satisfaction"; Mani et al., "Poverty Impedes Cognitive Function"; Mullainathan and Shafir, *Scarcity*, 47, 64–67; Quinlan et al., "The Global Expansion of Precarious Employment, Work Disorganization, and Consequences for Occupational Health."

11. Kohn et al., "Hassles, Health and Personality"; Smith, *Psychology*, 467.

12. Taylor, *Health Psychology*, 200.

13. Taylor, *Health Psychology*, 201.

14. Smith, *Psychology*, 487.

15. Cohen and Edwards, "Personality Characteristics as Moderators of the Relationship between Stress and Disorder"; Smith, *Psychology*, 474–75.

16. Dean, *Social Policy*, second edition, 119–20; Marmot, *Fair Society, Healthy Lives*, 24, 32–33; Torry, *A Modern Guide to Citizen's Basic Income*, 103–6.

17. Smith, *Psychology*, 367.

18. Weiner, *Human Motivation*, 1.

19. Deci and Ryan, *Intrinsic Motivation and Self-determination in Human Behavior*, 11.

needs for "competence, autonomy, and relatedness" are met,[20] intrinsic motivation is enhanced, but it is "vulnerable to the continued encroachment of environmental forces."[21] So we would expect insecure housing, insecure employment, and challenging family relationships, to reduce intrinsic motivation,[22] and secure employment, secure housing, and positive family relationships, to enhance it. The less pressured environment that a level of unconditional income would foster would increase intrinsic motivation. "Extrinsic motivation," on the other hand, is driven by external causes rather than by our longer-term psychological needs.[23] So, for instance, research has shown that

> children who are expected by their teachers to gain intellectually in fact do show greater intellectual gains after one year than do children of whom such gains are not expected.[24]

In many practical circumstances both intrinsic and extrinsic motivations will be working either together or against each other to influence our decisions and actions. So, for instance, we might experience an intrinsic motivation to seek employment, and once in employment we find that the external negative motivation of difficult working conditions is demotivating and that the financial reward of the wage is an external positive motivation.[25]

Experiments have shown that if we were being rewarded for something that we were doing for its own sake, and the extrinsic reward was then withdrawn, then motivation might drop, and might fall below the level that it was at before the rewards were offered.[26] However, if we experience rewards as recognition of performance, rather than as an incentive to undertake a future task, then rewards can be motivating; and rewards can also be motivating if a task is initially undertaken for reward.[27] All of these psychological effects are quite small, they often depend on the context, and the connections between

---

20. Ryan and Deci, "Self-determination Theory and the Facilitation of Intrinsic Motivation, Social Development, and Well-being."

21. Deci and Ryan, *Intrinsic Motivation and Self-determination in Human Behavior*, 43.

22. Reeve and Deci, "Elements of the Competitive Situation that Affect Intrinsic Motivation."

23. Pittman and Heller, "Social Motivation."

24. Rosenthal and Jacobson, *Pygmalion in the Classroom*, 121.

25. Bryson and MacKerron, *Are you Happy while you Work?*

26. Brehm et al., *Social Psychology*, 62; Lepper and Greene, eds, *The Hidden Costs of Reward*, xi; Smith, *Psychology*, 369.

27. Brehm et al., *Social Psychology*, 62; Cameron and Pierce, "Reinforcement, Reward, and Intrinsic Motivation"; Smith, *Psychology*, 370.

motivation and the activities described have been contested:[28] but what research has shown is that

> widely differing external constraints will undermine creativity, as long as those constraints can lead people to view their work as extrinsically motivated rather than intrinsically ... positive effects of reward ... appear when intrinsic motivation is kept salient, when extrinsic motivation becomes less salient ... and when rewards signify competence or enable performance of interesting new activities—rather than signifying external control of behavior ... A considerable body of ... evidence suggests that constraint placed on task engagement has consistent negative effects on creativity.[29]

To take a particular example: research has shown that the level of the wage or salary is not a significant motivator, and that "only procedural justice [is] related to intrinsic work motivation ... how people's compensation is determined and communicated has implications for employees' need satisfaction."[30] [31]

In one sense there is nothing special about motivation: "an internal process that influences the direction, persistence, and vigor of goal-directed behavior."[32] It is a process in the brain that influences other processes in the brain and that is itself influenced by other processes in the brain. The result is a diverse and constantly changing tangle of changing patterns of action involving our brain, our muscles, our senses, and our environment. What *is* special about motivation, and the reason for the conceptual boundary that we place around it, is that it influences goal-directed behavior: that is, motivation is changing patterns of action that are future-oriented and outward-oriented. As with all subsets of action in changing patterns, the boundary around the changing patterns of action that we term "motivation" is both individually and socially constructed, so there is nothing intrinsic about it, and different individuals will locate the boundary in different places. So, for instance, whilst the wage level might be motiving or demotivating, should we regard the fact of being paid as a motivator, or simply as a requirement without which we would not be able to accept the paid employment? Either way, payment, doing the work, being ourselves, the motivations that we experience: all of it is action in changing patterns.

28. Eisenberger and Cameron, "Detrimental Effects of Reward: Reality or Myth?"; Tang and Hall, "The Overjustification Effect."
29. Amabile, *Creativity in Context*, 171, 177.
30. Olafsen et al., "Show them the Money?" 455.
31. Torry, *A Modern Guide to Citizen's Basic Income*, 95–100.
32. Smith, *Psychology*, 367.

Social norms

In the Zimbardo prison study college students were allocated roles as guards and prisoners and began to behave in ways that aligned with their perceptions of those roles, showing how much "social systems exert profound influences on our thoughts, emotions, attitudes, and behavior."[33] They were following social norms: patterns of behavior that we absorb from the societies in which we live.[34] A particularly prevalent social norm is that of reciprocity: a bidirectional pattern with four variants: "ante/required," in which a resource will only pass from person A to person B if the required condition is met; "ante/expected," in which a contribution is expected from person B before person A extends the resource to them, but that contribution is not required; "post/required," in which B has to reciprocate once A has provided the resource; and "post/expected" in which B is expected to reciprocate after A has provided the resource but is not required to do so.[35] Stuart White gives an example of post/expected reciprocity:

> where institutions governing economic life are otherwise sufficiently just, e.g., in terms of the availability of opportunities for productive participation and the rewards attached to these opportunities, then those who claim the generous share of the social product available to them under these institutions have an obligation to make a decent productive contribution, suitably proportional and fitting for ability and circumstances, to the community in return. I term this the fair-dues conception of reciprocity.[36]

The reciprocity social norm, like any other, is constituted by diverse patterns of action entangled with multiple other personal, interpersonal, and social patterns of action, and the label "reciprocity" that we ascribe to a set of changing patterns of action is simply a recognition that we have noticed a family resemblance between them, an important characteristic of which is bidirectionality.

Changing our minds

In the United Kingdom and in other countries public opinion appeared to shift quickly from rejection of the possibility of same sex marriage to significant

---

33. Smith, *Psychology*, 570.

34. Haslam and Reicher, "When Prisoners take over the Prison"; Staerklé, et al., "A Normative Approach to Welfare Attitudes," 81–83; Zimbardo, "Pathology of Imprisonment."

35. Dean, *Social Policy*, second edition, 51; Torry, *A Modern Guide to Citizen's Basic Income*, 64–66, 108–9.

36. White, *The Civic Minimum*, 59.

levels of acceptance. How did such a rapid change in the patterns of action that constitute our minds come about?

Our attitudes are shaped by the social norms discussed above, by people around us, by our upbringings and education, and so on, and they can become deeply embedded:[37] that is, significantly entangled with the changing patterns of action that constitute who we are. However, persuasive alternatives can dissolve and reshape these patterns of action, and such change can either be localized to a particular set of understandings, or radical and wide-ranging, reshaping every changing pattern of action that constitutes our minds and activities.[38]

Group and societal conversion experiences can be more complicated. A member of a family, group, community, or society, will generally be seeking public approval, so even if a minority opinion persuasively and consistently expressed has prompted them to think through an issue and to change their mind about it, they might be hesitant to reveal that change for fear of disapproval: but one member of the family, group, community, or society, explaining that they have been converted to the formerly minority opinion, can enable all of those members of the former majority to reveal their conversions to the minority opinion, and the formerly minority opinion can be found to have become the majority opinion. This is probably what has happened in relation to same sex marriage. A lot of people appear to have changed their minds on the subject without saying so, and a few public declarations of similar mind-changing, particularly among much-watched television personalities, has enabled families and communities to discover widespread mind-changing.[39]

BEHAVIORAL ECONOMICS

Behavior is what we do: it is patterned human action, and so is intrinsically actological—but where does the study of human behavior belong? The science that studies human behavior in relation to the economy is sometimes called "behavioral economics," and in some cases there is a reason for that: but because it is human behavior that we are studying, its natural home is

---

37. Hogg and Vaughan, *Social Psychology*, 152–53; Smith, *Psychology*, 578–80; Staerklé et al., "A Normative Approach to Welfare Attitudes," 114.

38. James, *The Varieties of Religious Experience*; Sargant, *Battle for the Mind*.

39. Moscovici, *Influence and Social Change*, 81, 109; Moscovici, "Toward a Theory of Conversion Behavior"; Moscovici, "Social Influence and Conformity," 348–49, 401; Nemeth et al., "Patterning of the Minority's Responses and their Influence on the Majority," 61; Nemeth et al., "Exposure to Dissent and Recall of Information"; Torry, *A Modern Guide to Citizen's Basic Income*, 117–20; Van Avermaet, "Social Influence in Small Groups," 408–10, 418.

within psychology.[40] To recognize that certain aspects of behavioral science are about both the economy and about how the human mind works, this section is called "behavioral economics" and is located within a chapter about psychology.

A focal concept in behavioral economics is "nudge," which represents the ways in which governments and other institutions attempt to influence behavior patterns in an era in which governments, companies, and other organizations are less trusted, and more direct educational methods can be counterproductive. In this situation, it can be more effective to alter the "choice architecture" that people face than to tell people what would be good for them. Instead of posters telling people to keep their doctors' appointments, they might tell people how much additional money would be available to the National Health Service if everyone was to keep their appointments. In a different context, telling employers to enrol everyone in an occupational pension, and then giving people the freedom to leave it if they wish, is a more effective way to enable workers to build their pensions than inviting them to opt in to occupational pension schemes. Sometimes simply framing a statistic differently can have an effect: for instance, more people are likely to agree to a medical operation if they are told that ninety per cent of people survive it than if they are told that ten per cent of people die during it.[41] In all of these cases the behavioral outcome depends on how the choice is framed.

> Framing works because people tend to be somewhat mindless, passive decision makers. Their Reflective System does not do the work that would be required to check and see whether reframing the question would produce a different answer. One reason they don't do this is that they wouldn't know what to make of the contradiction. This implies that frames are powerful nudges, and must be selected with caution.[42]

Is such framing ethical? We rightly criticize the surreptitious media bias that nourishes unevidenced conspiracy theories, so why should we not criticize surreptitious government and corporate framing that is designed to influence behavior? At the very least this is a "new paternalism,"[43] and it has been understandably accused of distracting government attention from the kind of evidence-based policy-making that can make a difference to people's lives.[44]

40. Egan, *A Macat Analysis*, 58–61.
41. Thaler and Sustein, *Nudge*, 37.
42. Thaler and Sustein, *Nudge*, 40.
43. Abdukadirov, "Introduction."
44. Egan, *A Macat Analysis*, 44–47, 65; Thierer, "Failing Better."

An important ethical factor will be the extent to which the nudge enables someone to choose and reach their own beneficial goals rather than fulfilling someone else's. An example of the former would be placing fruit next to the supermarket checkout; and an example of the latter would be placing sweets there.[45] And to ask an old political question: Who will nudge the nudgers, and with what agendas?[46]

In our chapter on economics we suggested that the classical economic model made a number of assumptions. One of those is that each individual is a utility-maximizing individual, which assumes that every individual understands the choices available to them and the differential utilities that they would deliver. Behavioral economics makes the opposite assumption: that we don't understand the choices available to us, and we don't understand their differential utilities.[47] As we have suggested, to abandon the rational utility-maximizing individual is to undermine the classical economic model, which the behavioral economics of "nudge" certainly does. However, that does not mean that we are left entirely without pattern to human action. For instance, an important experimental result is the "endowment effect": that the loss of something already possessed is more keenly felt than the gain of something of the same value in all respects.[48] [49]

As with all of the aspects of our psychology that we have studied in this chapter, this section on behavioral economics again shows just how interconnected everything is: or rather, how interconnected are changing patterns of action throughout the cosmos. We are constituted by the action in changing patterns that we are and by the changing patterns of action that impinge on us. Nothing escapes.

CONCLUSION

Whether we are asking about a healthy society, motivation, stress, social norms, or behavioral economics, we find ourselves understanding the ways that our minds work in terms of action in changing patterns, and particularly as changing patterns of action entangled with a potentially infinite number of

---

45. Citizen's Basic Income Trust, "Book Review: Peter John, *How Far to Nudge?*"; John, *How Far to Nudge?*; Rizzo, "The Four Pillars of Behavioral Paternalism"; White, "Overview of Behavioral Economics and Policy."

46. Smith, and Zywicki "Nudging in an Evolving Marketplace," 245; Williams, "Conclusion," 326.

47. Thaler, *Misbehaving*, 50.

48. Thaler, *Misbehaving*, 33–34; Thaler and Sustein, *Nudge*, 36–37.

49. Torry, *A Modern Guide to Citizen's Basic Income*, 100–103.

changing patterns of action that impinge on us. In the context of an actology there is a sense in which the human mind has no boundary. It is simply impossible to conceive of the mind as restricted to the human brain, which is changing patterns of action around which we can more easily locate a boundary. To understand the mind actologically reveals psychology to be a fascinating field of study with fewer limits than we might previously have thought.

Chapter 8

Actological politics

Politics: The science or study of government and the state.[1]

INTRODUCTION

POLITICS CROSSES BOUNDARIES INTO society, the economy, individual and social psychologies, language, history, and multiple other fields, so, as we would expect, the study of politics crosses boundaries into sociology, economics, psychology, social psychology, language, history, and multiple other fields of study. In this chapter we shall study a variety of aspects of politics and of the ways in which they are studied, and we shall also study a particular variant of politics: social policy. Social policy is a variant of politics that meets human needs, and rather than restricting itself to "government and the state" it seeks to understand how a wide diversity of social institutions contribute to the meeting of need: so the discipline that we call "social policy" studies human need and asks how social institutions meet it. As readers will see, it is not always easy to decide that a subject belongs to social policy rather than to politics more generally. Study of the concept of poverty is a case in point: discussion of the meaning of poverty and ways to address it are clearly both social policy issues and significantly political.

1. Oxford English Dictionary.

POLITICAL IDEOLOGIES

Paul Spicker suggests that ideologies are "inter-related sets of ideas and values which shape the way that problems are understood and acted on";[2] Botterill and Fenna that they drive social change;[3] and Robert Garner that they are

> action-orientated in the sense that they seek to promote a particular social and political order for which they urge people to strive ... all ideologies have different strands or schools, and sometimes there is considerable overlap between one ideology and another ... it is possible to distinguish between concepts at the core of an ideology from those which are further away from the centre and those which are at the periphery ... ideologies reflect, as well as shape, the social and historical circumstances in which they exist.[4]

An ideology is constituted by ideas, which means that in practical terms it is constituted by words both spoken and written. An ideology is an example of language, so in relation to speech it is changing patterns of action entangled with multiple other changing patterns of action—organizations, individuals, events, and so on; and in relation to text it is patterns with which the reader then engages, and the pattern of the text tangles with the action in changing patterns that constitute the reader and creates change in the reader's thought-forms and actions. And so, for instance, the relationship between social policy and any particular ideology will always be historically determined, with every social policy being the result of a variety of ideological pressures, leading to multiple compromises and therefore complexity, and every ideology being influenced by the evolutions of social policies associated with it.[5]

Whilst words such as "liberalism" and "socialism" might remain the same in terms of the pattern constituted by the letters, their meanings, like the meanings of all words, change constantly, which means that connections with other words change, and the ways in which the labels affect individuals' and institutions' ideas and actions change constantly. Abrupt change might be represented by an adaptation of the label: for instance, from "liberalism" to "neoliberalism"—a change that we might describe as a shift from rule-based

---

2. Spicker, *Social Policy*, 190.
3. Botterill and Fenna, *Interrogating Public Policy Theory*, 45, 110.
4. Garner et al., *Introduction to Politics*, 115–16.
5. Dean, *Social Policy*, second edition, 25.

market freedom for the common good[6] to an evisceration of the State's ability to make rules for the market.[7]

As well as changing constantly, the meaning of an ideological label or of the name of a political party will always be highly diverse, with the diversity rooted in the ideology's history. For instance, in the UK, the Labour Party emerged out of the trade union movement and succeeded in gaining parliamentary representation for industry's employees and eventually an electoral majority and the ability to found a more robust welfare state and to extract more of the proceeds of production for workers. The Labour Party has also attracted socialists, for whom a more egalitarian and co-operative society is the aim. These two groups, with their somewhat different ideas, have often been the reason for the Labour Party's electoral success and for its internal tensions. And socialism itself has often experienced a pendulum effect along a spectrum between communism and social democracy, the former envisaging the abolition of the State, private property, and the free market, and the latter the regulation of private property and of the market, and the extraction of resources from them to fund public services.[8]

All of liberalism, neoliberalism, socialism, and what we might call the "labourism" of industry's workers gaining more power over the proceeds of production, envisage a changing society. They might be seeking different goals and therefore different trajectories, but they are all dynamic, both in terms of the meanings of their descriptions, and in terms of the ways in which all of them generate change in the changing patterns of action that constitute society and the economy.[9]

One ideology that might look as if it is not dynamic in these senses is classic conservatism. The UK's Conservative Party used to be genuinely conservative: that is, it aimed to preserve tried and tested institutions. However, in a changing social and economic environment, doing that required change so that institutions might evolve in order to continue to serve society's changing needs in a constantly changing context. More recently the Conservative Party has actively sought to change social and economic institutions, and under Margaret Thatcher even to abolish society:

---

6. Brittan, *Towards a Humane Individualism*, 11, 42; Fleischer and Lehto, "Libertarian Perspectives on Basic Income"; Garner et al., *Introduction to Politics*, 117; Spicker, *Social Policy*, 196.

7. Mead, *The New Politics of Poverty*; Murray, *Losing Ground*; Murray, *Charles Murray and the Underclass*.

8. Garner et al., *Introduction to Politics*, 119, 123; Marx and Engels, *The Communist Manifesto*, 96, 99, 104; Spicker, *Social Policy*, 194–95;

9. Torry, *A Modern Guide to Citizen's Basic Income*, 198–205.

There is no such thing as society. There is living tapestry of men and women and people and the beauty of that tapestry and the quality of our lives will depend upon how much each of us is prepared to take responsibility for ourselves and each of us prepared to turn round and help by our own efforts those who are unfortunate.[10]

The claim to be "conservative" is now wearing rather thin.[11]

POVERTY

Poverty is a political issue, and a far from simple one. First of all, it has multiple dimensions: low income, poor housing, poor health, poor quality employment or no employment, inadequate education, and so on, all of which are incommensurable: that is, it would be difficult to decide that someone in poor housing was more or less poor than someone with inadequate education. And then there are complete incommensurables such as poor early socialization, abusive parenting, and so on, that both constitute poverty and cause additional poverties. To take just one aspect of poverty: Who is the poorest: someone without enough income who might be able to find additional employment and whose disposable income would rise by the amount of the additional earned income, or someone with more initial income and who might be able to find additional employment but for whom benefits withdrawal would mean that their disposable income would rise by only a small proportion of the additional earned income? The latter is initially less poor, but the former would find it easier to climb out of poverty. How might we be able to compare those two scenarios? It is no surprise that there is little consensus over the definition of "poverty."[12] For instance: Brian Abel-Smith and Peter Townsend understand poverty to mean simply income poverty,[13] whereas other authors include substandard housing, inadequate healthcare, poor educational provision, insufficient public transport, and so on.[14] This lack of consensus over the definition of poverty can mean that researchers, politicians, think tank personnel, journalists, and so on, can find themselves using the same word but meaning very different things. Family resemblances between the assumed

10. Thatcher, Interview for *Woman's Own*, 31 October 1987.
11. Garner et al., *Introduction to Politics*, 125; Giddens, *The Third Way*, 8, 13; Torry, *A Modern Guide to Citizen's Basic Income*, 205–8.
12. Spicker, *Social Policy*, 90–91; Torry, *Money for Everyone*, 161–68.
13. Abel-Smith and Townsend, *The Poor and the Poorest*.
14. Donnison, *The Politics of Poverty*; Seebrook, *Landscapes of Poverty*.

definitions might be rather distant. Suggesting that poverty should be defined in terms of some other broad concept—for instance, as "unmet needs"— merely shifts the definitional difficulty elsewhere.

Not only are definitions of poverty diverse and often insufficiently specified, but because we compare our own situation with those of people in social contexts close to our own,[15] each of us effectively develops our own definition of relative poverty, perhaps of the variety "The family next door can afford a holiday abroad and we can't." This suggests that whilst we might be able to describe someone with no home and no income as being in absolute poverty, much of our discussion of poverty assumes that poverty is relative poverty: relative, that is, to social norms, with "poverty" understood to mean "exclusion from ordinary living patterns"[16] or "social exclusion."[17] On this basis we can understand an individual or household being in poverty if they do not possess the resources required for a decent life in contemporary society, with those resources defined by a survey designed to discover what a representative sample of the population believe to be the resources required for that.[18] Attempts have been made to assess human need in a more objective way,[19] but these methods too end up delivering significantly socially constructed definitions of poverty, with the construction undertaken by academics rather than by focus groups.[20] Unfortunately it is often policies designed to alleviate poverty that construct the social meaning of it. For instance, benefits that are means-tested and therefore paid only to people with low or zero earned incomes define "poverty" as "on means-tested benefits": a process that does not occur with such unconditional benefits as the UK's Child Benefit, which therefore tend to dissolve the category of "the poor."

The fundamental problem with the definitions of poverty that we have discussed is that they tend to be static: that is, they create a category in which individuals and households are put. However, we have already discussed the difference between someone with a low income who is able to increase their disposable income and therefore climb out of poverty and someone on a higher income whose benefit withdrawal rate traps them in poverty. A further

15. Jordan et al., *Trapped in Poverty?*; Runciman, *Relative Deprivation and Social Justice*, 18.
16. Townsend, *Poverty in the UK*, 131.
17. Hills et al. eds, *Understanding Social Exclusion*.
18. Bailey and Bramley, "Introduction"; Davis et al., *A Minimum Income Standard for the United Kingdom in 2024*; Dermott, "Introduction"; Mack, "Fifty Years of Poverty in the UK"; Lansley and Mack, *Breadline Britain*; Lansley Mack, *Breadline Britain*.
19. Maslow, "A Theory of Human Motivation"; Spicker, *Social Policy*, 88–108; Townsend, *Poverty in the UK*, 32–34.
20. Dean, *Understanding Human Need*, 46–47; Dean, *Social Policy*, 89.

relevant characteristic of household incomes is that a household's disposable income can vary wildly from month to month.[21] It is such income characteristics that Ruth Lister has in mind when she defines poverty as a process: we would say, actologically. She understands individuals as agents with varying degrees of ability to climb out of poverty, with each person's practical ability to do that being partly determined by socially constructed rules and institutions.[22] This definition of poverty is helpful as it encourages policymakers to seek policies that will enable people to climb out of poverty and exercise their capabilities[23] rather than policies that will keep them in poverty and restrict their agency. And of course even better than policies that enable us to climb out of poverty are policies that keep us from falling into it in the first place: policies such as healthcare free at the point of use, and unconditional incomes.[24]

An unfortunate dynamic related to poverty is the ever-increasing inequality experienced by the world's nations' societies:[25] unfortunate not only because of the divisive effects that inequality has, and the ways in which it hands both economic and political power to a small group of wealthy individuals, but also because inequality restricts economic growth and increases poverty.[26] Globalization and technological change, and a consequent reduction in the proportion of the proceeds of production going to labor income, are major drivers of increasing inequality,[27] as are an employment market increasingly divided globally between high-paid, high-skilled jobs and low-paid, low-skilled jobs, and also wealthy individuals' ability to shift their assets into tax havens.[28] In 2009 Richard Wilkinson and Kate Pickett found correlations between education, health, income, and other inequalities, but they had not proved causality, and further research showed that it is deep social structures that are at the root of all of the different inequalities:[29] so it is those

21. Hills, *Good Times, Bad Times*; Tomlinson, *Irregular Payments*.

22. Lister, *Poverty*, 94–97, 145–46, 178–83; Lister, *Poverty*, second edition.

23. Sen, *The Idea of Justice*, 225–52, 370–71.

24. Burchardt and Vizard, *Developing a Capabilities List*; Rosner, *The Economics of Social Policy*, xiv–xv; Torry, *A Modern Guide to Citizen's Basic Income*, 209–13; Torry, *Unconditional*.

25. Atkinson, *Inequality*, 105; Deaton, ed., *Dimensions of Inequality*.

26. Hills et al., *Understanding the Relationship between Poverty and Inequality*; Lansley, "Tackling Inequality is an Economic Imperative."

27. Crocker, "Funding Basic Income by Money Creation"; Piketty, *Capital in the Twenty-First Century*.

28. Atkinson, *Inequality*, 82; Evans and Williams, *A Generation of Change, a Lifetime of Difference?* 313; Graeber, *Bullshit Jobs*.

29. Bergh et al., *Sick of Inequality?* **70**; Dean, *Social Policy*, second edition; Dorling,

deep structures that need to change.³⁰ This suggests that inequality will not be reduced by increasing the incomes of poorer households by increasing the levels of means-tested benefits. All this achieves is more poor households trapped in poverty.³¹ The prescription is the same as that for poverty, because to reduce poverty would reduce inequality: so what is required is the ability to climb out of poverty, which suggests healthcare free at the point of need, high quality and free education for everyone, and an income structure based on an unconditional income that would not be withdrawn however much additional income might be earned.³² Whether income should be redistributed more or less than it is at the moment is a subsidiary question: what matters is people's ability to reduce their own poverty and for them not to be prevented from doing so.³³ Both poverty and inequality are diverse and dynamic and are processes, and so are best studied through an actological lens.

CITIZENSHIP

A citizen is a "legally recognized subject or national of a state, commonwealth, or other polity, either native or naturalized, having certain rights, privileges, or duties,"³⁴ and a discussion of citizenship is appropriate in a chapter about politics because politics is "the science or study of government and the state"³⁵, citizens are citizens of a state, and citizens elect governments.

Citizenship is both diverse and dynamic. First of all, it is different in different places. Take the UK as an example. The establishment of separate governments in Northern Ireland, Scotland, and Wales, all with differing devolved powers in relation to a variety of public services, and all elected by voters in the relevant parts of the UK, has given to people living in Northern Ireland, Scotland, and Wales, layered citizenships different from the citizenship experienced by people living in England. The addition of citizenship of

---

Injustice; Spicker, *Social Policy*, 43–57; Torry, "Review Article: *The Spirit Level*, by Richard Wilkinson and Kate Pickett"; Wilkinson and Pickett, *The Spirit Level*.

30. Dorling, *The Equality Effect*, 84, 93.

31. Edmiston, "Review Article: Welfare, Austerity and Social Citizenship in the UK," 267; Edmiston, "Introduction."

32. Dorling, *Injustice*, 245; Lo Vuolo, "Piketty's *Capital*, his Critics and Basic Income"; Torry, *A Modern Guide to Citizen's Basic Income*, 213–16; Torry, *Two Feasible Basic Income Schemes for the UK, and a Feasible Pilot Project for Scotland*; Wilkinson and Pickett, *The Spirit Level*, 263–64.

33. Torry, *A Modern Guide to Citizen's Basic Income*, 216–20.

34. Oxford English Dictionary.

35. Oxford English Dictionary.

the European Union appears to have constituted a little too much complexity for a majority of UK referendum voters in 2016. Whilst citizenships broader than the nation state might be coming under pressure, citizenships internal to the nation state are growing in salience and putting nation state citizenship under pressure.[36] As David Held puts it,

> The study of citizenship has to concern itself with all those dimensions which allow or exclude the participation of people in the communities in which they live and the complex pattern of national and international relations and processes which cut across them.[37]

And then there is the legislative change that constantly moves the boundaries around who is and who is not permitted to reside in the UK: and whilst the UK might offer a particularly extreme example of constant change to rules about visas, asylum, and refugee status, similar, albeit slower, change occurs elsewhere.[38] Citizenship is both diverse and dynamic: it is actological.

Citizenship rights have been as dynamic as citizenship itself in the sense that they have evolved through time and remain diverse. Citizenship rights have evolved through three stages: civil rights, such as rights relating to contracts; political rights, such as the right to participate in elections and to stand for election; and social rights, such as access to the public services of a welfare state.[39] As T.H. Marshall described social rights in 1950:

> By the social element I mean the whole range from the right to a modicum of economic welfare and security to the right to share to the full in the social heritage and to live the life of a civilized being according to the standards prevailing in the society.[40]

Not every evolution of citizenship rights has happened in the order proposed by Marshall. Sometimes modest welfare rights have preceded civil and political rights,[41] and it is perfectly possible for the evolution to go into reverse, and for social rights to wither, which in turn compromises citizens' ability to exercise civil and political rights:[42] but there has always been diversity and a dynamic

36. Aneesh, "Differentiating Citizenship"; Purdy, "Citizenship, Basic Income and Democracy."
37. Held, *Political Theory and the Modern State*, 203.
38. Dean, "The Ethics of Migrant Welfare," 25–26.
39. Heywood, *Political Theory*, 210–13.
40. Marshall, *Citizenship and Social Class and Other Essays*, 10–11.
41. Golding, "The Primacy of Welfare Rights," 135–136; Standing, "Why You've Never Heard of a Charter that's as Important as Magna Carta."
42. Coote, "Social Rights and Responsibilities"; Heywood, *Political Theory*, 213–15;

process, again suggesting that, as with citizenship itself, an actological lens might be the best approach to the study of citizenship rights. The study of citizenship rights has also been dynamic. For instance, whether economic rights should be regarded as a category of citizenship rights in their own right, or should rather be understood as a subcategory of social rights, has been a matter of debate. Here again we have action in changing patterns, so an actological lens would be helpful here, too.[43]

Just as dynamic as citizenship rights have been citizenship duties: not surprisingly, as to grant a right implies that some individual or institution has a duty to ensure that the right can be exercised, which will generally require the provision of resources. So, for instance, paying taxes is a citizenship duty that enables citizens to exercise their social rights by accessing public services. A citizenship duty that has changed radically during the past fifty years, and that continues to change, is the duty to undertake paid employment in order to provide the worker with an income that enables them to ensure that they and their dependents can exercise civil, political, and social rights, and that they can pay the taxation required for others to exercise the same rights. However, a duty implies that it can be exercised, and the globalization of employment markets, increasing automation, and companies' ability to move production to wherever in the world they can produce most cheaply, has meant a collapse in full-time stable skilled and semi-skilled employment in manufacturing and extractive industries. This problematizes the ability to exercise a citizenship duty, and thus compromises the duty itself.[44] One option is to see unpaid labor as an equivalent means of fulfilling citizenship duties, and for that to happen a number of social policies will have to change, particularly in relation to income provision.[45]

Reynolds and Healy, eds, *New Frontiers for Full Citizenship*, 8; Roche, *Rethinking Citizenship*, 4, 16, 167; Torry, *A Modern Guide to Citizen's Basic Income*, 220–23.

43. Heywood, *Political Theory*, 211; Marshall, *Citizenship and Social Class and Other Essays*, 10–11; Melden, "Are there Welfare Rights?" 276.

44. Culpit, *Welfare and Citizenship*; Heywood, *Political Theory*, 216–18; Plant, "Needs, Agency, and Welfare Rights," 73; Sherman and Jenkins, *Licensed to Work*, 57; Standing, *Work after Globalization*.

45. Pettinger, *What's Wrong with Work?* 39–47; Reynolds and Healy, *New Frontiers for Full Citizenship*, 69; Purdy, "Citizenship, Basic Income and Democracy"; Sherman and Jenkins, *Licensed to Work*, 156; Torry, *A Modern Guide to Citizen's Basic Income*, 223.

ACTOLOGICAL SOCIAL POLICY

> Public policy: Policy, esp. of government, that relates to or affects the public as a whole; social policy.[46]
>
> Policy science: The systematic study of the making and implementation of policy, esp. social policy; any of the academic disciplines which deal with this study.[47]
>
> Social administration is the study of the development, structure and practices of the social services... the social services are mainly understood to include social security, housing, health, social work and education...[48]

There is no entry for "social policy" in the Oxford English Dictionary, although the entry for "public policy" refers to "social policy" as if the reader is bound to know what that means. The London School of Economics defines social policy like this:

> Social policy is concerned with the ways societies across the world meet human needs for security, education, work, health and wellbeing. Social policy addresses how states and societies respond to global challenges of social, demographic and economic change, and of poverty, migration and globalisation. Social policy analyses the different roles of: national governments, the family, civil society, the market, and international organisations in providing services and support across the life course from childhood to old age. These services and support include child and family support, schooling and education, housing and neighbourhood renewal, income maintenance and poverty reduction, unemployment support and training, pensions, health and social care. Social policy aims to identify and find ways of reducing inequalities in access to services and support between social groups defined by socio-economic status, race, ethnicity, migration status, gender, sexual orientation, disability and age, and between countries.[49]

For our purposes, the relevant words here are "is concerned with... addresses ... analyses ... aims to identify ... find ways of reducing ..." Social policy is

---

46. Oxford English Dictionary.
47. Oxford English Dictionary.
48. Spicker, *Social Policy*, 477, 1.
49. London School of Economics, "What is Social Policy?"

a process, so is appropriately described by using verbs; and the study of social policy is similarly best described by using verbs.

Making social policy

In an actological context both social policy and the study of social policy will be action in changing patterns, among those changing patterns will be perspectives, strategies, national economies, participants in the policy process, institutional formal and informal structures,[50] the ideological, electoral, and career interests of individuals involved,[51] the commercial interests of computer companies with government contracts,[52] and so on, and those changing patterns of action will be different in every time and place.[53] New and changing social policy will influence the economy, communities, families, individuals, organizations, and much more, and those will influence governments, think tanks, trades unions, and other institutions in the policy process, and so will influence social policy.[54] All of this means that any study of social policy will have to ask about the *changing* patterns of action that constitute social policy, and therefore the changing patterns of action that constitute all of the institutions and individuals in any way engaged with it.[55] For instance, in the UK context it would be particularly important to study the changing relationship between the "heroic" policymaking of government ministers and the more "humdrum" contributions of civil servants.[56]

The problem for anyone engaged with policy-making is that everything changes all the time. Social problems are socially constructed on the basis of lived experience, and both the lived experience and the associated narratives will change constantly; and any solutions implemented will be constantly

50. Dunn, "'Stage' Theories of the Policy Process," 115.
51. Ham and Hill, *The Policy Process in the Modern Capitalist State*, 124, 146; Hill, *The Public Policy Process*, 19, 90, 102, 105; Majone, *Evidence, Argument, and Persuasion in the Policy Process*, 76; Marcello Natili, *The Politics of Minimum Income*.
52. French, and Raven, "The Bases of Social Power"; Hill, *The Public Policy Process*, 191.
53. Blomquist, "Policy and Socioeconomic Characteristics."
54. Birkland, *An Introduction to the Policy Process*, 97–103; Ham and Hill, *The Policy Process in the Modern Capitalist State* 124; Hill, *The Public Policy Process*, 4; Hodge and Lowe, *Understanding the Policy Process*, 160; Smith, *Psychology*; Spicker, *Social Policy*, 137–50; Torry, *The Feasibility of Citizen's Income*, 226; Zahariadis, "Ambiguity, Time, and Multiple Streams," 74.
55. Bartels, "Policy as Practice."
56. Page, "'Whatever Governments Choose to Do or Not to Do'"; Diamond, *The End of Whitehall*.

changed by both relevant and irrelevant factors: irrelevant, that is, in relation to social problems, but highly relevant in relation to political exigences.[57] The process by which social policy is constantly made and constantly changed would be difficult to understand as a rational system: a mistake too often made by thinktanks.[58] The process might best be compared to a "primeval soup"[59] that evolves in unpredictable directions in such a way that any part of the changing complex process can enhance, negate, or corrupt any other part of it.[60]

Whilst the policy process is changing patterns of action, those changing patterns will always exhibit family resemblances: hence the experience of "path dependency"[61] in policy-making: that is, the policy process is likely to continue in the same direction even if radical change would benefit society and every individual within it. Paradigm shifts are difficult enough for individuals: for complex institutions they can seem impossible[62]—until they happen, that is. After the event, radical change can appear obvious and sensible, an important example being the UK's 1942 Beveridge Report on the future of the welfare state, and the National Health Service and unconditional Family Allowance (later Child Benefit) that emerged from it.[63] Important reasons for path dependency are that different members of policy communities might pull in different directions; policy networks—communication networks relating to policy fields—might be full of contradictory evidence, contradictory theory, and contradictory framings of social problems;[64] and we understand

---

57. Anglund, "American Core Values and Policy Problem Definition," 151; Dean, *Social Policy*, second edition, 99; Gregory, "Political Rationality or Incrementalism?" 189; Minogue, "Theory and Practice in Public Policy and Administration," 12, 15; Spicker, *Social Policy*, 63–69; Turnbull, "Policy as (Mere) Problem-solving."

58. Birkland, *An Introduction to the Policy Process*, 191; Botterill and Fenna, *Interrogating Public Policy Theory*, 63, 78; Garnett and Garnett, *British Think-tanks and the Climate of Opinion*, 195.

59. Gordon et al., "Perspectives on Policy Analysis"; Hill, *The Public Policy Process*, 88, 108, 157.

60. Colebatch, "Linkage and the Policy Process"; Morçöl, *A Complexity Theory for Public Policy*; Hill, *The Public Policy Process*, 6, 73.

61. Majone, *Evidence, Argument, and Persuasion in the Policy Process*, 77; Zahariadis, "Ambiguity, Time, and Multiple Streams," 90.

62. Hill, *The Public Policy Process*, 159; Jacobs and Shapiro, "The Media Reporting and Distorting of Public Opinion towards Entitlements," 136.

63. Beveridge, *Social Insurance and Allied Services*; Torry, *Unconditional*, 173–80, 182–84.

64. Hill, *The Public Policy Process*, 58–66; Hodge and Lowe, *Understanding the Policy Process*, 155, 160–61.

the way things work,[65] so changing a complex system can look like a risk not worth taking:[66] so we "satisfice";[67] that is, policy-makers study only a small number of minor tweaks to the existing system rather than consider options for radical change.[68] It might be true that policy pendulums and gyrations are becoming more common as political values bifurcate under pressure from social media silos and politicians, and political parties follow suit:[69] but it is still true that we "muddle through."[70] [71]

The fact that social policy is a *complex* network of entangled patterns of action suggests that complexity studies might be helpful as we study it. Complex physical systems frequently exhibit both chaos and self-organization.[72] An obvious example is living organisms: "the result of the unfolding of many developmental mechanisms that have become integrated with one another ... such integrated complexity generally yields simplicity."[73] The same is true of both social policy and the study of social policy. So, for instance, households are agile entrepreneurs that seek the most advantageous routes around a complex social policy landscape;[74] and tax and benefits systems in countries with more developed economies tend to be complex, and if they are to be able to evolve along with their environment then they will need to remain diverse and not over-controlled by any one element. This suggests that simplification of the system is not required, but that a mixture of unconditional, social insurance, and means-tested provisions is what is required.[75]

It is already clear that social policy is a complex network of entangled changing patterns of action. It is intrinsically actological and so must be studied as such, which means that any study of social policy needs to be focused on the policy process, and that particular policies should be discussed more

65. Richardson, "Interest Group, Multi-arena Politics and Policy Change"; Rose, "Inheritance before Choice in Public Policy," 51; Smith, *Psychology*, 56–65.

66. Smith and May, "The Artificial Debate between Rationalist and Incrementalist Models of Decision Making," 166; Rose, "Inheritance before Choice in Public Policy," 51.

67. Richardson and Jordan, *Governing Under Pressure*, 21–22.

68. Barkai, *The Evolution of Israel's Social Security System*, 199; Hill, *The Public Policy Process*, 156–57, 164, 188.

69. Botterill and Fenna, *Interrogating Public Policy Theory*, 96, 110.

70. Botterill and Fenna, *Interrogating Public Policy Theory*, 82.

71. Torry, *A Modern Guide to Citizen's Basic Income*, 148–54.

72. Davies, in *The New Physics*, 4; Nicolis, "Physics of Far-from-equilibrium Systems and Self-organisation"; Prigogine and Stengers, *Order out of Chaos*.

73. Kauffman, *The Origins of Order*, 642.

74. Jordan et al., *Trapped in Poverty?*

75. Hodgson, *Evolution and Institutions*, 13; Torry, "A New Agenda: Complexity Theory, Tax and Benefits"; Torry, *A Modern Guide to Citizen's Basic Income*, 154–55.

in terms of the ways in which they change than in relation to any aspects that appear not to do so.

Social administration

Just as social policy changes constantly, so the study of social policy changes, both in relation to changing social policy and in relation to other factors that affect the academic and thinktank worlds. In the early days of the London School of Economics, what we now call "social policy" was called "social administration": a term usually now reserved for a particular aspect of the discipline of social policy.

> Social administration is the study of the development, structure and practices of the social services ... the social services are mainly understood to include social security, housing, health, social work and education ... [76]

Social administration as a subdiscipline usually concerns itself with the administrative minutiae of public services. To take an example: the UK's Child Benefit is paid to the main carer for every child in the UK, at the same rate for every first child in the family and at the same rate for every subsequent child. It is still unconditional, regardless of the fact that high-earners living in households that receive Child Benefit are charged additional Income Tax. Administration of Child Benefit is radically simple. The administration of a Basic Income—an unconditional income for every individual—would be equally simple once the required database was in place.[77] Means-tested benefits are at the other end of the spectrum: the amount that someone receives depends on their household structure, earned and other income, responsibilities for dependents, employment status, and so on. Detailed enquires have to be made into claimants' circumstances, and changes in those circumstances can cause their benefits to gyrate wildly and their domestic budgets likewise. Fraud and error are rife, and it is often difficult to tell the difference between them.[78] Equally complex would be a proposed "Participation Income": an income that would depend on fulfilling a "social participation" condition but otherwise unconditional. Certain individuals, such as individuals over a retirement age, people with disabilities, and so on, would be exempt from having to fulfil the

76. Spicker, *Social Policy*, 477, 1.

77. Torry, *A Modern Guide to Citizen's Basic Income*, 172–77, 187–90.

78. Morris, "The Structure of Personal Income Taxation and Income Support," 210–18; Parker, *Instead of the Dole*, 6; Spicker, "Five Types of Complexity"; Torry, *A Modern Guide to Citizen's Basic Income*, 177–78, 185–87.

participation condition, but everyone else who wished to receive the income would have be in employment or self-employment, studying full-time, caring for others, or undertaking approved voluntary work. In order to test a recipient's right to the Participation Income detailed enquiry would have to be made. Research shows that just one per cent of the UK's population would be likely to be excluded from receipt of the Participation Income, so the effort spent on administration would cost more than the money saved. Such an income would either not be implemented in the first place or would be quickly abandoned.[79]

A significant test of how complicated a particular kind of benefits system might be is how easy it is to administer, an important indicator of which is how easy it is to computerize. Child Benefit was computerized decades ago without any problems, and the same would be true of a Basic Income. When this author was working as a Clerical Officer on the public counter of Brixton's Supplementary Benefits office during the late 1970s we made the system work for claimants. Many of their family structures and other circumstances did not fit the complicated regulations, so we had to make sure that they did. Computerization of means-tested benefits has always been problematic for both administrators and claimants. Administration and computerization of a Participation Income would rapidly collapse.[80]

CONCLUSION

A significant factor in relation to the different kinds of income discussed in the section above on social administration has been what is *done*, and in particular the enquiries that have to be made when the amount of the benefit to be paid to an individual or a household is calculated. What has to be done by the claimant, and what has to be done by the benefits administration, are both elements of the complexity or otherwise of the system, and a result of it. What therefore matters when we study social administration is the changing patterns of action of the individuals and institutions involved. We have seen that the same has been true of the other aspects of politics and social policy and of the study of them that we have explored in the earlier sections of the chapter. Politics and social policy are inherently actological, so any study of them must be actological and must treat them as action in changing patterns.

---

79. Atkinson, "The Case for a Participation Income"; Torry, *The Feasibility of Citizen's Income*, 134–39; Torry, *A Modern Guide to Citizen's Basic Income*, 179–83.
80. Torry, *A Modern Guide to Citizen's Basic Income*, 183–84.

Chapter 9

Actological organizational behavior

Organization: The condition of being organized; systematic ordering or arrangement; . . . the way in which particular activities or institutions are organized . . . The action or process of organizing, ordering, or putting into systematic form; the arrangement and coordination of parts into a systematic whole; *spec.* the action of banding together or gathering support for a political cause . . . An organized body of people with a particular purpose, as a business, government department, charity, etc.

Behavior: An organized body of people with a particular purpose, as a business, government department, charity, etc.

Institution: A law, custom, convention, etc., that is widely recognized and accepted within the political or social life of a community, society, or civilization . . . An organization or association established for a social purpose, typically educational, charitable, or scholarly in nature . . . any social or political organization of considerable size or influence. [1]

INTRODUCTION

Much of this chapter relies on research into management theory conducted while the author was researching the characteristics and management of

---

1. Oxford English Dictionary.

religious organizations between 2000 and 2016,[2] and particularly while he was writing the two volume *Managing Religion: The Management of Christian Religious and Faith-Based Organizations*.[3] Where those two volumes contain more developed treatments of management theory than will be found here, references to *Managing Religion* will appear in the footnotes.

In this chapter, as in the book *Mediating Institutions: Creating Relationships between Religion and an Urban World*,[4] an institution will be understood in actological terms as changing patterns of action, and organizations as a subset of institutions. So, for instance, both marriage and money are action in changing patterns, and so are institutions, but they are not organizations, and a company limited by guarantee is action in changing patterns and is both an institution and an organization.[5]

The science of organizational behavior is a social science like sociology, economics, and social policy: it studies organizations in order to develop testable theories, and, like any scientific theory, because organizations are always dynamic and diverse, any theory will be local and temporary and might not apply in a different place or at a different time. This means that theories developed and tested in one type of organization might not apply in another type, and in particular it is why religious and faith-based organizations require their own treatment and we cannot assume that theory developed elsewhere will necessarily apply to them.[6]

In Chapters 6 and 7 we have alluded to the way in which the institution of marriage has changed, and Chapter 6 on social sciences treats the institution of money as action in changing patterns, so we do not need to study non-organizational institutions here. What we shall be doing in this chapter is studying organizations as changing patterns of action, so we shall be looking for management theory that coheres with that understanding.

---

2 Harris and Torry, *Managing Religious and Faith-based Organisations*; Rochester and Torry, "Faith-based Organizations and Hybridity"; Torry, "The Practice and Theology of the South London Industrial Mission"; Torry, ed. *The Parish*; Torry, *Managing God's Business*; Torry, ed. *Diverse Gifts*; Torry, ed. *Regeneration and Renewal*; Torry, "Voluntary, Religious and Faith-based Organizations"; Torry, "On Building a New Christendom"; Torry, *Bridgebuilders*; Torry, "Is there a Faith Sector?"; Torry and Heskins, eds. *Ordained Local Ministry*; Torry and Thorley, eds. *Together and Different*; Torry, *Managing Religion*, volumes I and II; Torry, *Mediating Institutions*.

3. Torry, *Managing Religion*, volumes I and II.

4. Torry, *Mediating Institutions*.

5. Torry, *Mediating Institutions*, 2–3.

6. Torry, *Managing God's Business*; Torry, *Managing Religion*, volumes I and II; Torry, *Mediating Institutions*.

SUPPLY RIVERS

An organization is "an organized body of people with a particular purpose, as a business, government department, charity, etc.,"[7] which means that it functions in society as a single entity as well as as its human and other constituents, and in that sense it can be understood as an alternative to market mechanisms. The market is frequently a highly efficient means for providing us with the goods and services that we need. So, for instance, if there is something wrong with my car then I might attempt to mend it myself and purchase any parts that I might need in the shop down the road; or if I am lacking either the skills or the time required then I might take the car to an organization that repairs cars and pay them to do it: that is, I am likely to choose either a market or an organizational solution in relation to my perception of the various costs of each of them. In a broader context, each individual cannot provide themselves with streetlighting by purchasing streetlamps in the market and installing them. Here an organizational approach is essential. As Ronald Coase suggested in 1937, organizations occur where market mechanisms would be either impossible or more expensive than organizations undertaking the task;[8] and because in a market competition and economies of scale are likely to be operating, if a market solution exists then it is likely to be the cheaper option.[9] A further factor might be frequency of transaction. If a transaction is to take place only once then a market transaction might be appropriate, whereas a frequent transaction might mean that it would be worth an organization establishing the infrastructure for creating the service or part so that they can be created inhouse. Yet another factor would be security of supply. If a particular part is crucial to the manufacture of a complex object such as a car, then it might not be worth taking the risk of purchasing them from another company that might fail to supply them. Inhouse production might therefore make sense even if it might be more expensive. And yet another factor might be the complexity of specifying the characteristics of a part or service, the cost of managing a contract in the market, and the cost of monitoring production quality in another organization. Even if inhouse manufacture might be more expensive per item, the total cost of inhouse production might prove to be lower.[10]

---

7. Oxford English Dictionary.
8. Coase, "The Nature of the Firm," 391.
9. Besanko et al., *Economics of Strategy*.
10. Besanko et al., *Economics of Strategy*; Coase, "The Nature of the Firm," 391; Powell and DiMaggio, *The New Institutionalism in Organizational Analysis*, 4; Torry, *Managing Religion*, volume I, 22–25; Williamson, "The Economics of Organizations."

The distinction between markets and organizations might be a somewhat false one, because no market transaction occurs without organizations being involved (for instance, banks, and government organizations that regulate weights and measures), and no organizations exist that do not engage in market transactions (for instance, markets for labor and for financial services). But the extent to which markets and organizations merge into each other will also depend on the conceptual framework within we study organizations. In an ontological context it might look as if the market and organizational approaches are radically different, because purchasing several objects in a market looks different from employing a single organization, whereas in an actological context the market and organizational approaches can begin to look rather more similar because then we are studying what is done rather than who or what does it. Take the example of car manufacture. Let us suppose that I have the skills to build my own car. I will then buy the raw materials, create the parts, and build the car. The same process would occur in a factory, although no doubt mainly undertaken by robots rather than by human beings. Some of those parts might be made by the company, and some, such as light bulbs, the company might buy in from other companies, because it would be cheaper for the company to buy those than to establish an entire light bulb manufactory of its own. Whether the various processes took place in the market or within an organization, the same things would be done, and in both cases a complex pattern of changing patterns of action would take place, the market and organizational solutions would bear substantial family resemblances to each other, and significant drivers of change in the patterns of action would be varying relative costs between market and organizational solutions and the relative extents of automation of both market and organizational processes. Rather than understanding the process as a supply chain, perhaps we ought to call it a supply river, and understand the river to be turbulent.

WORK PROCESSES

Perhaps the most important contract in any organization is that between employer and employee. As Frederick Taylor put it in 1911:

> What the workmen want from their employers beyond anything else is high wages, and what employers want from their workmen most of all is a low labor cost of manufacture.[11]

---

11. Taylor, *Scientific Management*, 22.

At the Bethlehem Steelworks in the United States Taylor broke down manual workers' activities into completely definable tasks, and then decided the best way to undertake them and the time that each task should take. The result was more efficient activity, higher profits, and higher wages.[12] A similar scientific approach, and one more humanizing, was taken by Lilian Gilbreth, who established experiments to discover the optimum amounts of work and leisure for efficient production, which led to paid holidays, a shorter working day, canteens, and better factory heating and lighting.[13] Again we are in the world of action in changing patterns, for that is what work is. If a human being is a complex changing pattern of changing patterns of action, and the industrial and service industry worlds are changing patterns of action with which the changing patterns of action that constitute the individual are entangled, then a proper understanding of the worker and of the company for which they work will require an actological approach that understands both the process by which the individual does the work required of them and the action in changing patterns within which that work is done.

ORGANIZATIONS AS NETWORKS OF PEOPLE

The previous section of this chapter has treated organizations as economic realities, with both individuals and organizations treated as at least to some extent engaged with economic changing patterns of action. Here we shall develop further our understanding of organizations' participants as changing patterns of action engaged with each other and with organizational activity, both within and without their own organizations, with all of it understood as action in changing patterns. In this respect every individual becomes a relatively autonomous agent engaging with other relatively autonomous agents, rather than being understood as an economic unit.[14] As Peter Abell puts it, we shall be studying "the structure and functioning and performance of organizations and the behavior of groups and individuals within them."[15] In Chapter 7 we have already studied how individuals can be socialized into roles—for instance, into "jailer" and "prisoner" roles:[16] and precisely the same happens to individuals working in organizations: that is, the changing patterns of

---

12. Huczynski and Buchanan, *Organizational Behavior*, 413–17; Taylor, *Scientific Management*, 29, 38.

13. Huczynski and Buchanan, *Organizational Behavior*, 418–20, 424; Torry, *Managing Religion*, volume I, 27–28.

14. Taylor and Bain, "'An Assembly Line in the Head,'" 110–13.

15. Abell, *Organisation Theory*, 10.

16. Zimbardo, "Pathology of Imprisonment."

action that constitute the individual are changed by those that constitute other individuals in the organization and by the communication and other action in changing patterns that constitute the organization.[17]

In terms of metaphors, we shall be treating organizations as "flux and transformation" and as "organisms"[18] and studying what happens rather than what is. For instance, early exercises in management theory found that management activity could be characterized as forecasting, planning, organizing, commanding, coordinating, and controlling, and that "esprit de corps" and initiative were as important as division of work, authority structures, discipline, and so on.[19] Even when we study the ubiquitous bureaucratic structures of organizations, what we are in fact studying are the ways in which communication travels between individuals in the organization, and how individuals in the organization internalize how the organization works: that is, the changing patterns of action that constitute who we are are changed by our engagement with the action in changing patterns that constitutes the complex network of communication around the organization.[20] A particularly interesting finding relates to the diverse lengths of time during which action in changing patterns at different levels of an organization can influence changing patterns of action throughout the organization. A particular pattern of action of a Chief Executive Officer might influence other changing patterns of action for twenty years; a supervisor, by writing rotas, might influence changing patterns of action for a week; and a call center telephonist might influence other changing patterns of action for three minutes.[21]

Diversity has been found across the organizational field as well as within individual organizations. Different kinds of industry require different technologies, and these generate organizations with different structures; and further factors that can influence organizational structure are the analyzability of tasks; the speed with which technology changes; the ways in which technological change changes employment;[22] how stable the marketing environment might be; and customers' ability to substitute alternative products.[23] A

17. Martin and Nicholls, *Creating a Committed Workforce*; Sherif, *The Psychology of Social Norms*, 25.
18. Morgan, *Images of Organizations*.
19. Fayol, *General and Industrial Management*.
20. Weber, *The Theory of Social and Economic Organization*, 328.
21. Jaques, Elliott, *Requisite Organization*, 1, 37–41.
22. Daugareilh et al., *The Platform Economy and Social Law*, 29; Mowshowitz, "Virtual organization," 267.
23. Bruun and Duka, "Artificial Intelligence, Jobs and the future of Work"; Brynjolfsson and McAfee, *The Second Machine Age*; Burns and Stalker, *The Management of Innovation*, 20; Daft, *The New Era of Management*, 375; Greve, *Technology and the Future*

similar diversity can be found in relation to the structures and activities of groups within organizations.[24] What we mean by "structure" is the ways in which changing patterns of action relate to each other and constitute an organization, so a general conclusion is that everything is contingent: that is, the characteristics of the changing patterns of action that constitute organizations are influenced by a wide variety of factors.[25]

ORGANIZATIONAL CULTURE

One of the "symbolic resources"[26] deployed by organizations to enable them to fulfil their purposes is their culture:[27]

> collective . . . emotionally charged . . . historically based . . . inherently symbolic . . . dynamic . . . inherently fuzzy . . . shared sets of beliefs, values, and norms, that both impel people to action and justify their actions to themselves and others:[28]

and particularly "dynamic." Organizations will often invest in their cultures as a contribution to "organizational capital" that can reap cultural and other dividends, and it might be particularly useful for both the organization and everyone involved in it for everyone to foster a culture of trust.[29] This is efficient for both markets and organizations because it means that little effort has to be expended on supervision, that contracts can be minimally specified, that long-term relationships can evolve seamlessly, and that rapid decisions can be made in fast-changing environments. But what do we mean by "trust" here? Indeed, what do we mean by "culture"?

The relevant definition of "culture" is

> the distinctive ideas, customs, social behaviour, products, or way of life of a particular nation, society, people, or period. Hence: a society or group characterized by such customs, etc. . . .[30]

---

of Work; Perrow, *Organizational Analysis*, 90; Woodward, *Industrial Organization*, 50, 57; Woodward, *Management and Technology*, 18.

24. Baron and Greenberg, *Behavior in Organizations*, 348.
25. Perrow, *Organizational Analysis*, 49; Torry, *Managing Religion*, volume I, 30–40.
26. Abell, *Organisation Theory*, 10.
27. Robins and Judge, *Organizational Behavior*, 585.
28. Trice and Beyer, *The Cultures of Work Organizations*, 5–7, 75.
29. Ghoshal and Moran, "Bad for Practice," 41–42; Tomer, *The Human Firm*, 2, 6.
30. Oxford English Dictionary.

In the context of an ontology, culture so defined is not a being and so has to be counted as less real than beings. In the context of an actology, we can understand culture as changing patterns of action and so as real as anything else. Ideas are changing patterns of action within our minds and communicated by language; customs are quintessential changing patterns of action; and social behavior and way of life similarly. As David Kreps puts it, an appropriately evolving culture is "an intangible asset carrying a reputation that is beneficial for efficient transactions, conferring that reputation upon whoever currently owns the asset":[31] and what is essential is that an organization's culture should be able to change as the organization and its context both change,[32] which means that organizational culture will vary from country to country and from organization to organization.[33] Culture is changing patterns of action, with the emphasis on both the pattern and the changing; and because organizations are complex changing patterns of action, with both formal and informal communication channels, within each organization we shall find multiple diverse cultures that are "multiple, dissenting, emergent, organic, counter, plural, resisting, incomplete, contradictory cultures,"[34] particularly where a management-imposed culture is experienced as oppressive and subcultures emerge at various points within the organization's structure.[35] An important organizational task will be not to reduce the number of different cultures within the organization but rather to help them to work together even if people see things very differently.[36] Boundary-spanners will be essential.[37] Similarly to culture more generally, trust is

> firm belief in the reliability, truth, or ability of someone or something; confidence or faith in a person or thing, or in an attribute of a person or thing . . . to believe or accept a statement, story, etc., without seeking verification or evidence for it . . . The quality or condition of being trustworthy; loyalty; reliability; trustworthiness

---

31. Kreps, "Corporate Culture and Economic Theory," 95.

32. Pearson, *The Rise and Fall of Management*, 165; Robins and Judge, *Organizational Behavior*, 591, 608-9.

33. Daft, *The New Era of Management*, 143-44, 466-83, 489; Guillen, *Models of Management*; Hofstede, *Culture's Consequences*, 393; Huang and Van de Vliert, "Where Intrinsic Job Satisfaction Fails to Work," 159; Robins and Judge, *Organizational Behavior*, 607.

34. McSweeney, "Hofstede's Model of National Culture Differences," 96.

35. Ray, "Corporate Culture," 289.

36. McSweeney, "Hofstede's Model of National Culture Differences," 96.

37. Mintzberg, *Mintzberg on Management*, 229; Trice and Beyer, *The Cultures of Work Organizations*, 225.

... Confident expectation of something; hope. Also occasionally: an instance of this.[38]

Again, in the context of an ontology, trust is not a being and so is less real than other beings; but in the context of an actology, trust is changing patterns of action, and in particular the making of statements that cohere with reality, believing the statements, and acting on them, finding that the statements were true to the reality expressed, again believing statements and acting on them, and so on. Trust is therefore changing patterns action that entangle with other changing patterns of action in a continuous reinforcing process. If trust is not betrayed then it will increase within the organization, but if it is then it will diminish, and hard work will have to be expended to increase it.[39]

ORGANIZATIONAL DYNAMICS

An organization is a complex changing pattern of changing patterns of action, which suggests that studying what actually happens might be more important than asking about bureaucratic structure. We have already recognized that informal communication pathways might be as important as formal ones (in a company, the Chief Executive Officer's secretary might be a more significant communication hub than the CEO), and the ways in which things are done might have little to do with statements about how things should be done. The author had some experience of this phenomenon when fifty years ago he worked on the public counter at Brixton's Supplementary Benefit Office administering means-tested benefits. The complex regulations frequently did not cohere with claimants' complex household structures, relationships, or income streams, so the calculation of how much they should be paid was frequently a matter of continuing negotiation involving the claimant and a number of members of staff. This was action in changing patterns and not a single point in time calculation.

As we shall see, a particularly important aspect of the dynamics of an organization is how groups form and behave. A group, like an organization as a whole, is a complex changing pattern of changing patterns of action as individual members join and leave and all of them change over time. Because each person is a complex changing pattern of changing patterns of action, we might understand a group as changing patterns of changing patterns of changing patterns of action, or as a particularly complex single changing

38. Oxford English Dictionary.
39. Kreps, "Corporate Culture and Economic Theory," 92; Torry, *Managing Religion*, volume I, 51–67.

pattern of action. Research has revealed a fairly common pattern: groups form (including a leader emerging), storm (conflict and bargaining over roles), norm (working rules and role allocations evolve[40]), perform (the group functions to get work done), and might adjourn or dissolve.[41] Similarly, research has discovered three main kinds of group task: additive (all members do the same thing); conjunctive (all members' abilities are required); and disjunctive (success depends on the most talented member). Examples might be a tug of war team, a relay race, and a pub quiz.[42] As we find these patterns of activity in both formal and informal groups, there might not be as much difference between them as an organizational chart might imply.[43] And so, for instance, "group think,"[44] goal displacement (the group satisfies its members' needs rather than those of the organization), power dynamics,[45] and norm development and maintenance,[46] can be found across a broad diversity of both formal and informal groups.

The importance of informal groups within an organization had already been recognized during the 1930s when during the Bank Wiring Observation room experiment at the Hawthorne Electrical Works researchers had discovered that informal groups operated across the boundaries of formal groups, and that these groups had established rules, norms, behavior patterns, and enforcement mechanisms. In particular, workers were keeping the work rate artificially low out of fear that a higher rate would result in redundancies.[47]

A further experiment at the same factory gave birth to "human relations" management theory. Researchers found that altering illumination levels made no difference to production levels, but that in the Relay Assembly Test Room, changing the length of breaks increased productivity whether the breaks were lengthened or shortened. The only conclusion to draw was that what was increasing production was someone showing an interest in the production process.[48] What these two experiments showed was that motives are diverse

40. Belbin, *Management Teams*, 37, 48, 78, 94–99.
41. Tuckman, "Developmental Sequence in Small Groups," 396.
42. Steiner, *Group Process and Productivity*, 17–18, 163.
43. Bales, *Interaction Process Analysis*, 11, 20, 136; Moreno, *Who Shall Survive?* 699.
44. Stoner, *A Comparison of Individual and Group Decisions Involving Risk*.
45. French and Raven, "The Bases of Social Power."
46. Feldmann, "The Development and Enforcement of Group Norms"; Goffman, *Stigma*, 231–32.
47. Homans, *The Human Group*, 67–79, 155; Huczynski and Buchanan, *Organizational Behavior*, 292, 315.
48. Acker and Van Houten, "Differential Recruitment and Control"; Mayo, *Management and the Worker*; Mayo, *The Human Problems of an Industrial Civilization*, 58–70; Mills and Tancred, *Gendering Organisational Analysis*.

across an organization; that communication is multidirectional; that the most significant communication channels might be informal ones; and that the many human beings who interact with each other to constitute the organization generate a

> web of calculations and technologies connecting macro-economic policy, the management of the enterprise, and the design of the labour process with human subjectivity itself.[49]

Particularly important will be "boundary-spanners"[50] who communicate across departmental and hierarchical boundaries, for it is as communication flows around a network composed of both formal and informal pathways that organizations can adapt to both internal and external change. This is as true of those who are nominally in charge, such as Chief Executive Officers, as it is of anyone else. CEOs spend as much time "networking," both within and outside the organization, and on keeping open both formal and informal communication channels,[51] as they spend on formal management tasks related to their job description.[52]

> Folklore: the manager is a reflective, systematic planner ... Fact: ... managers work at an unrelenting pace, and their activities are characterised by brevity, variety and discontinuity, and they are strongly oriented towards action and dislike reflective activities.[53]

This suggests that an organization will only find itself on its stated desired trajectory if work and other processes cohere with the action in changing patterns that constitute the human beings who relate to the organization as workers, managers, customers, clients, and so on;[54] that workers' interests, sense of achievement, recognition, self-development, desire for variety and change, creativity, power and influence, social contact, tangible rewards, relationships, and physical conditions, are as important as remuneration;[55] and that in gen-

---

49. Rose, *Governing the Soul*, 60.
50. Cross and Prusak, "The People who Make Organizations Go, or Stop."
51. Barnard, *The Functions of the Executive*, 227.
52. Cross and Prusak, "The People who Make Organizations Go, or Stop," 112; Mintzberg, "The Manager's Job."
53. Mintzberg, "The Manager's Job," 418–19.
54. Barnard, *The Functions of the Executive*, 46, 115; Huczynski and Buchanan, *Organizational Behavior*, 387; Mayo, *The Human Problems of an Industrial Civilization*, 94; Mayo, *The Social Problems of an Industrial Civilization*, 55, 110; Rose, *Governing the Soul*, 101, 104; Woodward, *Industrial Organization*, 243–44.
55. Ritchie and Martin, *Motivation Management*, v, xiii, 131, 204.

ACTOLOGICAL ORGANIZATIONAL BEHAVIOR

eral we have to understand organizations as complex changing patterns of action rather than as static structures.[56]

Whilst an individual's motivation—the changing patterns of action in the mind that propel someone along a trajectory in a particular direction, perhaps towards an organization's stated aims, or towards their own chosen goals—will to some extent be internal to the individual mind, they will always be action in changing patterns that are constantly influenced by other changing patterns of action—those that constitute organizations, and those that constitute other individuals—and they in turn will influence multiple external changing patterns of action.[57] Boundaries are ubiquitously porous and always socially constructed, so always subject to change. So although individual rewards might or might not motivate someone to work towards an organizational goal,[58] it will be the communication and other processes within the organization that will determine the extent to which an organization can establish a trajectory and then follow it. Douglas McGregor's "Theory X" and "Theory Y" distinction, perhaps unintentionally, reveals an important correlation: Theory X assumes that workers cannot be trusted, so disciplinary procedures are required to motivate them to work, whereas Theory Y assumes that workers can be trusted and can be motivated by increasing autonomy, co-operative working practices, and generally increasing involvement in the organization as a whole.[59] Theory X looks inwards to the individual worker, whereas Theory Y looks outwards to the organization in which they find themselves. It is Theory Y that coheres with an action in changing patterns understanding of organizations, because within an actological conceptual framework we understand the individual worker as action in changing patterns intimately engaged with the changing patterns of action that constitute another individual worker,[60] a work group, and the organization as a whole and its many and varied participants. Decisions are made at all of these relationship levels,[61] and all of those decisions will be made in relation to a changing economic and social environment, adding complexity to complexity: so

---

56. Torry, *Managing Religion*, volume I, 89–95.

57. Douma and Schreuder, *Economic Approaches to Organizations*, 248; Mullins, *Management and Organisational Behavior*, 405–8; Powell and DiMaggio, *The New Institutionalism in Organizational Analysis*, 3.

58. Locke, "Personnel Attitudes and Motivation," 458, 463–67, 473; Vroom, *Work and Motivation*, 15–18.

59. McGregor, *The Human Side of Enterprise*, 47–48; Vaill, "The Purposing of High-performance Systems," 25.

60. Huczynski and Buchanan, *Organizational Behavior*, 349.

61. Vroom and Yetton, *Leadership and Decision Making*, 12–35.

"good enough" rather than optimal decisions will always be made,[62] simply because is impossible for anyone to take account of all of the factors at the same time, especially as all of them change all of the time. By employing "successive limited comparisons" we "muddle through,"[63] so we "satisfice" rather than satisfy the complex and constantly changing web of desires and aims.[64] The alternative to the dynamic is the static, so any organization that does not change will stagnate, and any structure will solidify rather than remain fluid.[65] But it is not only change that is needed. Only if an organization remains diverse will it have the capacity to evolve into the future as its own needs and those of the individuals and organizations in its environment change: hence the management theory concept of a "balanced scorecard": an attempt to take into account the diversity of an organization's aims and objectives: a diversity that will be different for every organization.[66] Some of those aims and objectives might need to be met immediately, whereas others might be met at some later date but activity now will be required if they are to be met when they are required to be.[67] Leadership in such a complex changing situation can be a challenge. What is required is leadership that listens, that takes into account the changing environment and the many changing levels of the organization, and that concentrates on facilitating an organization in which decisions can be made at every level and in which those diverse and changing decisions will cohere with changing organizational trajectories.[68]

STRATEGY

If we study an organization ontologically then we shall understand it as a being that changes and so will understand a strategy as a plan for the way in which the organization will change: that is, as a set of ideas in managers' heads that will guide their actions as they attempt to steer the organization in the way in which they wish it to go. However, if we understand an organization

62. Vroom and Yetton, *Leadership and Decision Making*, 198.
63. Lindblom, "The Science of Muddling Through."
64. Daft, *The New Era of Management*, 312–13; Moher, *Explaining Organizational Behavior*, 167.
65. Burns and Stalker, *The Management of Innovation*, xv; Carroll and Hannan, *The Demography of Corporations and Industries*, 5.
66. Barnard, *The Functions of the Executive*, 199; Kaplan and Norton, "The Balanced Scorecard"; Keyt, "Beyond Strategic Control."
67. Daft, *The New Era of Management*, 534; Drucker, *Management Challenges for the Twenty-first Century*, 22; Kaplan and Norton, "The Balanced Scorecard," 71.
68. Homans, *The Human Group*, 425–40.

actologically—as changing patterns of action—then we shall understand strategy as changing patterns of action in particular changing directions; and we shall understand that to manage strategy is "to craft thought and action, control and learning, stability and change."[69] An important skill will be the ability to understand how fast the patterns of action that constitute the organization should change and in which directions if they are to continue to cohere with a changing organizational, market, economic, and social environment.[70] This requires the manager to be a "pattern recognizer . . . who manages a process in which strategies (and visions) can emerge as well as be deliberately conceived."[71] The difficulty is that organizations have multiple stakeholders: if a private sector organization then it might have shareholders, customers, managers, employees, and so on; if a public sector organization it might have electors, elected representatives, employees, clients, and so on; and if a voluntary organization it might have trustees, employees, volunteers, clients, donors, and so on. In a changing environment, strategy will have to change constantly, but if all of an organization's stakeholders are to understand and work with the strategy then there must be sufficient stability in the changing patterns of action to enable all of an organization's stakeholders to understand and cohere with the strategy. The changing patterns of action that constitute the organization must entangle with the changing patterns of action that constitute all of the stakeholders in such a way as to generate a single complex changing pattern of action that can navigate its way through the complex network of changing patterns of action that constitute the organization's environment.

All of this raises a question about long-term strategies, published mission statements, and so on.[72] We might think that a certain level of relative permanence in these might enable stakeholders to engage with the organization, but that is not necessarily the case. Every stakeholder is action in changing patterns, and the environment as a whole is a complex network of changing patterns of action, so only if an organization and everything about it is changing patterns of action will the organization be able to connect with its environment. This suggests that any mission statements or stated goals, aims, or objectives, should be constantly reviewed and frequently changed so that they can continue to connect the changing organization with its changing environment. It means that planning will have to be "contingency planning": that is, at every point in time multiple new and different plans will

69. Mintzberg, *Mintzberg on Management*, 38.
70. Mintzberg, *Mintzberg on Management*, 40–41.
71. Mintzberg, *Mintzberg on Management*, 38.
72. Daft, *The New Era of Management*, 241–42, 245.

have to be made at each level of an organization so that as the organization and the environment and their attendant risks and uncertainties change, the most appropriate plans can be chosen and then rapidly changed as yet more change emerges.[73] This suggests that any managers who decide that creating a long-term strategy might be a good idea should ask themselves whether they have understood what an organization is. What is required is "emergent" and rapidly changing strategy, if any.[74]

Organizations are changing *patterns* of action, and sometimes, even at the risk of temporary disconnection from a rapidly changing environment, organizational change might have to be slowed down so that stakeholders can catch up:[75] but then the patterns of action might have to change rapidly if the organization is to cohere with its changing environment. There can be no let-up.

Here the structure of an organization is relevant. A rigid hierarchical bureaucracy that sends information up the hierarchy and control down it to employees is going to struggle to change as its environment changes, but a more decentralized and therefore diverse organization that can change more easily in relation to diverse environments will be more difficult for owners and managers to control. There will always be slowly changing hierarchical aspects and more quickly changing devolved aspects to an organization—that is, both pattern and change: and research shows that different technologies—whether that is understood in the industrial or broader sense—require different levels of hierarchy and devolution. In an extremely diverse and rapidly changing environment the organization might have to abandon almost all hierarchy and devolve maximum levels of authority to the individual employee.[76] As Lawrence and Lorsch have discovered, there is a relationship

> among external variables (the certainty and diversity of the environment, and the strategic environmental issue), internal states of differentiation and integration, and the process of conflict resolution.[77]

Such "contingency theory" is entirely appropriate to organizations understood actologically, and an important conclusion to draw is that there is no single

---

73. Daft, *The New Era of Management*, 250.
74. Mintzberg, *Mintzberg on Management*, 33–34, 333, 358, 362, 386.
75. Perrow, *Organizational Analysis*, 121–24.
76. Burns, "Industry in a New Age"; Lawrence and Lorsch, *Organization and Environment*, 104–6, 212; Morgan, *Creative Organization Theory*, 64; Woodward, *Management and Technology*, 4.
77. Lawrence and Lorsch, *Organization and Environment*, 156–57.

best way of running an organization. It all depends . . .[78] A further conclusion that we might draw from an understanding that an organization, its structure, its strategy, and everything else about it, is changing patterns of action, is that everything affects everything else. So structure affects strategy, strategy affects structure, devolution affects market activity, market activity affects devolution, and so on.[79] The changing patterns of action that constitute the organization in its environment are circular, complex, and best understood as a constantly changing network of changing patterns of action within which what we understand as the organization has no effective boundaries.

RELIGIOUS AND FAITH-BASED ORGANIZATIONS

Religion is its organizations as much as it is anything else, and religious organizations constitute an organizational category of their own that is populated by congregations gathered for the primary purpose of public worship.[80] Private, public, and voluntary organizations all have their authority structures within themselves, whereas for religious organizations the primary authority is always God, and every other authority structure is therefore secondary and able to appeal beyond the organization to the primary authority.[81] So within a private, public, or voluntary organization, hierarchical structures are appropriate and effective and can be recognized as primary authorities, whereas in a religious organization hierarchies can only ever be secondary authorities, so can be brought into question by any other part of the organization; and because the primary authority that belongs to God is always mediated authority, and every congregation member can regard their religious experience and their interpretation of sacred texts as mediations of God's authority, every individual member of every congregation becomes a secondary authority.[82] The result is what we might call network accountability.[83]

Take, for example, the clergy of the Church of England. They are accountable to the Bishop, the Archdeacon, the Parochial Church Council,

78. Woodward, *Management and Technology*, 10.
79. Chandler, *Strategy and Structure*, 3, 13, 383.
80. Beckford, "Religious Organizations"; Dulles, *Models of the Church*, 27; Dunlap, *Religion*, 257; Durkheim, *The Elementary Forms of the Religious Life*, 47; Torry, *Managing God's Business*, 14–17; Von Campenhausen, *Ecclesiastical Authority and Spiritual Power in the Church of the First Three Centuries*, 74.
81. Von Campenhausen, *Ecclesiastical Authority and Spiritual Power in the Church of the First Three Centuries*, 295–300.
82. Torry, *Managing God's Business*, 70.
83. Torry, *Managing Religion*, volume I, 1–19.

the Churchwardens, every congregation member, canon law, the Deanery Chapter, the Deanery Synod, decisions by the General and Diocesan Synods, diocesan pastoral regulations, and ultimately to God. It is this network accountability that makes their office-holder status appropriate, whereas an employee status would require hierarchical line management that would subvert network accountability and arguably compromise the religious nature of the organizations served by the clergy. Where diocesan structures become hierarchical, and behave in line management fashion, we have to assume that even though individual congregations might continue to be religious organizations, the diocesan organization has ceased to be one.[84]

The fact that a religious organization's primary authority is external, and that the organization's purpose is public worship, generates a variety of additional unique characteristics: for instance, that the clergy exhibit a greater diversity of roles and characteristics than professionals in other sectors; that members of a congregation are neither volunteers nor members of a clearly defined membership structure; and that the religious organization's main purpose, public worship, coincides with its main activity, which is not necessarily the case with other kinds of organization.[85] There are of course ways in which religious organizations *are* like other kinds of organization, and particularly voluntary organizations: for instance, they are generally managed by volunteer trustees, and they might provide welfare and other services for their own members and for the wider community:[86] but the significant unique characteristics of religious organizations clearly locate them in a category of their own:[87] a category of organizations that exhibit often extreme internal and external diversity and sources of change.

Faith-based organizations are organizations that exhibit some of the characteristics of a religious organization and some of private, public, or voluntary organizations, usually because of a history related to a religious organization followed by relating to other kinds of organization. For instance, a housing association might have been established by a congregation, but as it grew it will have taken on staff from the public and voluntary sectors, and will have established contracts with organizations in a variety of sectors, and so will have had to adapt its policies and activities to those sectors. Travel along

---

84. Torry, *Managing Religion*, volume I, 198–213.
85. Torry, *Managing God's Business*, 58–59, 69–71, 123–32, 135–47; Torry, *Managing Religion*, 10–11.
86. Harris, "Seeing Churches as Voluntary Associations," 39.
87. Torry, "Is there a Faith Sector?"

the spectrum from religious to secular organizations is a normal process when this occurs.[88]

As we can see from these brief descriptions, religious organizations experience an internal diversity and capacity for change way beyond those of private, public, or voluntary organizations, because the network accountability experienced by every individual and organization within a religious organization represents considerably greater diversity of lines of authority than the kinds of hierarchical authority structures found within other kinds of organization; and the fact that authority can be exercised everywhere within a religious organization means that change can begin anywhere, and so to see a religious organization as action in changing patterns is entirely appropriate. The further a faith-based organization has travelled along the spectrum towards secular organizations, the less will it experience such radical diversity and opportunity for change, but the fact that movement along the religious-secular spectrum is always possible until all vestiges of religious organization have been lost suggests that faith-based organizations experience elements of diversity and change not available to the purely religious organization constituted by a congregation gathered for public worship. To understand a faith-based organization in terms of diversity and of action in changing patterns is also entirely appropriate.

CONCLUSIONS

Throughout this chapter we have found organizations to be action in changing patterns, which suggests that a "process theory" approach might be the most appropriate as it recognizes that change is ubiquitous, that every changing pattern of action is contingent on a wide variety of other changing patterns of action, that prediction is difficult in the short term and impossible in the longer term,[89] that a "garbage can" might be the best metaphor for what goes on both inside an organization, where both formal and informal processes are active,[90] and in relation to external individuals and organizations: and that an evolutionary understanding might best represent the ways in which organizations evolve in relation to their changing surroundings,[91] and in which

---

88. Torry, *Managing God's Business*, 117–21; Torry, *Managing Religion*, volume II, 50–70, 79–86.
89. Moher, *Explaining Organizational Behavior*, 50, 173.
90. Weber, *The Theory of Social and Economic Organization*, 328.
91. Moher, *Explaining Organizational Behavior*, 50, 173.

organizational cultures likewise evolve. We have been led to an understanding of an organization as

> a loosely structured and incompletely shared system that emerges dynamically as cultural members experience each other, events, and the organization's contextual features:[92]

and as Lawrence suggests, we should understand organizations

> in terms of isolated motives, limited models, under-the-surface mechanisms, evolutionary forces, constrained situations, probabilistic arrangements, and other concepts that lead in theoretically amenable directions.[93]

Within any such dynamic organization we should expect to find that

> ambiguity is the essence of organizational culture. Consensus and dissensus are issue-specific and constantly fluctuating. No stable organization-wide or subcultural consensus exists. Clear consistencies and clear inconsistencies are rare.[94]

Just as no individual is isolated from other people and from the changing patterns of action that constitute their community, their society, the planet Earth, and the cosmos, so no organization is isolated from its social, economic, planetary, and cosmic environments: and all of it is action in changing patterns.

---

92. Huczynski and Buchanan, *Organizational Behavior*, 643.
93. Moher, *Explaining Organizational Behavior*, 101.
94. Martin, *Cultures in Organizations*, 12.

Chapter 10

Conclusions

IN THE VARIOUS CHAPTERS of this book previous treatments of philosophy, metaphysics, cosmology, anthropology, and theology, have been complemented by explorations in language, the humanities, ethics, mathematics, the natural sciences, social sciences, psychology, politics, and organizational behavior. In each case we have asked about the actological character of the discipline: that is, how we might understand the discipline as action in changing patterns. But this book has a second aim: that is, to ask how the different disciplines, studied actologically, might contribute towards the creation of an actology. This dual agenda has driven the research that has given birth to the previous books in the "Actological Explorations" series: and so, for instance, we have asked how different authors' philosophies might be understood actologically—as action in changing patterns—and how their philosophies might contribute towards the construction of an actology: an understanding of reality as action in changing patterns. Here we shall review our treatments of the different disciplines as action in changing patterns, and shall then ask how the different disciplines, understood actologically, might contribute towards the construction of an actology.

In Chapter 1 we have concluded that language is actological: it is action in changing patterns, both in relation to the human activity of speaking a language, and in relation to the connections between words. The patterns change all the time: nothing remains the same. We have discovered that linguistics is a spiral science because it uses language to study language; and because it uses evolving language to study evolving language it will change and it will change language, so a highly complex process of change occurs, suggesting that, if reality is action in changing patterns, then linguistics is the most real of all of the sciences.

In Chapter 2, about the humanities, we have understood the arts as action in changing patterns: as creative acts, often with a pure-pattern intermediary—the "work of art"—between the creating of the work and the performance or appreciation of it. The history book and play script are pure pattern, and so less than real until they are read or performed, when the pattern influences the action in changing patterns that constitutes the reader's reading and the actor's performance.

In our third chapter we have studied ethics, which, although often regarded as a subdiscipline of philosophy or one of the humanities, we have treated as a discipline in its own right. Ethics is the study of moral action, and so of a significant aspect of human action. Not only is ethical human action changing patterns of action, but the discipline of ethics is action in changing patterns in which different ethical theories evolve and entangle with each other, creating an exploration characterized by change and diversity.

Mathematics might initially appear to be a not very obvious candidate for an actological discipline, but once we understand logical and mathematical laws as local and contingent, we can begin to see the potential for an actological understanding of mathematics. Mathematics is diverse, it constantly evolves, it might be different in different places and at different times, and whilst mathematical texts and formulae might be pure pattern, and thus less than real, the creation or discovery of them is action in changing patterns, and our appreciation and use of them is equally changing patterns of action. As with the other disciplines, it is where mathematics *is* action in changing patterns that it is real, and that is where the doing of mathematics entangles with the action in patterns that constitutes the cosmos and ourselves. Mathematics is actological when it is as diverse and active as is the cosmos to which it relates. The relatively new mathematical field of topos theory, that studies varieties of mathematical fields within categories, would seem to be ripe for actological understanding and treatment.

In Chapter 5 we have studied the natural sciences through an actological lens and have found this to be an approach to these sciences more in tune with the action in changing patterns that constitutes the cosmos than an ontological approach to the sciences could ever be. All of the realities that the sciences study: energy, acceleration, velocity, distance, mass, light, "particles," and so on, can all be interpreted actologically, and some of them struggle to be understood ontologically. We now understand space and time to be changing patterns of action rather than rigid grids, so in relation to these aspects of our cosmos in particular an actological approach is now essential. We have

CONCLUSIONS

suggested that because an actology is constituted by change and diversity, we should expect explanation to be diverse and changing, so an actology actually invites an ontological explanation: something not true in reverse because ontology privileges the unitary and the unchanging. We have also suggested that we might seek even more diversity and change: so not only new actologies, but also new members of the category of explanatory conceptual frameworks that now contains ontology and actology. In the meantime, an actological approach to the natural sciences might encourage us to think multidimensionally, to understand momentum as a fundamental reality, and to undertake multiple experiments in conceptual frameworks.

In Chapter 6 we studied sociology and economics, both of which study realities—society and the economy—highly characterized by change and diversity, suggesting that an actological approach is the natural one to take, so that each of the sciences coheres with the reality that it studies. Theories are constructed, tested, changed, and so on, as in any other science. What doesn't seem to fit an actological approach to the social sciences, and to society and the economy, is the kind of classical economic theory that thinks about economic relationships in rather static and unitary terms: for instance, by regarding an individual as utility-maximizing in relation to two statically-related goods. Neither society nor the economy is like that. Each of us is changing patterns of action entangled with a myriad of other changing patterns of action: the change and the diversity are ubiquitous and intense. So what is required is theory attuned to the diversity and dynamism of the economy, to the potentially infinite number of changing relationships that constitute it, and to an understanding of money as action in changing patterns. All of it is emergent, self-organizing, and dynamic complex systems, among which relationships are nonlinear, and within which relationships between different aspects are co-evolutionary.[1] A narrative approach to economics is clearly appropriate in such a context, in much the same way as a narrative approach to sociology is usually appropriate: but whether a more mathematical approach might also be possible must be a subject for a future discussion.

When in Chapter 7 we have studied psychology, we have found that whether we discuss motivation, stress, norms, or any of the other subjects normally studied by psychologists, it has been natural to understand the mind as changing patterns of action entangled with a myriad of other changing patterns of action. Any limits that we might place on the field that psychology studies are social constructs, which of course change constantly.

In Chapter 8 we studied politics, and in particular how social policy is made. All of it is action in changing patterns, and any apparent stabilities are

1. Morçöl, *A Complexity Theory for Public Policy*, 266.

local and contingent. All of the individuals and institutions involved in politics and social policy are action in changing patterns within vast and changing diverse networks: hence the attraction of heuristics and of path dependency in order to reduce the risks involved in making political and policy changes. Politics and social policy are inherently actological, so any study of them must be actological and must treat them as action in changing patterns.

We found the same to be true in Chapter 9 about organizational behavior. An organization is action in changing patterns, and change and diversity are ubiquitous, with every changing pattern of action being contingent on other changing patterns of action. Prediction beyond the immediate context is therefore impossible,[2] and a "garbage can" model might therefore be the best way to understand what is going on in an organization, whether we are considering the formal or informal processes that constitute an organization.[3] Organizations evolve in relation to their changing surroundings,[4] and organizational cultures and everything else about organizations evolve together.

We have discovered that all of the disciplines that we have discovered might best be understood actologically: both the fields that they study, and the disciplines themselves.

To return to the second question that we have asked in each of the books in the "Actological Explorations" series: How does what we have studied contribute to the construction of an actology? What we can now say with more confidence is that however we have studied the reality of the cosmos, ourselves, and potentially everything else, whatever that might be, we have found nothing that cannot be understood actologically, and no way of studying it that cannot be understood actologically. We might therefore wish to propose the hypothesis that there is nothing that cannot be understood actologically, and no way of studying reality that cannot be understood actologically. Of course, such a hypothesis could never be proved, but we might legitimately regard it as a scientific theory because it would be possible to falsify it. What might be of interest is that the discipline that we have thought would have been difficult to treat actologically, mathematics, in fact was not.

The previous six volumes in the "Actological Explorations" series explored philosophical, metaphysical, cosmological, and theological contributions to an actological understanding of reality, and asked how an actological lens might contribute to philosophy, metaphysics, cosmology, and theology. This seventh volume has filled some gaps by asking the same

2. Moher, *Explaining Organizational Behavior*, 50, 173.
3. Weber, *The Theory of Social and Economic Organization*, 328.
4. Moher, *Explaining Organizational Behavior*, 50, 173.

questions in relation to language, the humanities, ethics, mathematics, the natural sciences, the social sciences, psychology, politics, and organizational behavior. Each of these chapters has only been able to scratch the surface of the discipline in question, so there is much more that could be written about each of these disciplines, about how they might contribute to an actological understanding of reality, and about how an actology might contribute to each of the disciplines. Perhaps this book might best be understood as an agenda for further research.

One conclusion that we can draw is that all of the disciplines studied here are intrinsically actological, that their subject matters are actological, and that their methods are actological. Everything is action, change, movement, diversity, and the generally dynamic. An ontological understanding of all of these disciplines, their subject matters, and their methods, will of course remain an option, but what this book has shown is that an actological understanding of them is now both legitimate and necessary, and that an actology is able to provide a conceptual framework within which potentially every aspect of reality can be understood.

Epilogue

For my wife Rebecca

WE ARE WHAT WE DO

You are what you do

You are what you do.
If you plant bulbs in the garden, or read a story to a child, or listen to a friend, then that is what you are.
You are your walking and your digging, your speaking and your hearing, your breathing and your looking, your reading and your welcoming.
These are what you are. And the way you change is what you are, and the way you move is what you are, and the way you love is what you are.

I am what I do

I am what I do.
If I kick leaves in a field, or push a child on a swing, or cook dinner, or play the piano, or go to see a bereaved friend, or walk with you, or walk alone, then that is what I am.
When we moved house, I carried things; before we moved in, I painted walls. These are what I am.
I am my walking and my speaking, my singing and my playing, my writing and my making, my listening and my reading.
These are what I am. And the way I change is what I am, and the way I move is what I am, and the way I love is what I am.

We are what we do

We are what we do.
If we look, if we smile, if we walk, if we work, then that is what we are.
If we grasp each other's hand, if we phone each other, if we bring each other gifts, then that is what we are.
If we listen to one another, if we change because the other is changing, then that is love, and love is what we do, and love is what we are, for we are what we do.

We are what we speak

To speak is to do, and to think is to speak within, so to think is to do. To decide is to think, and so to decide is to speak within, and to decide is to do, and deciding, thinking, and speaking, are what we are.

To speak is to move, to act, to shake the air, and to move another's ear and their brain and to ask them to listen. To speak and to hear are entangled actions, and the speaking and the listening and the hearing are what we do.

To speak is to utter a new word—the old words in new places and new times and in new company. To listen is to hear a new word—and the action that comes is changed by our listening. So every speaking and every hearing is a new action and a new being, and we are something new, for we are what we do.

And just as we change as we use language, and just as language changes as we use it, so language changes as the world changes and we see everything anew. So maybe now we need a new language, a language based on verbs, rather than on nouns, so that our language can be an expression of a reality which is action rather than static substance.

But there are still things. A "thing" is a relatively stable pattern of activity, and we use nouns to refer to things. And because the patterns change, nouns constantly change their meaning, just as verbs do.

So there is only ever analogy, a likeness fleetingly expressed as the words we use change their connections yet again—for there is only difference and likeness, never sameness.

Every person, every institution, every word, is its changing, is the action which it is, is its changing diversity.

EPILOGUE

We are what we think

To think is to speak within, so to think is to do and to think is what we are.

There is no thinking without words, and to think is to do—even if the words come uninvited.

Our thoughts sometimes arrive as images, and these too are words spoken within, words to us that we make and to which we listen as they jostle with other words and change and create change.

As the words and the images emerge from the depths, we discover what we are doing in the subterranean depths of our minds, and we discover that our minds are action upon action, never still, and our minds, which are our thoughts, are what we are.

There is no stillness. The images and the words are constantly created and they constantly create. To submerge a word or an image, or to submerge all words and images, is itself a word, an image, an action, and constantly changing.

We think, and this is what we are.

We are what we choose

To decide is to think, so to decide is to speak within, and to decide is to do, and to decide is what we are.

There is no deciding without words, and to decide is to do, even though we might not know from where within ourselves the deciding comes.

The thoughts are actions and they coalesce into decision, and the doing is the deciding—it is not merely the evidence for our deciding. A seamless web of action enfolding both the speaking within and the doing amongst the people and the world around us—this is the deciding, and this is what we are.

And because the doing, the speaking, the thinking, and the deciding are a web of action, a network of action in changing patterns, every action constantly in flux, every action connected with every other, it is all *our* doing, *our* deciding, *our* speaking, *our* doing. Never someone else's, however much we might have been changed by others. And never merely our own.

And our choosing is real choosing: it is one change rather than another, one movement rather than another. That is what choice is, although, as always, there are only choices, never choice, for every choosing is different.

The deciding is what we are

Choosing the good

There is love and there is hatred. There is good and there is evil. They are different patterns of action, and the meanings of "love" and "hatred" and of "good" and "evil" change, for all language changes, as do all patterns of action: but there is still a stability, a likeness between one good and another, between one love and another, between one evil and another, and between one hatred and another. We have created the words, and they are about different patterns of activity, and the activity is reality and the patterns are real, so good, evil, love, and hatred, are real.

And we must choose what to call "good" and what to call "evil," what to call "love" and what to call "hatred." The deciding will change, and to decide is to change ourselves and is to change the world that is action in changing patterns.

So let us choose which patterns of action we shall call "love" and "good," and let us steer clear of those patterns that we call "evil" and "hatred," except to change them.

Love is what we do

Our love for one another is what we do for one another.

When we listen patiently to one another, that is love. When we decide not to be rude or not to be selfish, when we decide not to be self-seeking or not to be easily angered, that is our love for one another. When we choose not to boast to one another, when we decide not to be proud, when we manage not to envy, when we choose not to mention those occasions when we felt we had been wronged, then that is love. When we tell each other the truth, and when we are kind to one another, that is our love for one another. For our love for one another is what we do for one another, for love is what we do.[1]

Our deciding, our thinking, our speaking, our action: if that is this kind of action, then it is love, and if it is not, then it is not.

For love is what we do.

Our love is what we do together

Our love is what we do together.

When together we create a garden, that is love. When together we walk with family members or friends in the park, that is love. When we make love

---

1. 1 Corinthians 13.

EPILOGUE

together, that is love. When together we invite friends to a meal, that is love. When together we visit an ailing family member or friend, that is love. When together we go to social events, that is love. When together we try to change the world, that is love.

What we do together is different from what each of us does, and it is more than the sum of its parts. It is an entwined set of actions that constitutes a deeper love than does the action of one person alone.

Our love is what we do together, for love is what we do, and to do things together is to love.

We are our activity

We are what we do. Indeed, there is no "we" apart from what we do. We are constantly in motion. From the electrons that are pure movement, to the cells that are constantly in flux, to the organs that move all the time, to the lungs that breathe and the heart that pumps and the brain that is a mass of pulses even when we are in the deepest sleep: that is who we are, because we are our activity. And if these actions are of the character of love, then we are love.

We are the thinking that is our minds, we are the speaking of words, we are the movements that are our hands, we are the walking that is our legs, we are the messages that are our nerves, and we are our laughing and our weeping: and if these are of the character of love, then we are love.

For we are what we do. We are our action, and there is no "we" apart from that action. And our love for one another and beyond one another is the activity that we are, and it is that activity tangled together.

The love which we are is the activity that we are together.

Patterns in our changing

Yes, there is stability too. You are predictable as well as changing. There is a pattern to your changing, and there are bits of you which don't change very fast, like your bones.

But still it all changes. Your language changes (as all language changes), your features change, your emotions change, your memories change, your thoughts change, your personality changes, and your decisions change.

And I change: though there are still some things which are relatively stable. And so between us we are a web of change, with some changes slow, and some faster, but still all constantly moving. Our speech-patterns, our wills, our faces, our abilities, our movements: they all change and they are all action in changing patterns.

So our relationship—which is our entwined actions—changes all the time, and our love for one another changes, and our love for others and for the universe changes. Our love for God changes too.

For we are actions.

Beliefs

What I believe changes all the time, as the world around me changes, as people around me change, and as I change; and even if my new beliefs are expressed in the same words as my old beliefs, they are still changed, for the words change their connections and so are new words, even if they look like the old ones.

And your beliefs change; and the relationships between your beliefs and my beliefs change; and the beliefs of every group of people change (for even if the new words are the same as the old words, the words are different, for they have new connections).

And this is right, it is good, it is inevitable, for we change, and the world changes, and God changes: we are our change, the world is its change, and God is the change that is God: and if our beliefs are to connect us then they must change, they must *be* change, without reserve, though we might find temporary patterns in them.

We are our action, so we are our believing, and by our belief we grasp reality, for reality is action in changing patterns and the believing is action in changing patterns that entangles with the action in changing patterns that constitutes the cosmos.

Reality

Reality is action and action is reality: not something which acts, but action. What is *real* about something is the change that constitutes it and that it brings about, not some kind of stability. It is the dynamic, not the static, which is the basic fact of life: it is the action that is reality, and it is the changing that is reality—and not, as some have thought, the unchanging.

So the deepest reality is the greatest change, though we find it hard to express pure action, unrelated to anything static, because our language simply won't let us.

There is nothing static underlying the change: there is no substance, there is only action. There might be an appearance of unchangeability, but it is merely an appearance, for the reality is the action, the movement, the change: and the dynamic is all that there is, although some of the change might be slow enough for us to regard the changing patterns of action as unchanging objects, which they are not.

The real me and the real you are the actions that constitute us: and the real me and the real you are constant change. There is the appearance of unchangeableness—for there are patterns of activity that we can identify—but the reality is the change. The world's reality is the action in changing patterns that constitutes it.

The universe is action

The universe, from one edge to the other—if it has edges—and from the whole of it to the smallest particle, is its action, for there is nothing that does not change. Yes, there is stability, and some things don't change as fast as other things; and yes, there is often a pattern to the changing: but it is change nevertheless, and the patterns change. The universe *is* action, and because patterns change the universe is action in changing patterns.

We try to speak of the universe, and we posit laws of nature, but they always break down, because the way the world works changes, and the way we are changes.

The part of the universe that we understand is those actions which have fallen into patterns with a degree of predictability: and maybe the "dark matter" is that which hasn't—it is the chaos of movements that are incommensurably diverse. And that part of the universe which we understand changes constantly, for anything else is no thing and is not real.

So our relationship with the universe changes, because the universe changes, and we change; and our love for other people changes, for we change, and they change—and there is nothing which does not change, and nothing that *is* not change.

Is the universe converging on a single point? If so, it will be a point of infinite movement. And did the universe spring from a single point? If so, it was a point of infinite movement.

And is the universe's character that of love? Yes, if the pattern of its moving has about it the character of love.

Time and space

There is no such thing as time. There is only movement: and because there are patterns of activity that are like other patterns, and because we can experience simultaneity, we define "time" as the movement of a particular kind of particle—although there are no particles: there is only movement—and we compare one movement to another and find that one type of movement takes twice as long as another. It is the movement of the hand of the clock that defines time, not vice-versa.

Space is not some separate "thing." Again, the movement of a particle—or rather, a particular kind of movement—defines space. Everything is movement, and within each movement other movements happen. We experience identity of place, and we can therefore compare movements with one another, so we can speak of distance. Having defined distance in relation to one kind of movement, we can speak of the distances traversed by other movements.

But both time and space are abstractions, they are movements of the mind as we try to understand relationships between changing patterns of action that impinge upon us. Time and space are relative and flexible, and both time and space change: in relation to each other, in relation to patterns of activity, and in relation to ourselves. My time is not your time; one clock goes faster than another; and the movements that work an atomic clock, and that offer us a so-called "accuracy," are different in different parts of the universe. On our particular planet in a particular galaxy at this particular stage of the universe's evolution, patterns of action look quite predictable: but this may be a small island of stability in a sea of chaos, although perhaps the sea isn't a useful image, as it is really quite predictable.

Everything is movement and different. There is no substance, nothing is still, and no movement is the same as any other. There is no time and no space: there is only action.

History, economics, science...

History changes because we change: nothing is ever the same, and we shall never do the same thing again.

Economics changes: there is not "capitalism," there are capitalisms, and today's are not the same as yesterday's—and the same goes for socialism, marxism, and all the other isms, just as it goes for money itself, which is a human invention and one constantly changing.

EPILOGUE

The sciences change too, and their reality is their change: and the same goes for mathematics, however stable it might look, because every change changes everything else.

And whether it is the humanities, linguistics, the social sciences, the natural sciences, politics, ethics, mathematics, philosophy, cosmology, theology, anthropology—whatever it is—the disciplines are action in changing patterns, and their subject-matter is action in changing patterns, and they and their subject-matter are changing patterns of action that intertwine with each other. The study of history, the study of economics, the study of mathematics, the study of theology, the study of literature, are all in flux and they are about flux, and there are no fixed boundaries between them, for what is literature today will be history tomorrow, and it will change in the process. And it is indeed the change in disciplines in which we are now interested: it's the books about the books that matter, it's the historical method that matters, and it's how it changes that matters: so let us call by the name "history" the shifting boundary and the shifting methods and the study of the change, and let us know that this too changes.

There is nothing fixed, and our means of studying the action changes too, so there is change upon change, and the more our changing minds grapple with the action, the more we shall know the real and the more we shall be real ourselves.

Truth

There is no such thing as truth, there are only truths.

I speak "the truth" when the pattern created in your mind by the words I speak bears a family resemblance to the pattern created by other movements that have affected your mind. An event will have an effect on you, and my words (informed by the event) will be "the truth" about that event if the pattern they create for you somehow fits with the patterns of action that constitute the concepts already in your mind.

But no truth is static, and every truth is a matter of choosing one thing rather than another. There is no such thing as "the whole truth."

We can use the same word "truth" of all of these "truths" because all of these pattern-matchings bear a family resemblance to each other: they are similar processes. But there is no "truth" which defines the family resemblance, and any such attempt at truth is bound to add simply another truth, or possibly an untruth: that is, where we find it impossible to relate the changing patterns of action that constitute a statement to other patterns in our minds.

A MULTIDISCIPLINARY ACTOLOGY

Truths are action in changing patterns, and they are real: real because they are action, and real because they change the patterns of action around them in the world and in ourselves. And the same goes for beauty, goodness, and so on: or rather, for beauties, goodnesses, and the like. Those too are most real when most active, when they change the changing world and our changing selves.

Art

Languages change, and you can't stop it happening: and to take in bits of other languages is to improve flexibility and communication. Similarly, there is no such thing as *art*: there are only arts, and they change. No performance is ever the same. And a picture's definition is the movement of the observer's mind. If the picture is "there" in any sense apart from the observer, then it is "there" as pure pattern, and as potential movement: as the potential action in changing patterns that constitutes light that creates the gallery visitor's relationship to the picture. As we look at pictures from the past or from the present, our minds are awakened to new action—or old actions are renewed, changed—which is why we go to look. There *are* patterns in art, but they change, and they change us, and we change them.

The visual arts *are* the movement of the artist's body and mind, and the movement of my eyes and mind, and the movement that is the surface of the painting, and the movement that is the light, creating ever-changing patterns. A painting, stored in a basement, is not real, and it is not art, for there is no action in changing patterns: just as a musical score is not art without its performance, and just as a text is not real and is not art without its being read.

The word is the action, the action of the mind, the action of reading. Marks on a page are not words: they merely connect words, the words of the writer with the words of the reader.

Music is the ultimate art form: it is pure movement.

Grace

By "grace" we mean that kind of action which is self-giving, which is a free giving, expecting nothing in return. It is a radical love, a love without compromise. It is a pattern of action unlike any other, for its character is self-giving and it gives without expecting an action in return.

EPILOGUE

This kind of love is unconditional, constant, nonwithdrawable: a kind of love that never asks for anything, a kind of love that does not need to be patient, for it demands nothing. It is a simple giving.

We never find it in its pure form; but we have glimpsed it, and we hope for it. For this grace, this kind of love, is our healing, and it is the renewing of the action that is who we are. And our response is a kind of grace, but a compromise, and never (yet) the purely unconditional, the love without end.

Some of us glimpse this grace, this kind of love, in the man Jesus: who is the action which he is. And some of us in other people. And some of us in the universe around us. And it is always action in changing patterns.

Happiness

Happiness is when the change around us—in our world, our job, our relationships—creates a symphony with the change that we are, that creates changing patterns and then new changing patterns, always on the move (for to cease to move is to die): always change relating to change.

But where one change fights another, where one change denies another, where lack of change contradicts our need to change, then there is no happiness: there is suffering, exhaustion, and frustration.

We cannot always judge beforehand what change will be life and what will be death, what will be joy and what will be sorrow: for we can never know beforehand the other changes that we shall experience, in ourselves and in the world around us.

But don't children need stability rather than change if they are to learn to change, and to understand their own changing. Yes: but it is not the static that they need. They still need the dynamic. It's not that there is no movement: it's that one kind of movement requires another kind. The context *does* change, but in somewhat predictable ways, creating patterns within which the child's changing patterns can relate: and the action in changing patterns that constitutes the people around the child will enable the child to evolve coherently with the world around them if those changing patterns of action cohere with the changing patterns of action that constitute the child.

Similarly, a stable marriage or partnership is one in which change in one person meshes with change in the other to create a changing relationship that does not change too fast or too slowly—for relationship is always action in changing patterns: a changing relationship that is an unconditional giving in relation to the world around the marriage or partnership.

So we need many different changes, many new actions, and never just one. We must never allow just one kind of change to dominate our changing, or allow just one pattern of action to determine the direction of other patterns of action.

It is diversity of change that will create the symphony: and the next, and the next.

Marriage

To marry is to enter the rapids. There is nothing still, there is only the change and the not knowing.

Don't let the vows mislead you. They are not an invitation to permanence or to finality. They are promises of constant newness within the binding intimacy, within the not letting go.

Remain in these eternal chains, for they will hold you in an embrace in which your love can melt the evil (for let us not deny it).

Stay with it, however hard it is, and be the love that will give birth to new people and to new worlds. Do not be fooled into letting go by shallow promises of change. The deepest change comes from staying.

It's fifty years since we married. An ordinary fifty years, no doubt, but mind-changing, changing everything. For our marriage has fostered love in all its meanings.

Yes, of course there are things about each other that we don't like. There are failures and anxieties. But not for long, for you are my life, you are my flesh, for we are what we do together and our love is what we do together. We have changed one another and we shall change one another, we have changed the world and we shall change the world, and we shall continue to give birth to a new universe.

As we grow older we shall each seek new experiences and shall bring them back into the changing world of our secrets. And as we approach death we shall long for that deeper intimacy of the ever-new grace of which our ever-changing love is the merest shadow.

Giving birth

To conceive and to give birth—be it a child, a song, an idea, a meal, a word—is to change the universe, for every action affects every other and nothing is ever the same again.

Every birth gives birth to new births and to possibilities of love and hatred, good and evil. Every birth gives birth to risk, to uncertainty, to change, and to an infinity of action, and so to life and to reality. And every birth is intimate with the birth of the universe and with the birth of every man and woman.

And so we give birth to an ever-changing universe, and we await the transforming of evil in the embrace of God and of the good, and we await the giving birth of the always-changing grace which is a constantly new giving birth.

Give birth to a child, to a song, to an idea, to a meal, to a word: for thus you give birth to a new universe.

Our children

Our children, when we gave birth to you we didn't know what we were doing, and it has been a wanted not knowing. For you are not us, and you change us, and we change you, and together we change the universe, we change the present, we change the future, and we change the past.

Yes, when we gave birth to you we gave birth to risk, to choosing, to good and to evil, to unpredictable and shifting patterns, to ideas and words and actions, let loose on a world of unimaginable complexity.

So give birth: give birth to grace, for thus the evil will be transfigured and the universe will be beautiful. And act and change, our children, for you are what you do, and you are your speaking and your choosing and your loving and your giving birth, whether it be another child, a friendship, an idea, a novel, a building, a computer program, a relationship, or a garden.

Be intimate with the universe. Join in the symphony of grace that shall be, and make it happen. Be grace.

My friend

My friend, you are so different from me. Different age, different tasks, different times of day, different culture, different most things.

So let us talk. That way we shall know and change one another. Not to deny the ways that we are, but to understand and to be new people, knowing ourselves (which is our changing) and knowing one another. For to know myself is to change. To observe something is to change it, and to study our depths is to be changed and is to influence those closest to us in new ways, to change the world in new ways, to change the universe.

For we are what we do, and to make new decisions is to become new people, to give birth to new selves who then begin again to speak, to listen, to understand, to know, and to give birth.

Cultures

My culture is an accident, just as I am. And your culture is an accident, just as you are. And neither of our cultures stays the same, and neither is ultimate.

And the same goes for your religion. It is an accident, and your attachment to it is an accident. My religion too is an accident, and my attachment to it likewise.

Let us not be afraid. Let's enjoy the ride, the new perspectives, the glimpses of grace, the promise of a new age, the new births: one after the other, constantly born anew into new understandings of ourselves, of one another, and of God.

Let's explore the strangest of cultures: strange because strange to us. For thus I shall become new and you will become new, and our cultures and our religions and our institutions will change, and together we shall become a new world, marveling at the new births which the old could neither glimpse nor promise.

For the future will not be more sameness, it will be more difference; and eternity will not be uniformity, but infinite diversity, a unity of infinite change.

Work

Work hard, with your hands and with your brain, for to work is to be like God.

Whether you create things or ideas, or look after other people and their things and ideas, whether you are paid or not, whether you decide what you do or whether someone else decides, give to your work a pattern that is grace-shaped. Let the creating and the product be beautiful. And where the product and the creating are evil and you still have to do it to feed your children, do not let your deciding die, do not let your mind be still: and when you have changed your corner of the world, change the next corner, so that your good shall transform the whole created order.

God's work is like this. So let yours be.

Dying

My friend, take care over your dying. Prepare for it, for it is the greatest change you will ever experience.

Of course you are afraid of dying. It is the deepest unknown, it is the most terrible separation. And your dying will change so many lives, and the web of changing patterns of action that is reality will be jarred and will take a long time to take on new patterns.

And as you don't know the date of your death, prepare for it every day. By action which is love, transform hatred; by good action remake evil into grace. Change constantly, for at your death the whole of your diverse life shall be transfigured, and not just its last accidental moment. And it will belong to the action which is the grace of God, and the corruption will be changed, and the suffering will be beautiful, and justice will be done: for if these things are not so then there is no justice and no hope.

The God who is grace has been this way, and so from eternity to eternity the action that is dying belongs to the action that is God. You are not alone.

Take care over your dying. It is both the least and the most significant action that you will ever do.

Grief

My friend, grieve your heart out. A death is precisely that: a death; and the gap will never be filled. Life is so utterly changed for you that the connections are difficult to find.

There are few greater changes. Of course you must look back and give thanks. Of course you must live in the present and love those others who grieve. But it is the future where the risk lies, it is the future where the suffering and the new birth will be.

The one you have loved and love still is dead. Their influence will not stop, but it will change. The one you have loved is gone, and no daily action will ever be the same, no friendship the same, no intimacy the same. You are launched on a cacophony of change, and it will be difficult to find your way.

Know that God has been there before, and that God is love and is intimate with your suffering: for if God has been there then God is there, participating in the action which is your suffering, and so experiencing suffering too. And know that God will go with you into the new birth that you are suffering.

We are what we do.

Bibliography

Abdukadirov, Sherzod. "Introduction: Regulation Versus Technology as Tools of Behavior Change." In *Nudge Theory in Action: Behavioral Design in Policy and Markets*, edited by Sherzod Abdukadirov, 1–11. Basingstoke: Palgrave Macmillan, 2016.

Abel-Smith, Brian, and Peter Townsend. *The Poor and the Poorest*. London: G. Bell and Sons Ltd., 1965.

Abell, Peter. *Organisation Theory: An Interdisciplinary Approach*. London: London School of Economics and Political Science, 2008.

Acker, Joan, and Donald R. Van Houten. "Differential Recruitment and Control: The Sex Structuring of Organisations." *Administrative Science Quarterly* 19 (2) (1991) 152–63.

Allejo, Irene. *Papyrus*. Translated by Charlotte Whittle. London: Hodder and Stoughton, 2022.

Alt, James E., and K. Alec Chrystal. *Political Economics*. Berkeley CA: University of California Press, 1983.

Amabile, Teresa M. *Creativity in Context*, Boulder, CO: Westview, 1996.

Aneesh, A. "Differentiating Citizenship." In *After Capitalism: Horizons of Finance, Culture, and Citizenship*, edited by Kennan Ferguson and Patrice Petro, 196–214. New Brunswick, NJ: Rutgers University Press, 2016.

Anglund, Sandra M. "American Core Values and Policy Problem Definition." In *The Policy Process*, edited by Stuart S. Nagel, 147–63. New York: Nova Science, 1999.

Aristotle. *Nicomachean Ethics*. In *Aristotle's Ethica Nicomachea*, edited by J. Bywater. Oxford: Clarendon, 1894. English translation from Aristotle, *Aristotle in 23 Volumes*, volume 19, translated by H. Rackham. Cambridge, MA and London: Harvard University Press and William Heinemann Ltd., 1934. www.perseus.tufts.edu/Texts/chunk_TOC.grk.html. References are given as book number followed by paragraph numbers.

Atkinson, A.B. "The Case for a Participation Income." *The Political Quarterly* 67 (1) (1996) 67–70.

Atkinson, A.B. and J.S. Flemming. "Unemployment, Social Security and Incentives." *Midland Bank Review*, Autumn 1978, 6–16.

Atkinson, Anthony B. *Inequality: What can be Done?* Cambridge, MA: Harvard University Press, 2015

Austin, J.L. *How to Do Things with Words*. Oxford: Clarendon, 1962.

———. "Performative Utterances." In *Philosophical Papers*, by J.L. Austin, edited by J.O. Urmson and G.J. Warnock, third edition, 233–52. Oxford: Clarendon, 1979.

BIBLIOGRAPHY

Bachelard, Gaston. "The Idea of the Epistemological Obstacle." Translated by Mary McAllester Jones. In Gaston Bachelard, *The Formation of the Scientific Mind: A Contribution to a Psychoanalysis of Objective Knowledge*, 24–32. Manchester: Clinamen, 2002. Originally published in 1934 as "La formation de l'esprit scientifique."

———. "Noumenon and Microphysics." *The Philosophical Forum* 27 (1) (2006) 75–84. https://doi.org/10.1111/j.1467-9191.2006.00230.x. Translated from Gaston Bachelard, "Noumène et Microphysique," in Gaston Bachelard, *Études*. Paris: J. Vrin. First published in *Recherches Philosophiques* (1931–32) 55–65.

———. "Objectivity and Rectification: The Role of Detail the Objective." Translated by David Webb in 2021 from chapter 14 of Gaston Bachelard, *Essai sur la Connaissance Approchée*. Paris: La Librairie Philosophique Vrin, 1928.

———. "La Philosophie Dialoguée." *Dialectica* 1 (1) (1947), *What is Dialectic/L'Idée de Dialectique/Die Dialektische Denkweise*, 11–20. https://www.jstor.org/stable/42963796.

Bailey, Nick, and Glen Bramley. "Introduction." In *Poverty and Social Exclusion in the UK: Volume 2—The Dimensions of Disadvantage*, edited by Glen Bramley and Nick Bailey, 1–23. Bristol: Policy Press, 2018.

Bales, Robert F. *Interaction Process Analysis: A Method for the Study of Small Groups*. Cambridge, MA: Addison-Wesley, 1950.

Bambrough, Renford. *Reason, Truth and God*. London: Methuen, 1969.

Barad, Karen. *Meeting the Universe Halfway*. Durham and London: Duke University Press, 2007.

Barkai, Haim. *The Evolution of Israel's Social Security System*. Aldershot: Ashgate, 1998.

Barnard, Chester. *The Functions of the Executive*, eighteenth edition. Cambridge, MA: Harvard University Press, 1968. First published in 1938.

Baron, Robert A. and Jerald Greenberg. *Behavior in Organizations: Understanding and Managing the Human Side of Work*, third edition. Boston: Allyn and Bacon, 1986.

Barr, Nicholas. *The Economics of the Welfare State*. London: Weidenfeld and Nicolson, 1987.

Bartels, Koen P.R. "Policy as Practice." In *Handbook on Policy, Process and Governing*, edited by Hal K. Colebatch and Robert Hoppe, 68–88. Cheltenham: Edward Elgar, 2018.

Beckford, J.A. "Religious Organizations." In *International Encyclopedia of the Social and Behavioral Sciences*, 2001. www.sciencedirect.com/science/article/pii/B0080430767 040201, pp 13127-32.

Bekker, M. H. et al. "Combining Care and Work: Health and Stress Effects in Male and Female Academics." *International Journal of Behavioral Medicine* 7 (1) (2000) 28–43.

Belbin, R. Meredith. *Management Teams: Why they Succeed or Fail*. London: Heinemann, 1981.

Bellah, Robert. "Christian Faithfulness in a Pluralist World." In *Postmodern Theology: Christian Faith in a Pluralist World*, edited by Frederic B. Burnham, 74–91. San Francisco: Harper and Row, 1989.

Benedict, Ruth. *Patterns of Culture*. London: Routledge and Kegan Paul, 1935.

Berger, John. *G*. London: Bloomsbury, 1972.

Berger, Peter. *Invitation to Sociology: A Humanistic Perspective*. Harmondsworth: Penguin, 1966.

Bergh, Andreas, et al. *Sick of Inequality? An Introduction to the Relationship Between Inequality and Health*. Cheltenham: Edward Elgar, 2016.

BIBLIOGRAPHY

Berghofer, Philipp. "Husserl's Conception of Experiential Justification. What it is and Why it Matters." *Husserl Studies* 34 (2) (2018) 145–70.

Bergson, Henri. *The Creative Mind*. Translated by M. L. Andison. Westport CT: Greenwood, 1946.

Berthoud, Richard, et al.. *Poverty and the Development of Anti-poverty Policy in the United Kingdom*. London: Policy Studies Institute/Heinemann, 1981.

Besanko, David et al. *Economics of Strategy*, Hoboken, NJ: John Wiley and Sons, 1996.

Beveridge, William. *Social Insurance and Allied Services*. Cmd 6404. London: Her Majesty's Stationery Office, 1942.

Birkland, Thomas A. *An Introduction to the Policy Process: Theories, Concepts, and Models of Public Policy Making*, second edition. Armonk, New York: M.E. Sharpe, 2005.

Blomquist, William. "Policy and Socioeconomic Characteristics." In *Handbook on Policy, Process and Governing*, edited by Hal K. Colebatch and Robert Hoppe, 438–56. Cheltenham: Edward Elgar, 2018.

Blumer, Herbert. *Symbolic Interactionism*. New Jersey: Prentice Hall, 1969.

Botterill, Linda Courtenay, and Alan Fenna. *Interrogating Public Policy Theory: A Political Values Perspective*. Cheltenham: Edward Elgar, 2019.

Boys Smith, John S. *Christian Doctrine and the Idea of Evolution*. D Society Pamphlets III. Cambridge: Bowes and Bowes, 1930.

———. "Do Men Gather Grapes of Thorns, or Figs of Thistles? Matthew 7:6." In *The Sermons of John Boys Smith*, edited by Malcolm Torry, 276–79. Cambridge: St. John's College, Cambridge/Aquila Books, 2003.

———. *The Sermons of John Boys Smith: A Theologian of Integrity*. Edited and with an introduction by Malcolm Torry. Cambridge: Aquila Books for St. John's College, Cambridge, 2003.

Brandt, Richard B. *A Theory of the Good and the Right*. Oxford: Clarendon, 1979.

Braunstein, Jean-François. "Historical Epistemology Old and New." In *Epistemology and History from Bachelard and Canguilhem to Today's History of Science*: Conference Proceedings, 33–40. Max Planck Institute for the History of Science, 2012. https://www.mpiwg-berlin.mpg.de/Preprints/P434.PDF.

Brehm, Jack W., and Elizabeth A. Self. "The intensity of Motivation." *Annual Review of Psychology* 40 (1) (1989) 109–31.

Brehm, Sharon et al.. *Social Psychology*, fourth edition. Boston, MA: Houghton Mifflin, 1999.

Brittan, Samuel. *Towards a Humane Individualism*. London: John Stuart Mill Institute, 1998.

Broadie, Sarah. *Ethics with Aristotle*. New York: Oxford University Press, 1991.

Brown, C.V., and E. Levin. "The Effects of Income Taxation on Overtime: The Results of a National Survey." *Economic Journal* 84 (336) (1974) 833–48.

Bruun, Edvard P.G., and Alban Duka. "Artificial Intelligence, Jobs and the Future of Work: Racing with the Machines." *Basic Income Studies* 13 (2) (2018). https://doi.org/10.1515/bis-2018-0018.

Brynjolfsson, Erik, and Andrew McAfee. *The Second Machine Age: Work, Progress, and Prosperity in a Time of Brilliant Technologies*. New York: W.W. Norton and Co., 2014.

Bryson, Alex, and George MacKerron. *Are you Happy while you Work?* CEP Discussion Paper No 1187. London: Centre for Economic Performance, London School of Economics, 2013. http://cep.lse.ac.uk/pubs/download/dp1187.pdf.

BIBLIOGRAPHY

Bub, Jeffrey. "The Entangled World: How Can It Be Like That?" In *The Trinity and an Entangled World: Rationality in Physical Science and Theology*, edited by John Polkinghorne, 15–31. Grand Rapids, Michigan: William B. Eerdmans, 2010.

Burchardt, Tania, and Julian Le Grand, *Constraint and Opportunity: Identifying Voluntary Non-employment*. CASEpaper 55. London: Centre for Analysis of Social Exclusion, London School of Economics, 2002.

Burchardt, Tania, and Polly Vizard. *Developing a Capabilities List: Final Recommendations of the Equalities Review Steering Group on Measurement*. CASE paper no.121. London: Centre for Analysis of Social Exclusion, London School of Economics, 2007.

Burns, T. "Industry in a New Age." *New Society*, 31st January 1963, 17–20, quoted in *Organization Theory: Selected Readings*, second edition, edited by D.S. Pugh, 40–51. Harmondsworth: Penguin, 1984.

Burns, Tom, and G.M. Stalker. *The Management of Innovation*. London: Tavistock, 1961.

Butterworth, P. I. et al. "The Psychosocial Quality of Work Determines Whether Employment has Benefits for Mental Health: Results from a Longitudinal National Household Panel Survey." *Occupational and Environmental Medicine* 68 (11) (2011) 806–12.

Callinicos, Alex. *The Revolutionary Road to Socialism: What the Socialist Workers Party Stands For*. London: Socialist Worker's Party, 1983.

Cameron, Judy, and W. David Pierce. "Reinforcement, Reward, and Intrinsic Motivation: A Meta-analysis." *Review of Educational Research* 64 (3) (1994) 363–423.

Canguilhem, Georges. *Knowledge of Life*. Translated by Stefanos Geroulanos and Daniela Ginsburg. New York: Fordham University Press, 2008.

———. *Writings on Medicine*. Translated by Stefanos Geroulanos and Todd Meyers. New York: Fordham University Press, 2012.

Carr, E., and H. Chung. "Employment Insecurity and Life Satisfaction: The Moderating Influence of Labour Market Policies Across Europe." *Journal of European Social Policy* 24 (4) (2014) 383–99.

Carroll, Glenn R., and Michael T. Hannan. *The Demography of Corporations and Industries*. Princeton, NJ: Princeton University Press, 2000.

Cartwright, Nancy. *The Dappled World: A Study of the Boundaries of Science*. Cambridge: Cambridge University Press, 1999.

Castelao-Lawless, Teresa. "Phenomenotechnique in Historical Perspective: Its Origins and Implications for Philosophy of Science." *Philosophy of Science* 62 (1) (1995) 44–59.

Centre for Economic Studies/Ifo Institute. *Bismarck Versus Beveridge: Social Insurance Systems in Europe*. Munich: Ifo Institute for Economic Research/Centre for Economic Studies, 2008. https://www.cesifo-group.de/DocDL/dicereport408-db6.pdf.

Centre for the Modern Family. *Family: Helping to Understand the Modern British Family*. Edinburgh: Scottish Widows, Centre for the Modern Family, 2011.

Chandler, Alfred D., Jr. *Strategy and Structure: Chapters in the History of the Industrial Enterprise*, Cambridge, MA: MIT Press, 1962.

Chimisso, Cristina. "The Tribunal of Philosophy and its Norms: History and Philosophy in Georges Canguilhem's Historical Epistemology." *Studies in History and Philosophy of Biological and Biomedical Sciences* 34 (2003) 297–327.

Cholbi, Michael, and Michael Weber, eds. *The Future of Work, Technology, and Basic Income*. New York: Routledge, 2020.

BIBLIOGRAPHY

Citizen's Basic Income Trust. "Book Review: Peter John, *How Far to Nudge?*" London: Citizen's Basic Income Trust, 2018. https://citizensincome.org/book-reviews/peter-john-how-far-to-nudge.

Clifford, Catherine. "What Billionaires and Business Titans Say about Cash Handouts in 2017 (Hint: Lots!)." https://www.cnbc.com/2017/12/27/what-billionaires-say-about-universal-basic-income-in-2017.html.

Coase, R.H. "The Nature of the Firm." *Economica* 4 (16) (1937) 386–405.

Cohen, Sheldon, and Jeffrey R. Edwards. "Personality Characteristics as Moderators of the Relationship Between Stress and Disorder." In *Advances in the Investigation of Psychological Stress*, edited by Richard W.J. Neufeld, 235–83. New York: John Wiley and Sons, 1989.

Colebatch, H.K. "Design as a Window on the Policy Process." In *Handbook on Policy, Process and Governing*, edited by Hal K. Colebatch and Robert Hoppe, 131–46. Cheltenham: Edward Elgar, 2018.

———. "Linkage and the Policy Process." In *Handbook on Policy, Process and Governing*, edited by Hal K. Colebatch and Robert Hoppe, 204–19. Cheltenham: Edward Elgar, 2018

Conen, Wieteke, and Joop Schippers, eds. *Self-Employment as Precarious Work: A European Perspective*. Cheltenham: Edward Elgar Publishing, 2019.

Coote, Anna. "Social Rights and Responsibilities." *Soundings,* issue 2, 203–12.

Crocker, Geoff. "Funding Basic Income by Money Creation." In *The Palgrave International Handbook of Basic Income*, edited by Malcolm Torry, 180–85. Cham: Palgrave Macmillan, 2019.

Cross, Rob, and Prusak, Laurence. "The People who Make Organizations Go, or Stop." *Harvard Business Review* 80 (60) (2002) 104–12.

Cuff, E.C. et al. *Perspectives in Sociology,* fourth edition. London: Routledge, 1998.

Culpit, Ian. *Welfare and Citizenship: Beyond the Crisis of the Welfare State*. Beverly Hills: Sage, 1992.

Daft, Richard L. *The New Era of Management*. Ohio: Thomson, 2006.

Daugareilh, Isabelle, et al. *The Platform Economy and Social Law: Key Issues in Comparative Perspective,* Brussels: European Trade Union Institute, 2006. https://www.etui.org/Publications2/Working-Papers/The-platform-economy-and-social-law-Key-issues-in-comparative-perspective.

Davies, Paul. In *The New Physics*, edited by Paul Davies, 4. Cambridge: Cambridge University Press, 1989.

Davis, Abigail, et al. *A Minimum Income Standard for the United Kingdom in 2024*. York: Joseph Rowntree Foundation, 2024. https://www.jrf.org.uk/a-minimum-income-standard-for-the-united-kingdom-in-2024.

Davis, Andrew M. "Whiteheadian Cosmotheology: Platonic Entities, Divine Realities and Shared Extraterrestrial Values." In *Process Cosmology*, edited by A.M. Davis et al., 423–52. Cham: Palgrave Macmillan, 2022.

Dean, Hartley. "The Ethics of Migrant Welfare." *Ethics and Social Welfare* 5 (1) (2011), 18–35.

———. *Social Policy*, second edition. Cambridge: Polity Press, 2012.

———. *Understanding Human Need*. Bristol: Policy Press, 2010.

———. *Understanding Human Need*, second edition, Bristol: Policy Press, 2020.

Deaton, Angus, ed. *Dimensions of Inequality: The IFS Deaton Review*. Supplement 1 to volume 3 of *Oxford Open Economics*. Oxford: Oxford University Press, 2024.

BIBLIOGRAPHY

———. *Understanding Consumption*, Oxford: Clarendon, 1992.
Deaton, Angus, and John Muellbauer. *Economics and Consumer Behaviour*. Cambridge: Cambridge University Press, 1980.
Deci, Edward L., and Richard M. Ryan. *Intrinsic Motivation and Self-determination in Human Behaviour*. New York: Plenum, 1985.
Dekker, S. W., and W.B. Schaufeli. "The Effects of Job Insecurity on Psychological Health and Withdrawal: A Longitudinal Study." *Australian Psychologist* 30 (1) (1995) 57–63.
Dermott, Esther. "Introduction: Poverty and Social Exclusion in the UK." In *Poverty and Social Exclusion in the UK: Volume 1—The Nature and Extent of the Problem*, edited by Esther Dermott and Gill Main, 1–15. Bristol: Policy Press, 2018.
Di Domenico, S. I., and M.A. Fournier "Socioeconomic Status, Income Inequality, and Health Complaints: A Basic Psychological Needs Perspective." *Social Indicators Research* 119 (3) (2014) 1679–97.
Diamond, Patrick. *The End of Whitehall*. Basingstoke: Palgrave Macmillan, 2018.
DiMaggio, Paul, and W. Powell. "The Iron Cage Revisited: Conformity and Diversity in Organisational Fields," *American Sociological Review* 48 (2) (1983) 147–60.
Donagan, Alan. *The Theory of Morality*. Chicago: University of Chicago Press, 1977.
Donnison, David. *The Politics of Poverty*. Oxford: Martin Robertson, 1982.
Dooley, D. "Unemployment, Underemployment, and Mental Health: Conceptualizing Employment Status as a Continuum." *American Journal of Community Psychology* 32 (1–2) (2003) 9–20.
Dorling, Danny. *The Equality Effect: Improving Life for Everyone*. Oxford: New Internationalist Publications, 2017.
———. *Injustice: Why Social Inequality Persists*. Bristol: Policy Press, 2010.
Douma, Sytse, and Hein Schreuder. *Economic Approaches to Organizations*, fourth edition. Harlow: Pearson, 2008.
Drucker, Peter. *Management Challenges for the Twenty-first Century*. New York: HarperBusiness, 1999.
Dulles, Avery. *Models of the Church*, expanded edition. New York: Doubleday, 2002.
Dunlap, Knight. *Religion: Its Functions in Human Life: A Study of Religion from the Point of View of Psychology*. Westport, Connecticut: Greenwood, 1970. First published in 1946.
Dunn, William N. "'Stage' Theories of the Policy Process." In *Handbook on Policy, Process and Governing*, edited by Hal K. Colebatch and Robert Hoppe, 112–30. Cheltenham: Edward Elgar, 2018.
Durkheim, Emile. *The Division of Labour in Society*. Basingstoke: Macmillan, 1984.
———. *The Elementary Forms of the Religious Life*. London: George Allen and Unwin, 1915.
———. *Moral Education*. New York: The Free Press, 1961.
———. *The Rules of Sociological Method*. Chicago: University of Chicago Press, 1938.
———. *Suicide*. London: Routledge, 1952.
Duverger, Timothée. *L'Invention du Revenu de Ba$€: La Fabrique d'une Utopie Démocratique*. Lormont: Le Bord de L'Eau, 2018.
Edmiston, Daniel. "Review Article: Welfare, Austerity and Social Citizenship in the UK." *Social Policy and Society* 16 (2) (2017) 261–70.
Edmiston, Daniel, et al. "Introduction: Austerity, Welfare and Social Citizenship." *Social Policy and Society* 16 (2) (2017) 253–59.

BIBLIOGRAPHY

Egan, Mark. *A Macat Analysis: Richard H. Thaler and Cass R. Sunstein's Nudge: Improving Decisions about Health, Wealth and Happiness.* London: Macat, 2017.
Eisenberger, Robert, and Judy Cameron. "Detrimental Effects of Reward: Reality or Myth?" *American Psychologist* 51 (11) (1996) 1153–66.
Ermisch, John. *The Political Economy of Demographic Change.* London: Heinemann, 1983.
Evans, Martin, and Lewis Williams. *A Generation of Change, a Lifetime of Difference? Social Policy in Britain since 1979.* Bristol: Policy Press, 2009.
Farmelo, Graham. *The Strangest Man: The Hidden Life of Paul Dirac, Quantum Genius.* London: Faber and Faber, 2009.
Fayol, H. *General and Industrial Management.* London: Pitman, 1916, 19-42. First published in 1916. Quoted in *Organization Theory: Selected Readings*, second edition, edited by D.S. Pugh, 135–56. Harmondsworth: Penguin, 1949.
Fée, David, and Anémone Kober-Smith, eds. *Inequalities in the UK: New Discourse, Evolutions and Actions.* Bingley: Emerald Publishing, 2018.
Feldmann, David C. "The Development and Enforcement of Group Norms." *Academy of Management Review* 9 (1) (1984) 47–53.
Ferguson, Iain et al. *Rethinking Welfare: A Critical Perspective.* London: Sage. 2002.
Fleischer, Miranda Perry, and Otto Lehto. "Libertarian Perspectives on Basic Income." In *The Palgrave International Handbook of Basic Income*, edited by Malcolm Torry, second edition, 509–28. Cham: Palgrave Macmillan, 2023.
Foucault, Michel. "Life: Experience and Science." In Michel Foucault, *Aesthetics, Method and Epistemology: The Essential Works of Michel Foucault, 1954-1984*, volume 2, edited by James D. Faubion, translated by Robert Hurley and others, 465–78. London: Penguin, 2000.
———. "What is Critique?" In Michel Foucault, *The Politics of Truth*, edited by Sylvère Lotringer, translated by Lysa Hochroth and Catherine Porter, 41–67. Los Angeles, CA: Simiotexte, 2007. A lecture given in 1978.
French, J. R. P. Jr., and B. H. Raven. "The Bases of Social Power." In *Studies in Social Power*, edited by D. Cartwright. Ann Arbor, MI: Institute for Social Research, 1959. Reprinted in *Organization Theory: Selected Readings*, second edition, edited by D.S. Pugh, 150–67. Harmondsworth: Penguin, 1984.
Fryer, D., and R. Fagan. "Towards a Critical Community Psychological Perspective on Unemployment and Mental Health." *American Journal of Community Psychology* 32 (1–2) (2003) 89–96.
Fryers, T. et al. "Social Inequalities and the Common Mental Disorders." *Social Psychiatry and Psychiatric Epidemiology* 38 (5) (2003) 229–37.
Galbraith, J.K. *Money: Whence it Came, Where it Went.* Harmondsworth: Penguin, 1976.
Garner, Robert, et al. *Introduction to Politics.* Oxford: Oxford University Press, 2009.
Gattei, Stefano. *Karl Popper's Philosophy of Science: Rationality Without Foundations.* New York and Abingdon: Routledge, 2009.
Gefter, Amanda. "Beyond Space-time." *New Scientist*, 6 August 2011, 34–37.
Giddens, Anthony. *Sociology*, fourth edition. Cambridge: Polity, 2001.
———. *The Third Way: The Renewal of Social Democracy.* Cambridge: Polity Press, 1998.
Ginn, Jay. "Pension Penalties: The Gendered Division of Occupational Welfare." *Work, Employment & Society* 7 (1) (1993) **47–70**.
Goffman, Erving. *Asylums: Essays on the Social Situation of Mental Patients and Other Inmates.* Harmondsworth: Penguin, 1968.
———. *The Presentation of the Self in Everyday Life.* London: Allen Lane, 1969.

BIBLIOGRAPHY

———. *Stigma: Notes on the Management of Spoiled Identity*. London: Penguin, 1990.
Golding, Martin P. "The Primacy of Welfare Rights." *Social Philosophy and Policy* 1 (2) (1972) 19–136.
Gordon, Ian, et al. "Perspectives on Policy Analysis." In *The Policy Process: A Reader*, edited by Michael Hill, 5–9. London: Prentice Hall/Harvester Wheatsheaf, 1997.
Gosling, R. and S. Taylor, eds. *Principles of Sociology*. London: London School of Economics and Political Science, 2005.
Gough, Ian. *Heat, Greed and Human Need: Climate Change, Capitalism and Sustainable Wellbeing*. Cheltenham: Edward Elgar, 2017.
Government of Canada. "Government of Canada Fighting Climate Change with Price on Pollution." 2018. https://pm.gc.ca/eng/news/2018/10/23/government-canada-fighting-climate-change-price-pollution.
Graeber, David. *Bullshit Jobs: A Theory*. London: Allen Lane, 2018.
Grayling, A.C. *Wittgenstein*. Oxford: Oxford University Press, 1988.
Gregg, Paul. "Job Guarantees—Easing the Pain of Long-term Unemployment." *Public Policy Research* 16 (3) (2009) 174–79.
Gregory, Robert. "Political Rationality or Incrementalism?" In *The Policy Process: A Reader*, edited by Michael Hill, 175–91. London: Prentice Hall/Harvester Wheatsheaf, 1997.
Greve, Bent. *Technology and the Future of Work: The Impact on Labour Markets and Welfare States*. Cheltenham: Edward Elgar Publishing, 2017.
Groenewegen, Peter. "Political Economy." In Palgrave Macmillan, eds, *The New Palgrave Dictionary of Economics*, Basingstoke: Palgrave Macmillan, 1987. https://link.springer.com/referenceworkentry/10.1057/978-1-349-95121-5_1365-2.
Groves, Peter *Grace*. Norwich: Canterbury Press, 2012.
Guggisberg, Adrian G., and Anaïs Mottaz. "Timing and Awareness of Movement Decisions: Does Consciousness Really Come Too Late?" *Frontiers of Human Neuroscience* 7 (385) (2013). https://pmc.ncbi.nlm.nih.gov/articles/PMC3746176/.
Guillen, Mauro. *Models of Management*. Chicago: University of Chicago Press, 1994.
Habermas, Jürgen. "Modernity versus Postmodernity." *New German Critique* 22 (1981) 3–14.
Ham, Christopher, and Michael Hill. *The Policy Process in the Modern Capitalist State*. Brighton: Wheatsheaf Books, 1984.
Hamilton, Peter. "The Enlightenment and the Birth of Social Science." In *Formations of Modernity*, edited by Hall, Stuart and Bram Gieben, 17–70. Milton Keynes: Open University, 1992.
Harari, Yuval Noah. *Nexus: A Brief History of Information Networks from the Stone Age to AI*. London: Fern Press, 2024.
Hare, R.M. *Freedom and Reason*. Oxford: Oxford University Press. . (1963),
———. *Moral Thinking: Its Levels, Method, and Point*. Oxford: Clarendon, 1981.
Harris, Margaret. "Seeing Churches as Voluntary Associations: Category Error or Insight for Practice?" In *Church Work and Management in Change*, edited by Kati Niemelä, 27–42. Finland: Church Research Institute, 2012.
Harris, Margaret, and Malcolm Torry. *Managing Religious and Faith-based Organisations: A Guide to the Literature*. Birmingham: University of Aston Business School, 2000.
Harrison, Robert, et al. "The Institutionalisation and Organisation of History." In *Making History: An Introduction to the History and Practices of a Discipline*, edited by Peter Lambert and Philipp Schofield, 9–25. Abingdon: Routledge, 2004.

BIBLIOGRAPHY

———. "Methodology: 'Scientific' History and the Problem of objectivity." In *Making History: An Introduction to the History and Practices of a Discipline*, edited by Peter Lambert and Philipp Schofield, 26–37. Abingdon: Routledge, 2004.

———. "The Primacy of Political History." In *Making History: An Introduction to the History and Practices of a Discipline*, edited by Peter Lambert and Philipp Schofield, 38–54. Abingdon: Routledge, 2004.

Haslam, S.A., and S.D. Reicher. "When Prisoners Take over the Prison: A social psychology of resistance," *Personal and Social Psychology Review* 16 (2) (2012) 154–79.

Held, David. *Political Theory and the Modern State*. Cambridge: Polity Press, 1984.

Hertog, Thomas. *On the Origin of Time: Stephen Hawking's Final Theory*. London: Torva, 2023.

Heywood, Andrew. *Political Theory: An Introduction*, second edition. Basingstoke: Palgrave Macmillan, 1999.

Hill, Michael. *The Public Policy Process*, fifth edition. Harlow: Pearson/Longman, 2009.

Hills, John. *Good Times, Bad Times: The Welfare Myth of Them and Us*. Bristol: Policy Press, 2014.

Hills, John, et al. *Understanding the Relationship between Poverty and Inequality: Overview Report*. London: International Inequality Institute, London School of Economics, 2014. http://sticerd.lse.ac.uk/dps/case/cr/casereport119.pdf.

———. *Understanding Social Exclusion*. Oxford: Oxford University Press, 2002.

Hodge, John, and Stuart Lowe. *Understanding the Policy Process: Analysing Welfare Policy and Practice*, second edition. Bristol: Policy Press, 2009.

Hodges, Andrew. *Alan Turing: The Enigma*. London: Vintage, 2012.

Hodgson, Geoffrey M. *Evolution and Institutions: On Evolutionary Economics and the Evolution of Economics*. Cheltenham: Edward Elgar, 1999.

Hofstede, Geert. *Culture's Consequences: International Differences in Work-Related Values*. Beverly Hills: Sage, 1980.

Hogg, Michael A., and Graham M. Vaughan. *Social Psychology*, seventh edition. Harlow: Pearson, 2014.

Homans, George C. *The Human Group*. London: Routledge, 1951.

Hoppe, Robert. "Choice v. Incrementalism." In *Handbook on Policy, Process and Governing*, edited by Hal K. Colebatch and Robert Hoppe, 398–417. Cheltenham: Edward Elgar, 2018.

Howard, Michael W. et al. "Ecological Effects of Basic Income." In *The Palgrave International Handbook of Basic Income*, second edition, edited by Malcolm Torry, 151–74. Cham: Palgrave Macmillan, 2023.

Huang, Xu and Evert Van de Vliert. "Where Intrinsic Job Satisfaction Fails to Work: National Moderators of Intrinsic Motivation." *Journal of Organizational Behavior* 24 (2) (2003) 159–79.

Huczynski, Andrzej A., and David A. Buchanan. *Organizational Behaviour*, sixth edition. Harlow: Pearson Education, 2007.

Husserl, Edmund. *Cartesian Meditations: An Introduction to Phenomenology*. Dordrecht: Springer Netherlands, 1999. Originally published in 1950.

———. *The Idea of Phenomenology*. Translated by Lee Hardy. Dordrecht: Kluwer Academic, 1999.

———. *Ideas Pertaining to a Pure Phenomenology and to a Phenomenological Philosophy: First Book, General Introduction to Pure Phenomenology*. Translated by F. Kersten. The Hague: Martinus Nijhoff, 1983.

BIBLIOGRAPHY

———. *Logical Investigations*, volume 1. Abingdon: Routledge, 2001. Translated by J.N. Findlay from Edmund Husserl, *Logische Untersuchungen*, Halle: M. Niemeyer, 1900/1901. References that give only the paragraph and page number refer to chapter 11 of the "Prolegomena" to the *Logical Investigations*; for other chapters of the "Prolegomena" the chapter number is given as well (for instance: 1, §6, 19); references to the "Introduction" between the Prolegomena and the Investigations are given as "I," followed by the paragraph and page numbers; and references to the first two Investigations are given as I1 or I2 respectively, followed by the paragraph and page numbers.

———. *Philosophy of Arithmetic: Psychological and Logical Investigations with Supplementary Texts from 1887-1901*. Translated by Dallas Willard. Dordrecht: Springer Netherlands, 2003.

Hutchinson, D. S. "Ethics." In *The Cambridge Companion to Aristotle*, edited by Jonathan Barnes, 195-232. Cambridge: Cambridge University Press, 1995.

Huyssen, Andreas. "The Search for Tradition." *New German Critique* 22 (1981) 23-40.

Jacobs, Lawrence R., and Robert Y. Shapiro. "The Media Reporting and Distorting of Public Opinion Towards Entitlements." In *The Policy Process*, edited by Stuart S. Nagel, 135-45. New York: Nova Science, 1999.

James, William. *The Varieties of Religious Experience: A Study in Human Nature*. Oxford: Oxford University Press, 1902. Reprinted in 2012.

Jaques, Elliott. *Requisite Organization: The CEO's Guide to Creative Structure and Leadership*. Arlington, VA: Cason Hall, 1989

John, Peter. *How Far to Nudge? Assessing Behavioural Public Policy*. Cheltenham: Edward Elgar, 2018.

Johnson, Mark. *Moral Imagination: Implications of Cognitive Science for Ethics*. Chicago: Chicago University Press, 1993.

Jones, Elizabeth, et al. *Family Stressors and Children's Outcomes*. London: Department of Education, 2013. http://dera.ioe.ac.uk/16415/1/DFE-RR254.pdf.

Jordan, Bill. *Paupers: The Making of the New Claiming Class*. London: Routledge and Kegan Paul, 1973.

Jordan, Bill, et al. *Trapped in Poverty? Labour-market Decisions in Low-income Households*. London: Routledge, 1992.

Juarrero, Alicia. "Intentions as Complex Dynamical Attractors." In *Causing Human Action: New Perspectives on the Causal Theory of Action*, edited by Jesús H. Aguilar and Andrea A. Buckareff, 253-75. Cambridge, MA: MIT, 2010.

Kant, Immanuel. *Groundwork for the Metaphysics of Morals*. Translated by Arnulf Zweig. Oxford: Oxford University Press, 2002. First published in 1785.

Kaplan, R.S. and D.P. Norton. "The Balanced Scorecard—Measures that Drive Performance." *Harvard Business Review* 70 (1) (1992) 71-79.

Kauffman, Stuart A. *The Origins of Order: Self-organisation and Selection in Evolution*. Oxford: Oxford University Press, 1993.

Keuth, Herbert. *The Philosophy of Karl Popper*. Translated by Herbert Keuth. Cambridge: Cambridge University Press, 2005.

Keyt, John C. "Beyond Strategic Control: Applying the Balanced Scorecard to a Religious Organization." *Journal of Nonprofit & Public Sector Marketing* 9 (1-2) (2001) 91-102.

Kitagawa, Kate, and Timothy Revell. *The Secret Lives of Numbers*. London: Penguin, 2024.

BIBLIOGRAPHY

Koenig-Robert, Roger, and Joel Pearson. "Decoding the Contents and Strength of Imagery before Volitional Engagement." *Scientific Reports* 9 (3504) (2019). https://doi.org/10.1038/s41598-019-39813-y.

Kohn, Paul M., et al. "Hassles, Health and Personality." *Journal of Personality and Social Psychology* 61 (3) (1991) 478–82.

Koopman, Colin. *Genealogy as Critique: Foucault and the Problems of Modernity.* Bloomington and Indianapolis: Indiana University Press, 2013.

Kotowicz, Zbigniew. *Gaston Bachelard: A Philosophy of the Surreal.* Edinburgh: Edinburgh University Press, 2016.

Kreps, David M. "Corporate Culture and Economic Theory." In *Perspectives on Positive Political Economy*, edited by James Alt and Kenneth Shepsle, 90–143. Cambridge: Cambridge University Press, 1990.

Kuhn, Thomas S. "A Function for Thought Experiments." In *Scientific Revolutions*, edited by Ian Hacking, 6–27. Oxford: Oxford University Press, 1981.

———. *The Structure of Scientific Revolutions.* Chicago: Chicago University Press, 1962.

Lambert, Peter, and Philipp Schofield, eds. *Making History: An Introduction to the History and Practices of a Discipline.* Abingdon: Routledge, 2004.

Lansley, Stewart. "Tackling Inequality is an Economic Imperative." In *Inequalities in the UK: New Discourse, Evolutions and Actions*, edited by David Fée and Anémone Kober-Smith, 39–57. Bingley: Emerald Publishing, 2018.

Lansley, Stewart, and Joanna Mack. *Breadline Britain.* London: London Weekend Television, 1983.

———. *Breadline Britain*, second edition. London, Oneworld, 2015.

Lawrence, Jon. "Political History." In *Writing History: Theory and Practice*, edited by Stefan Berger et al., 183–202. London: Hodder Arnold, 2003.

Lawrence, Paul R. and Jay W. Lorsch. *Organization and Environment: Managing Differentiation and Integration.* Boston: Harvard University Press, 1967.

Lemke, Thomas. "Critique and Experience in Foucault." *Theory, Culture and Society* 28 (4) (2011) 26–48.

Lepper, Mark R., and David Greene, eds. *The Hidden Costs of Reward: New Perspectives on the Psychology of Human Motivation.* Hillsdale, NJ: Lawrence Erlbaum Associates, 1978.

Lévinas, Emmanuel. *Entre Nous: Essays on Thinking-of-the-other.* New York: Columbia University Press, 2000. First published in French in 1991.

Lindblom, C.E. "The Science of Muddling Through." *Public Administration Review* 19 (2), quoted in *Organization Theory: Selected Readings*, second edition, edited by D.S. Pugh, 238–55. Harmondsworth: Penguin, 1959.

Lipsey, Richard G., and K. Alec Chrystal. *Economics*, tenth edition. Oxford: Oxford University Press, 2004.

Lister, Ruth. *Poverty.* Cambridge: Polity, 2004.

———. *Poverty*, second edition. Cambridge: Polity Press, 2020.

Lo Vuolo, Rubén M. "Piketty's *Capital*, his Critics and Basic Income." *Basic Income Studies* 10 (1) (2015) 29–43.

Locke, Edwin. "Personnel Attitudes and Motivation." *Annual Review of Psychology* 26 (1975) 457–80.

London School of Economics. "What is Social Policy?" London: London School of Economics and Social Science, 2025. https://www.lse.ac.uk/social-policy/about-us/What-is-social-policy.

BIBLIOGRAPHY

Lyotard, Jean-François. *La Condition Postmoderne*. Paris: Les Éditions de Minuit, 1979.

Mack, Joanna. "Fifty Years of poverty in the UK." In *Poverty and Social Exclusion in the UK: Volume 2—The Dimensions of Disadvantage*, edited by Glen Bramley and Nick Bailey, 27–55. Bristol: Policy Press, 2018.

Majone, Gian Domenico. *Evidence, Argument, and Persuasion in the Policy Process*. New Haven: Yale University Press, 1989.

Mani, Anandi, et al. "Poverty Impedes Cognitive Function." *Science* 341 (6149) (1989) 976–80.

Mappes, Thomas A., and Jane S. Zembaty. *Social Ethics: Morality and Social Policy*. New York: McGraw-Hill, 1997.

Marion, Jean-Luc. *Being Given: Toward a Phenomenology of Givenness*. Stanford, CA: Stanford University Press, 2002.

———. *Étant Donné : Essai d'une Phénoménologie de la Donation*. Paris: Presses Universitaires de France, 1997.

Marmot, Michael. *Fair Society, Healthy Lives*. Firenze: Leo S. Oslchlei, 2013.

Marshall, T.H. *Citizenship and Social Class and Other Essays*. Cambridge: Cambridge University Press, 1950.

Martin, Joanne. *Cultures in Organizations: Three Perspectives*. New York: Oxford University Press, 1992.

Martin, P., and J. Nicholls. *Creating a Committed Workforce*. London: McGraw-Hill, 1987.

Marx, Karl, and Friedrich Engels. *The Communist Manifesto*. Translated by Samuel Moore. Reprinted 1967. Harmondsworth: Penguin, 1888.

Maslow, Abraham. "A Theory of human motivation." *Psychological Review* 50 (4) (1943) 370–96.

Mason, Paul. *PostCapitalism: A Guide to our Future*. London: Allen Lane/Penguin Random House, 2015.

Maxwell, James Clerk. "God and Molecules." In *The Faber Book of Science*, edited by John Carey, 167–68. London: Faber and Faber, 1995.

Mayo, Elton. *The Human Problems of an Industrial Civilization*. New York: The Viking Press, 1960.

———. *The Social Problems of an Industrial Civilization*. London: Routledge and Kegan Paul, 1949.

Mayo, George Elton et al. *Management and the Worker*. Cambridge, MA: Harvard University Press, 1939.

McArthur, Daniel. "Why Bachelard is not a Scientific Realist." *The Philosophical Forum* 33 (2) (2002) 159–72.

McGregor, Douglas. *The Human Side of Enterprise*. New York: McGraw-Hill, 1960.

McHenry, Leemon B. *The Event Universe: The Revisionary Metaphysics of Alfred North Whitehead*. Edinburgh: Edinburgh University Press, 2015.

McSweeney, Brendan. "Hofstede's Model of National Culture Differences and their Consequences: A Triumph of Faith—A Failure of Analysis." *Human Relations* 55 (1) (1996) 89–118.

Mead, Lawrence. *The New Politics of Poverty: The Non-working Poor in America*. New York: Harper Collins, 1992.

Melden, A.I. "Are There Welfare Rights?" In *Income Support: Conceptual and Policy Issues*, edited by Peter G. Brown et al., 259–78. New Jersey: Rowman and Littlefield, 1981.

Mellor, Mary. *Money: Myths, Truth and Alternatives*. Bristol: Policy Press.

BIBLIOGRAPHY

Mideros, Andrés, and Cathal O'Donoghue. "The Effect of Unconditional Cash Transfers on Adult Labour Supply: A Unitary Discrete Choice Model for the Case of Ecuador." *Basic Income Studies* 10 (2) (2019) 225-55.

Mill, John Stuart. *Utilitarianism*, reprinted in 1993. London: Everyman/Dent, 1861.

Miller, Edward J. "Demand Side Economics and its Consequence: The National Dividend." Paper presented at the 2014 BIEN Congress, Montreal, 26-29 June 2014. https://basicincome.org/bien/pdf/montreal2014/BIEN2014_Miller.pdf.

Miller, James B. "The Emerging Postmodern World." In *Postmodern Theology: Christian Faith in a Pluralist World*, edited by Frederic B. Burnham, 1-19. San Francisco: Harper and Row, 1989.

Mills, Albert J., and Peter Tancred. *Gendering Organisational Analysis*. Newbury Park: Sage, 1979.

Minogue, Martin. "Theory and Practice in Public Policy and Administration." In *The Policy Process: A Reader*, edited by Michael Hill, 10-29. London: Prentice Hall/Harvester Wheatsheaf, 1997.

Mintzberg, H. "The Manager's Job: Folklore and Fact." *Harvard Business Review*, July-August 1975. Quoted in *Organization Theory: Selected Readings*, second edition, edited by D.S. Pugh, 417-40. Harmondsworth: Penguin, 1984.

Mintzberg, Henry. *Mintzberg on Management: Inside our Strange Model of Organizations*. New York: The Free Press, 1989.

Moher, Lawrence B. *Explaining Organizational Behavior*. San Francisco: Jossey-Bass, 1982.

Morçöl, Göktuğ. *A Complexity Theory for Public Policy*. New York: Routledge, 2012.

Morgan, Gareth. *Creative Organization Theory: A Resourcebook*. Newbury Park: Sage, 1989.

———. *Images of Organizations*. Newbury Park: Sage, 1986.

Moreno, J.L. *Who Shall Survive? Foundations of Sociometry, Group Psychotherapy and Sociodrama*. Beacon, New York: Beacon House Inc. 1953.

Morris, C.N. "The Structure of Personal Income Taxation and Income Support. *Fiscal Studies*, 3 (3) (1982) 210-18.

Moscovici, Serge. *Influence and Social Change*. London: Academic Press, 1976.

———. *Social Influence and Conformity*. In *Handbook of Social Psychology*, volume II, third edition, edited by Gardner Lindzey and Elliot Aronson. New York: Random House, 1985.

———. "Toward a Theory of Conversion Behavior. New Plant." In *Advances in Experimental Social Psychology*, edited by Leonard Berkowitz, 209-39. New York: Academic Press, 1980.

Mowshowitz, Abbe. "Virtual Organization: A Vision of Management in the Information Age." *The Information Society* 10 (4) (1994) 267-88.

Mullainathan, Sendhil, and Eldar Shafir, *Scarcity: Why Having Too Little Means So Much*. London: Macmillan, 2013.

Mullins, Laurie J. *Management and Organisational Behaviour*, seventh edition. Harlow: Pearson, 2005.

Murali, Vijaya, and Femi Oyebode. "Poverty, Social Inequality and Mental Health." *Advances in Psychiatric Treatment* 10 (3) (2004) 216-24.

Murphy, Gregory C. and James A. Athanasou. "The Effect of Unemployment on Mental Health." *Journal of Occupational and Organizational Psychology* 72 (1) (1999) 83-99.

Murray, Charles. *Losing Ground: American Social Policy, 1950–1980*. New York: Basic Books, 1984.
———. *Charles Murray and the Underclass: The Developing Debate*. London: Institute of Economic Affairs, 1996.
Nagel, Thomas. *The Possibility of Altruism*. Oxford: Clarendon, 1977.
Natili, Marcello, *The Politics of Minimum Income: Explaining Path Departure and policy Departure in the Age of Austerity*. Cham: Palgrave Macmillan, 2019.
Nemeth, Charlan et al. "Patterning of the Minority's Responses and their Influence on the Majority." *European Journal of Social Psychology* 4 (1) (1974) 53–64.
———. "Exposure to Dissent and Recall of Information." *Journal of Personality and Social Psychology* 58 (3) (1990) 429–37.
Neufeld, Richard W.J. and Randolph J. Paterson. "Issues Concerning Control and its Implementation." In *Advances in the Investigation of Psychological Stress*, edited by Richard W.J. Neufeld, 43–67. New York: John Wiley and Sons, 1989.
Nicolis, Gregoire. "Physics of Far-from-equilibrium Systems and Self-organisation." In *The New Physics*, edited by Paul Davies, 316–47. Cambridge: Cambridge University Press, 1989.
Niebuhr, Reinhold. *Christian Realism and Political Problems*. London: Faber and Faber, 1954.
———. *The Godly and the Ungodly: Essays on the Religious and Secular Dimensions of Modern Life*. London: Faber and Faber, 1958.
———. *An Interpretation of Christian Ethics*. London: SCM, 1936.
———. *Moral Man and Immoral Society: A Study in Ethics and Politics*. New York: Charles Scribners' Sons, 1936.
Nozick, Robert. *The Normative Theory of Individual Choice*. New York: Garland, 1990.
Olafsen, Anja H. et al. "Show them the Money? The Role of Pay, Managerial Need Support, and Justice in a Self-determination Theory Model of Intrinsic Work Motivation." *Scandinavian Journal of Psychology* 56 (4) (2015) 447–57.
Oxford English Dictionary, www.oed.com
Page, Edward. "'Whatever Governments Choose to Do or Not to Do'". In *Handbook on Policy, Process and Governing*, edited by Hal K. Colebatch and Robert Hoppe, 16–31. Cheltenham: Edward Elgar, 2018.
Pahl, Jan. "The Allocation of Money and Structuring of Inequality within Marriage. *Sociological Review* 31 (2) (1983) 237–62.
Palermo Kuss, Ana Helena, and K.J. Bernhard Neumärker. "Modelling the Time Allocation Effects of Basic Income." *Basic Income Studies* 13 (2) (2018) https://doi.org/10.1515/bis-2018-0006.
Papanicolaon, Andrew, and Peter Gunter, eds. *Bergson and Modern Thought*. London: Harwood Academic, 1987.
Parker, Hermione. *Instead of the Dole: An Enquiry into Integration of the Tax and Benefit Systems*. London: Routledge, 1989.
Paterson, Randolph J. and Richard W.J. Neufeld. "The Stress Response and Parameters of Stressful Situations." In *Advances in the Investigation of Psychological Stress*, edited by Richard W.J. Neufeld, 7–42. New York: John Wiley and Sons, 1989.
Peacocke, Arthur, and Ann Pederson. *The Music of Creation*. Minneapolis: Fortress Press, 2006.
Pearson, Gordon. *The Rise and Fall of Management: A Brief History of Practice, Theory and Context*. Farnham: Gower, 2009.

BIBLIOGRAPHY

Penrose, Roger. *The Road to Reality: A Complete Guide to the Laws of the Universe*. London: Vintage, 2005.
Perrow, Charles. *Organizational Analysis: A Sociological View*. London: Tavistock, 1970.
Peters, B. Guy. *Policy Problems and Policy Design*. Cheltenham: Edward Elgar, 2018.
Pettinger, Lynne. *What's Wrong with Work?* Bristol: Policy, 2019.
Phillips, Anthony. *God B.C.: God's Grace in the Old Testament*. Durham: Sacristy Press, 2018.
Piketty, Thomas. *Capital in the Twenty-First Century*. Cambridge, MA: The Belknap Press of Harvard University Press, 2014.
Pittman, Thane S. and Jack F. Heller. "Social Motivation." *Annual Review of Psychology* 38 (1987) 461–89.
Plant, Raymond. "Needs, Agency, and Welfare Rights." In *Rights and Welfare: The Theory of the Welfare State*, edited by T. Donald Moon, 55–74. Boulder, CO: Westview, 1988.
Polkinghorne, John. *Science and Providence: God's Interaction with the World*. London: SPCK, 1989.
———. *Science and Theology: An Introduction*. London: SPCK, 1998.
Popper, Karl. *Conjectures and Refutations: The Growth of Scientific Knowledge*. Third edition. London: Routledge and Kegan Paul, 1969.
———. *The Logic of Scientific Discovery*. London: Hutchinson, 1959.
———. *Objective Knowledge: An Evolutionary Approach*. Second edition. Oxford: Clarendon Press, 1979.
Powell, Walter W. and Paul J. DiMaggio. *The New Institutionalism in Organizational Analysis*. Second edition. Chicago: University of Chicago Press, 1991.
Prigogine, Ilya, and Isabelle Stengers. *Order out of Chaos: Man's New Dialogue with Nature*. London: Heinemann, 1984.
Privitera, Walter. *Problems of Style: Michel Foucault's Epistemology*. New York: State University of New York Press, 1995.
Psychologists for Social Change. *Universal Basic Income: A Psychological Impact Assessment*. London: Psychologists Against Austerity, 2017. http://www.psychchange.org/basic-income-psychological-impact-assessment.html.
Purdy, David. "Citizenship, Basic Income and Democracy." *BIRG Bulletin*, no. 10, Autumn/Winter 1990, 9–13.
Quinlan, Michael, et al. "The Global Expansion of Precarious Employment, Work Disorganization, and Consequences for Occupational Health: A Review of Recent Research." *International Journal of Health Services* 31 (2) (2001) 335–414.
Rawls, John. *A Theory of Justice*. Cambridge, MA: Harvard University Press, 1971.
Ray, Carol Axtell. "Corporate Culture: The Last Frontier of Control." *Journal of Management Studies* 23 (3) (1986) 287–97.
Reeve, Andrew, and Andrew Williams, eds. *Real Libertarianism Assessed: Political Theory after Van Parijs*. London: Palgrave Macmillan, 2002.
Reeve, John Marshall, and Edward L. Deci. "Elements of the Competitive Situation that Affect Intrinsic Motivation." *Personality and Social Psychology Bulletin* 22 (1) (1996) 24–33.
Reynolds, Brigid, SM, and Sean Healy, SMA, eds. *New Frontiers for Full Citizenship*. Dublin: Conference of Major Religious Superiors of Ireland, 1993.
Richardson, J.J. and A.G. Jordan. *Governing Under Pressure: The Policy Process in a Post-parliamentary Democracy*. Oxford: Basil Blackwell, 1979.

BIBLIOGRAPHY

Richardson, Jeremy. "Interest Group, Multi-arena Politics and Policy Change." In *The Policy Process*, edited by Stuart S. Nagel, 65–99. New York: Nova Science, 1999.

Ricoeur, Paul. *Du Texte à l'Action: Essais d'Herméneutique, II*. Paris: Éditions du Seuil, 1986.

———. *From Text to Action: Essays in Hermeneutics, II*. Translated by Kathleen Blamey. London: Continuum, 2008.

Ritchie, Sheila, and Peter Martin. *Motivation Management*. Aldershot: Gower, 1999.

Rizzo, Mario J. "The Four Pillars of Behavioral Paternalism." In *Nudge Theory in Action: Behavioral Design in Policy and Markets*, edited by Sherzod Abdukadirov, 37–63. Basingstoke: Palgrave Macmillan, 2016.

Robins, Stephen P. and Timothy A. Judge. *Organizational Behavior*, New Jersey: Pearson, 2009.

Roche, Maurice. *Rethinking Citizenship: Welfare Ideology and Change in Modern Society*. Cambridge: Polity, 1992.

Rochester, Colin, and Malcolm Torry. "Faith-based Organizations and Hybridity: A Special Case?" In *Hybrid Organizations and the Third Sector: Challenges for Practice, Theory and Policy*, edited by David Billis, 114–33. Basingstoke: Palgrave Macmillan, 2010.

Room, Graham. *Complexity, Institutions and Public Policy: Agile Decision-making in a Turbulent World*. Cheltenham: Edward Elgar, 2011.

Rosch, Eleanor. "Reclaiming Concepts." In "Reclaiming Cognition," edited by Walter J. Freeman and Rafael Núñez, *Journal of Consciousness Studies* 6 (11–12) (1999) 61–77.

Rosch, Eleanor, and Barbara B. Lloyd. *Cognition and Categorization*. Mahwah, NJ: Lawrence Erlbaum, 1978.

Rose, Nicholas. *Governing the Soul: The Shaping of the Private Self*. London: Routledge, 1989.

Rose, Nikolas. "Brains Matter." *LSE Connect*, Summer 2011, 10–11.

Rose, Richard. "Inheritance Before Choice in Public Policy." In *Making Policy Happen*, edited by Leslie Budd et al., 51–64. London: Routledge, 2006.

Rosenthal, Robert, and Lenore Jacobson. *Pygmalion in the Classroom: Teacher Expectations and Pupils' Intellectual Development*. Williston, VT: Crown House, 1992.

Rosner, Peter G. *The Economics of Social Policy*. Cheltenham: Edward Elgar, 2003.

Runciman, W.G. *Relative Deprivation and Social Justice: A Study of Attitudes to Social Inequality in Twentieth-century England*. London: Routledge and Kegan Paul. 1966.

Ryan, Richard M. and Edward L. Deci. "Self-determination Theory and the Facilitation of Intrinsic Motivation, Social Development, and Well-being." *American Psychologist* 55 (1) (2000) 68–78.

Sager, Lutz. "Income Inequality and Carbon Consumption: Evidence from Environmental Engel Curves." London: Grantham Research Institute on Climate Change and the Environment, 2017. https://www.lse.ac.uk/granthaminstitute/publication/income-inequality-and-carbon-consumption-evidence-from-environmental-engel-curves/.

Sargant, William. *Battle for the Mind: A Physiology of Conversion and Brain-washing*. London: Heinemann, 1976.

Scanlon, T.M. "Contractualism and Utilitarianism." In *Utilitarianism and Beyond*, edited by Amartya Sen and Bernard Williams, 103–28. Cambridge University Press, 1982.

Schelling, Friedrich Wilhelm Joseph. *The Unconditional in Human Knowledge: Four early essays, 1794–1796*. Translated by Fritz Marti. Lewisburg: Bucknell University Press, 1980.

BIBLIOGRAPHY

Schneewind, J.B. *Sidgwick's Ethics and Victorian Moral Philosophy*. Oxford: Clarendon Press, 1977.

Schofield, Philipp. "The Emergence of British Economic History, c.1870 to c. 1930." In *Making History: An Introduction to the History and Practices of a Discipline*, edited by Peter Lambert and Philipp Schofield, 65–77. Abingdon: Routledge, 2004.

Seebrook, Jeremy. *Landscapes of Poverty*. Oxford: Basil Blackwell, 1985.

Sen, Amartya. *The Idea of Justice*. London: Allen Lane/Penguin, 2009.

Serres, Michel. *The Birth of Physics*. Translated by David Webb and William Ross. London: Rowman and Littlefield, 2018.

———. *The Incandescent*. Translated by Randolph Burks. London: Bloomsbury, 2018.

———. *The Natural Contract*. Translated by Elizabeth MacArthur and William Paulson. Ann Arbor: University of Michigan Press, 1995.

———. *The Parasite*. Translated by Randolph Burks, based on a translation by Lawrence Schehr. 2021. https://www.academia.edu/45684409/The_Parasite_by_Michel_Serres_translated_by_Randolph_Burks_and_Lawrence_Schehr.

Sherif, Muzafer. *The Psychology of Social Norms*. New York: Harper and Row, 1936.

Sherman, Barrie, and Phil Jenkins. *Licensed to Work*, London: Cassell, 1995.

Sherry, Patrick. *Religion, Truth and Language Games*. London and Basingstoke: Macmillan, 1977.

Shone, Ronald. *Applications in Intermediate Microeconomics*. Oxford: Martin Robertson, 1981.

Simons, Massimiliano. "The Many Encounters of Thomas Kuhn and French Epistemology." *Studies in History and Philosophy of Science* 61 (2017) 41–50.

Skinner, Quentin. "Meaning and Understanding in the History of Ideas." *History and Theory* 8 (1) (1969), 3–53.

Sloman, Peter. "Universal Basic Income in British politics, 1918–2018: From a "Vagabond's Wage" to a Global Debate. *Journal of Social Policy*, 47 (3) (2018) 625–42.

———. *Transfer State: The Idea of a Guaranteed Income and the Politics of Redistribution in Modern Britain*, Oxford: Oxford University Press, 2019.

Smart, J.J.C. and Bernard Williams. *Utilitarianism: For and Against*. Cambridge: Cambridge University Press, 1973.

Smith, Adam C. and Todd J. Zywicki. "Nudging in an Evolving Marketplace: How Markets Improve their Own Choice Architecture." In *Nudge Theory in Action: Behavioral Design in Policy and Markets*, edited by Sherzod Abdukadirov, 225–50. Basingstoke: Palgrave Macmillan, 2016.

Smith, Gilbert, and David May. "The Artificial Debate between Rationalist and Incrementalist Models of Decision Making." In *The Policy Process: A Reader*, edited by Michael Hill, 163–74. London: Prentice Hall/Harvester Wheatsheaf, 1997.

Smith, Ronald E. *Psychology*. Menneapolis: West Publishing Company, 1993.

Smolin, Lee. *Time Reborn: From the Crisis in Physics to the Future of the Universe*, London: Penguin, 2014.

Spicker, Paul. "Five Types of Complexity." *Benefits* 13 (1) (2005) 5–9.

———. *Social Policy: Theory and Practice*. Third edition. Bristol: Policy, 2014.

Staerklé, Christian, et al. "A Normative Approach to Welfare Attitudes." In *Contested Welfare States: Welfare Attitudes in Europe and Beyond*, edited by Stefan Svallfors, 81–118. Stanford, CA: Stanford University Press, 2012.

Standing, Guy. *Work after Globalization: Building Occupational Citizenship*. Cheltenham: Edward Elgar, 2009.

BIBLIOGRAPHY

———. "Why You've Never Heard of a Charter that's as Important as Magna Carta." *Open Democracy*, 2017. https://www.opendemocracy.net/uk/guy-standing/why-youve-never-heard-of-charter-thats-as-important-as-magna-carta.

Stedman Jones, Gareth. "Rethinking Chartism." In *Languages of Class: Studies in English Working Class History, 1832–1982*, by Gareth Stedman Jones, 90–178. Cambridge: Cambridge University Press, 1983.

Steiner, Ivan D. *Group Process and Productivity*. New York: Academic, 1972.

Stocker, Michael. *Plural and Conflicting Values*. Oxford: Clarendon, 1990.

Stoner, J.A.F.. *A Comparison of Individual and Group Decisions Involving Risk*. Unpublished master's degree thesis. Boston, MA: Massachusetts Institute of Technology, 1961, quoted in Andrezej A. Huczynski and David A. Buchanan, *Organizational Behaviour*, sixth edition, 744. Harlow: Pearson Education, 2007.

Sverke, Magnus, et al. "No Security: A Meta-analysis and Review of Job Insecurity and its Consequences." *Journal of Occupational Health Psychology* 7 (3) (2002) 242–64.

Tang, Shua-Hua, and Vernon C. Hall. "The Overjustification Effect: A Meta-analysis." *Applied Cognitive Psychology* 9 (5) (1995) 365–404.

Taylor, Frederick Winslow. *Scientific Management*. New York: Harper, 1911.

Taylor, Phil, and Peter Bain. "'An Assembly Line in the Head': Work and Employer Relations in the Call Centre." *Industrial Relations Journal* 30 (2) (1999) 101–17.

Taylor, Shelley. *Health Psychology*. Fourth edition. Boston, MA: McGraw Hill, 1999.

Taylor, Steve. *Durkheim and the Study of Suicide*. Basingstoke: Macmillan, 1982.

Teilhard de Chardin, Pierre. *L'Avenir de l'Homme*. Paris: Éditions du Seuil, 1959.

———. *The Future of Man*. Translated by Norman Denny from *L'Avenir de l'Homme*. London: Collins, 1969.

———. *Le Phénomène Humain*. Paris: Éditions du Seuil, 1955.

———. *The Phenomenon of Man*. Translated by Bernard Wall from *Le Phénomène Humain*. London: Fontana/Collins, 1970. Subsequent editions were published under the title *The Human Phenomenon*.

Thaler, Richard H. *Misbehaving: How Economics Became Behavioural*. London: Allen Lane, 2015.

Thaler, Richard H. and Cass R. Sustein. *Nudge: Improving Decisions about Health, Wealth and Happiness*. Revised edition. London: Penguin, 2009.

Thatcher, Margaret. Interview for *Woman's Own*, 31 October 1987. https://www.margaretthatcher.org/document/106689.

Thierer, Adam. "Failing Better: What we Learn by Confronting Risk and Uncertainty." In *Nudge Theory in Action: Behavioral Design in Policy and Markets*, edited by Sherzod Abdukadirov, 65–94. Basingstoke: Palgrave Macmillan, 2016.

Tiles, Mary. "Technology, Science, and Inexact Knowledge: Bachelard's Non-Cartesian Epistemology." In *Continental Philosophy of Science*, edited by Gary Gutting, 157–75. Malden, MA: Blackwell, 2005.

Titmuss, Richard. *The Gift Relationship: From Human Blood to Social Policy*. London: Allen and Unwin, 1970.

Tomer, John F.. *The Human Firm*. London: Routledge, 1999.

Tomlinson, Daniel. *Irregular Payments: Assessing the Breadth and Depth of Month to Month Earnings Volatility*. London: Resolution Foundation, 2018. https://www.resolutionfoundation.org/app/uploads/2018/10/Irregular-payments-RF-REPORT.pdf.

BIBLIOGRAPHY

Torry, Malcolm. "Action, Patterns and Religious Pluralism." *Theology* 106 (830) (2003) 107–118.
———. *Actological Readings in Continental Philosophy*. Eugene, OR: Resource/Wipf and Stock, 2023.
———. *Actology: Action, Change, and Diversity in the Western Philosophical Tradition*. Eugene, OR: Resource/Wipf and Stock, 2020.
———. *An Actological Metaphysic*. Eugene, OR: Resource/Wipf and Stock, 2023.
———. *An Actology of the Given*. Eugene, OR: Resource/Wipf and Stock, 2023.
———. *Basic Income—A History*. Cheltenham: Edward Elgar, 2021.
———. *Bridgebuilders: Workplace Chaplaincy—A History*. Norwich: Canterbury, 2010.
———. "On Building a New Christendom: Lessons from South London Parishes." *Theology* CXII (870) (2009) 435–43.
———. ed. *Diverse Gifts: Varieties of Lay and Ordained Ministries in the Church and Community*. Norwich: Canterbury, 2006.
———. *The Feasibility of Citizen's Income*. New York: Palgrave Macmillan, 2016.
———. "Is there a Faith Sector?" *Voluntary Sector Review* 3 (1) (2012) 111–17.
———. "'Logic' and 'Action': Two New Readings of the New Testament." *Theology* 111 (860) (2008) 93–101.
———. *Managing God's Business: Religious and Faith-Based Organizations and their Management*. Aldershot: Ashgate, 2005.
———. *Managing Religion: The Management of Christian Religious and Faith-based Organizations: Volume I, Internal Relationships*. Basingstoke: Palgrave Macmillan, 2014.
———. *Managing Religion: The Management of Christian Religious and Faith-based Organizations: Volume II, External Relationships*. Basingstoke: Palgrave Macmillan, 2014.
———. *Mediating Institutions: Creating Relationships between Religion and an Urban World*. London: Palgrave Macmillan, 2016.
———. *A Modern Guide to Citizen's Basic Income: A Multidisciplinary Approach*. Cheltenham: Edward Elgar, 2020.
———. *Money for Everyone: Why we Need a Citizen's Income*. Bristol: Policy, 2013.
———. "A Neglected Theologian: John Sandwith Boys Smith." *Theology* 107 (836) (2004) 89–104.
———. "A New Agenda: Complexity Theory, Tax and Benefits." *Citizen's Income Newsletter*, issue 3 for 2002, 2–3. https://citizensincome.org/news/citizens-income-newsletter-2002-issue-3/.
———. "On Completing the Apologetic Spectrum." *Theology* 103 (812) (2000) 108–15.
———. ed. *The Parish: People, Places and Ministry: A Theological and Practical Exploration*. Norwich: Canterbury, 2004.
———. "The Practice and Theology of the South London Industrial Mission." Unpublished PhD thesis. London: University of London, 1990.
———. "Primary Care, the Basic Necessity." Part I: "Explorations in Economics"; and Part II: "Explorations in Ethics." In *Handbook of Primary Care Ethics*, edited by Andrew Papanikitas and John Spicer, 369–84. Boca Raton, FL: CRC/Francis and Taylor, 2017.
———. ed. *Regeneration and Renewal: The Church in New and Changing Communities*. Norwich: Canterbury, 2007.

―――. "Research Note: The Utility – or Otherwise – of Being Employed for a Few Hours a Week." *Citizen's Income Newsletter*, issue 1 for 2008, 14–16. https://citizensincome.org/wp-content/uploads/2016/02/CIT_Newsletter_2008_Issue_1.pdf.

―――. "Review Article: *The Spirit Level*, by Richard Wilkinson and Kate Pickett." *Citizen's Income Newsletter*, issue 1 for 2010, 4–7. https://citizensincome.org/wp-content/uploads/2016/02/CIT_Newsletter_2010_Issue_1.pdf.

―――. "Testing Torry's Model." *Theology* 109 (851) (2006) 343–52

―――. *Two Feasible Ways to Implement a Revenue Neutral Citizen's Income Scheme*. EUROMOD Working Paper EM6/15. Colchester: Institute for Social and Economic Research, 2015. https://iser.essex.ac.uk/research/publications/working-papers/euromod/em6-15.

―――. *Unconditional: Towards Unconditionality in Social Policy*. Cheltenham: Edward Elgar, 2024.

―――. "Voluntary, Religious and Faith-based Organizations: Some Important Distinctions." In *Words in Action: Finding the Right Words*, 13–26. The Institute Series: 11. London: Heythrop Institute for Religion, Ethics and Public Life, 2008.

Torry, Malcolm, and Jeffrey Heskins, eds. *Ordained Local Ministry: A New Shape for the Church's Ministry*. Norwich: Canterbury, 2006.

Torry, Malcolm, and Sarah Thorley, eds. *Together and Different: Christians Engaging with People of Other Faiths*. Norwich: Canterbury, 2008.

Townsend, Peter. *Poverty in the UK*. Harmondsworth: Penguin, 1979.

Trice, Harrison M., and Janice M. Beyer. *The Cultures of Work Organizations*. Englewood Cliffs, NJ: Prentice Hall, 1993.

Trivasse, Keith M. "May the Prophet Muhammad Be a Prophet to Christianity?" *Theology* 107 (840) (2004) 418–26.

Tuckman, Bruce Wayne. "Developmental Sequence in Small Groups." *Psychological Bulletin* 63 (6) (1965) 384–99.

Turnbull, Nick. "Policy as (Mere) Problem-solving." In *Handbook on Policy, Process and Governing*, edited by Hal K. Colebatch and Robert Hoppe, 53–67. Cheltenham: Edward Elgar, 2018.

Understanding Society. "Employment." Colchester: Institute for Social and Economic Research, University of Essex, 2024. https://www.understandingsociety.ac.uk/topic-page/employment/.

―――. "Family and Households." Colchester: Institute for Social and Economic Research, University of Essex, 2024. https://www.understandingsociety.ac.uk/topic-page/family-and-households/.

Unger, Roberto and Lee Smolin. *The Singular Universe and the Reality of Time: A Proposal in Natural Philosophy*. Cambridge: Cambridge University Press, 2015.

University of Cambridge. "The Medieval University," 2018. https://www.cam.ac.uk/about-the-university/history/the-medieval-university.

Vaill, Peter. "The Purposing of High-performance Systems." *Organizational Dynamics* 11 (2) (1982) 23–39.

Van Avermaet, Eddy. "Social Influence in Small Groups." In *Introduction to Social Psychology*, third edition, edited by Miles Hewstone and Wolfgang Stroebe, 403–443. Oxford: Blackwell, 2001.

Van Parijs, Philippe. "A Short History of the Basic Income Idea." In *The Palgrave International Handbook of Basic Income*, edited by Malcolm Torry, second edition, 43–59. Cham: Palgrave Macmillan, 2023.

BIBLIOGRAPHY

Van Parijs, Philippe, and Yannick Vanderborght. *Basic Income: A Radical Proposal for a Free Society and a Sane Economy*. Cambridge, MA: Harvard University Press, 2017.

Van Trier, Walter. *Every One a King: An Investigation into the Meaning and Significance of the Debate on Basic Incomes with Special Reference to Three Episodes from the British Inter-War Experience*. Leuven: Katholieke Universiteit Leuven Faculteit Sociale Wetenschappen Departement Sociologie, 1995.

von Below, Georg. "Über Historische Periodisierungen, mit Besonderem Blick auf die Grenze zwischen Mittelalter und Neuzeit." *Archiv für Politik und Geschichte*, 4 (1925) 1–29; 22 (1925) 170–214. Quoted in Robert Harrison et al. "Methodology: 'Scientific' History and the Problem of Objectivity," in Peter Lambert and Philipp Schofield, eds, *Making History: An Introduction to the History and Practices of a Discipline*, 26–37. Abingdon: Routledge, 2004.

Von Campenhausen, Hans. *Ecclesiastical Authority and Spiritual Power in the Church of the First Three Centuries*. Translated by J.A. Baker. London: Adam and Charles Black, 1969. First published in German, 1953.

Vroom, Victor H. *Work and Motivation*. New York: John Wiley and Sons, 1964.

Vroom, V.H. and P.W. Yetton. *Leadership and Decision Making*. Pittsburgh: University of Pittsburgh Press, 1973.

Waters, Malcolm. *Globalization*, London: Routledge, 2001.

Webb, David. *Foucault's Archaeology: Science and Transformation*. Edinburgh: Edinburgh University Press, 2013.

———. "Microphysics: From Bachelard and Serres to Foucault." *Angelaki: Journal of the Theoretical Humanities*, 10 (2) (2005) 123–33. https://www.tandfonline.com/doi/full/10.1080/09697250500417332.

Weber, Max. *The Protestant Ethic and the Spirit of Capitalism*. London: Routledge, 1992. Previously published in 1930 by Allen and Unwin.

———. *The Sociology of Religion*. London: Methuen, 1963.

———. *The Theory of Social and Economic Organization*. Translated by A.M. Henderson and T. Parsons. Glencoe, IL: Free Press, 1947.

Weiner, Bernard. *Human Motivation: Metaphors, Theories, and Research*. Newbury Park, CA: Sage, 1992.

Welskopp, Thomas. "Social History." In *Writing History: Theory and Practice*, edited by Stefan Berger et al., 203–22. London: Hodder Arnold, 2003.

White, Mark. "Overview of Behavioral Economics and Policy." In *Nudge Theory in Action: Behavioral Design in Policy and Markets*, edited by Sherzod Abdukadirov, 15–36. Basingstoke: Palgrave Macmillan, 2016.

White, Stuart. *The Civic Minimum: On the Rights and Obligations of Economic Citizenship*. Oxford: Oxford University Press, 2003.

———. *Equality*. Cambridge: Polity, 2007.

Whitehead, Alfred North. *Science and the Modern World*. New York: Free Press, 1967.

Whitehead, Alfred North, and Bertrand Russell. *Principia Mathematica*, volume I. Cambridge: Cambridge University Press, 1910.

Widerquist, Karl. "Three Waves of Basic Income Support." In *The Palgrave International Handbook of Basic Income*, first edition, edited by Malcolm Torry, 31–44. Cham: Palgrave Macmillan, 2019.

Wildiers, N.M. *An Introduction to Teilhard de Chardin*. Translated by H. Hoskins. London: Fontana/Collins, 1968.

BIBLIOGRAPHY

Wilkinson, Richard, and Kate Pickett. *The Spirit Level: Why More Equal Societies Almost Always Do Better*. London: Allen Lane/Penguin Books, 2009. Second edition published in 2010.

Williams, Bernard. *Ethics and the Limits of Philosophy*. London: Fontana/Collins, 1985.

Williams, Richard. "Conclusion: Behavioral Economics and Policy Interventions." In *Nudge Theory in Action: Behavioral Design in Policy and markets*, edited by Sherzod Abdukadirov, 317–29. Basingstoke: Palgrave Macmillan, 2016.

Williams, Rowan. *Grace and Necessity: Reflections on Art and Love*. London: Continuum, 2005.

Williamson, Oliver E. "The Economics of Organizations: The Transaction Cost Approach." *American Journal of Sociology* 87 (3) (1981) 548–77.

Wittgenstein, Ludwig. *Philosophische Untersuchungen / Philosophical Investigations*: the German text with a revised English translation. Third edition. Translated by G.E.M. Anscombe. Oxford: Basil Blackwell, 2001. The first edition was published in 1953. (References record the paragraph number followed by the page number.)

Woodhead, Linda, et al. eds. *Religions in the Modern World*. London: Routledge, 2002.

Woodward, Joan. *Industrial Organization: Theory and Practice*. London: Oxford University Press, 1965.

———. *Management and Technology*. London: Her Majesty's Stationery Office, 1958.

World Health Organization and Calouste Gulbenkian Foundation. *Social Determinants of Mental Health*. Geneva: World Health Organization, 2014.

Wrightson, Keith, and David Levine. *Poverty and Piety in an English Village, Terling 1525–1700*. London: Academic, 1979.

Zahariadis, Nikolaus. "Ambiguity, Time, and Multiple Streams." In *Theories of the Policy Process*, edited by Paul A. Sabatier, 73–93. Boulder, CO: Westview, 1999.

Zimbardo, Philip G. "Pathology of Imprisonment." *Society* 9 (6) (1972) 4–8.

Index

Abel-Smith, Brian, 110
Action (action itself), vii–x, xiii–xiv, xviii, 15, 56, 70
action, vii, x, xiii, 3–4, 15, 22, 48–49, 52, 56, 70, 85, 108, 122, 128, 145, 148–58, 161
   at a distance, 74
   gap, 7
   human, 5, 22–24, 29, 31, 35–37, 75, 103, 105, 142
   in patterns/changing patterns, vii–x, xiii–xvi, 1–8, 11–12, 14–17, 19–21, 24, 28, 34–37, 39–43, 45–46, 48–49, 53–57, 60, 63, 65–77, 79–83, 85, 91, 94–95, 98–99, 101–3, 105–6, 108–9, 115, 117–19, 121, 123, 125–33, 135–37, 139–44, 150, 152–58, 161
   unpatterned, 68, 77
   see also crystallization; society
actology, x, xiii–xviii, 11, 14, 22–28, 31, 34–38, 42–48, 52, 55–56, 60–61, 64–65, 70, 74–76, 79–83, 85, 91, 94–95, 97, 103, 106, 112–15, 119, 121, 123, 125–26, 129–30, 133, 135–36, 141–45
   see also context, actological
administration, xv–xvi, 18–19, 116, 120–21, 130
agency, 97–98, 112
agenda, 16–17, 21, 105, 141, 145
agriculture, 18

alienation, 80, 82
analogy, 5–6, 41, 148
anomaly, 61–62
apple, 2–3, 39–44, 47
approximation, 29–43, 52–53, 62, 69, 71, 73, 76
archives, 16–17, 21
argument, 27, 46, 56
Aristotelian ethics, *see* ethics, Aristotelian, 23, 31, 33–34, 36
arithmetic, xv, 38, 45
art, 6, 13–17, 22, 36, 142, 156
artist, 14, 156
assumption, 25, 28–29, 33, 59, 64, 69, 71, 88–91, 105
   see also presupposition
astronomy, xv
atom, 49–50, 58, 66, 72, 74–75, 154
Austin, J.L. 4, 61
author, xiv, 8, 17, 20–21, 79, 110, 121–22, 130, 141
authority, 27–28, 136
   legitimate/recognized, 9–10, 39
   structure, 127, 137–39
   types, 81–82
automation, 93–94, 115, 125
axiom, 23, 32–33, 50, 55–56

Bachelard, Gaston, 48–52, 58–59, 61
Bambrough, Renford, xi, 70
Basic Income, ix–xi, xvii, 10, 20–21, 90, 93, 98, 100, 111–13, 118–21
becoming, 36, 49, 73–76, 160

INDEX

behavior, 23–26, 43, 50, 68, 72–73, 79, 82, 85, 90–91, 94, 96–97, 99, 101
  organizational, xi, xiv, xviii, 122–41, 144–45
  social, 26, 30, 36, 82, 96–97, 102
behavioral economics, *see* economics, behavioral
Being (being itself), vii–viii, x, 13, 69, 91
being, vii, x, xiii–xv, 4, 26, 43, 45, 50, 52, 69, 75, 91, 94, 129–30, 134, 148
  human, 32–34, 56, 62, 83, 89, 91, 94, 114, 125–26, 132
belief, 128–29, 152
benefits, ix, 18–19, 27–28, 88, 110–13, 118–21, 130
Bergson, Henri, 54
Bethlehem Steelworks, 126
Beveridge Report, 19, 118
big crunch, 53
biology, xvi, 55–57, 62, 79, 83, 97
biosphere, 65
birth, 21, 44, 68, 79, 131, 141, 158–61
Blondel, Maurice, xvii
blood donation, 32
Blumer, Herbert, 80, 82
body, 62–63, 74–76, 96, 156
boundary, xvi, 2–3, 12, 32, 34, 56, 63, 71–72, 75, 80, 94–95, 99, 101, 106–7, 114, 131–33, 137, 155
  spanners, 129, 132
Boys Smith, John, viii, 30
brain, 2, 5–7, 35, 39, 45, 48, 75, 96, 101, 106, 148, 151, 160
budget constraint, 87–89
bureaucracy, 81, 99, 127, 130, 136

calculus, 43
Canada, 20, 93
Canguilhem, Georges, 55, 61–63, 65
canon, 7, 12, 14
capital, 80, 94, 128
capitalism/capitalist, 80–82, 154
carbon tax, *see* tax, carbon
Cartwright, Nancy, 71, 90

categorical imperative, 24–26, 32, 36
category, vii, xiii, 9–11, 13, 47, 56, 74, 111, 115, 137–38, 142–43
causality, 7, 16, 68, 72–73, 75, 81–82, 92–94, 100, 110, 112, 120
centralization, 18, 136
change, vii–ix, xiii–xv, 1, 3, 5, 8–11, 14–19, 24–26, 34–37, 42–43, 45–46, 48–54, 60–65, 68–70, 72–74, 80–85, 89, 91–95, 99, 101–3, 108–9, 112–20, 123, 125, 127–39, 141–45, 147–61
changing patterns of action, *see* action, in patterns/changing patterns
chaos, 24, 67–68, 119, 153–54
characteristic, xv, 3, 6, 9–11, 39, 47, 57, 62, 88, 102, 112, 122, 124, 128, 138
charisma, 81
chemistry, xvi, 55–57, 62
Chief Executive Officer, 127, 130, 132
child, 19, 83, 89, 97, 100, 116, 120, 147, 157–60
Child Benefit, 111, 118, 120–21
choice, xvi, 27, 30, 37, 51, 65, 86, 104–5, 149
  see also decision
Christian Faith, vii–viii, 32
circle, 42, 92
circulation, 91–93
circumstances, 18, 25–26, 35–36, 71, 73, 88–90, 96, 98–100, 102, 108, 120–21
citizenship, 81, 113–15
  rights, *see* rights, citizenship
civil rights, *see* rights, civil
civil servant, 117
class, 38–40, 45, 80, 82
client, 132, 135
clinamen 67–68
Coase, Ronald, 124
computer/computerization, 6, 117, 121, 159
cognitive capacity, 98–99

INDEX

communication, 7, 17, 38, 71, 75, 101, 118, 127, 129–30, 132–33, 156
community, xv, 8, 10–11, 34, 36–37, 98, 102–3, 114, 117
  mathematical, 45
  policy, 118
  scientific, 11, 56, 58–59, 61, 70
company, 84, 104, 115, 117, 123–26, 130
competition, 124
complexity, 15–17, 21, 27, 41, 52, 56–57, 65, 67, 71, 73–75, 78, 83, 85, 89–90, 93–96, 98, 108, 114, 118–21, 124–27, 129–30, 133–35, 137, 141, 143, 159
composer, 22
concept, x, xiv, 23–24, 32, 34, 36, 39, 43–46, 73, 75, 80, 89–90, 101–2, 104, 107–8, 111, 134, 140, 155
conceptual framework/structure, ii, vii–viii, 45, 73, 75, 125, 133, 143, 145
conditions, 6, 27, 47, 55–56, 68–69, 81, 85, 100, 102, 120–21, 129, 132
  see also unconditionality
conflict, 37, 66, 131
  resolution, 136
conjecture, 58, 61
connection, xvi, 3, 8–9, 11, 13, 15, 35, 41, 46, 56–58, 66, 69–70, 72, 97–98, 100, 108, 132, 136, 141, 148, 152, 161
consciousness, 46–47, 65, 75, 96–97
consequentialism, 23, 28, 34, 37
  see also utilitarianism
Conservative Party, 109–10
consumption, xv, 85–86, 93
context, vii, 3–4, 7, 9, 21, 24, 34–35, 37, 39, 45, 48–49, 62, 64, 75–76, 95–96, 100, 104, 109, 111, 117, 124–25, 129–30, 140, 143–44, 157

actological, ii, x, xiv–xvi, xviii, 14–15, 24, 34, 47, 56, 80, 82, 85, 91, 106, 117, 125, 129–30
contingency, 45–46, 50–54, 62–65, 128, 135–36, 139, 142, 144
continuity, viii, 69, 73
  see also discontinuity
contract, 66, 81, 83, 114, 117, 124–25, 128, 138
  natural, 67
  social, 10
conversion experience, 103
Copernicus, 73
coping, 9, 99
corroboration, 13, 57, 59, 61, 66, 94
cosmology, x, xiv, xviii, 53, 65, 141, 144, 155
cosmos, xiii, 22, 37, 41, 44, 52, 54, 57, 66, 71–73, 75, 91, 105, 140, 142, 144, 152
  see also universe
counting, 2–3, 39–42, 44–47, 60
creativity, 22, 33, 101, 132, 142
critique, 44, 49, 64–65
crystallization, 15–16, 21, 42, 53
  see also fixation
culture, 6, 13, 34, 75, 84–85, 159–60
  organizational, 128–30, 140, 144
custom, 81, 122
customer, 2–3, 39, 42, 81, 127, 132, 135

death, 157–58, 161
decentralization, 136
decision, xvi, 25–26, 29–31, 35, 37, 67, 79, 96, 100, 104, 128, 133–34, 138, 149, 151, 159
  see also choice
definition, xvi, 2, 5–6, 8–11, 13–14, 21, 37–39, 50, 58, 70–71, 79, 110–12, 128, 156
demand, 92, 95
deontological ethics, *see* ethics, deontological
depression, 92, 97
desire, 33, 36–37, 89, 132, 134
dialectic, 80, 82

187

dictionary, 5–6, 9, 13, 37, 70, 116
dimension, 15–16, 52, 64, 75–76,
    110, 143
Dirac, Paul, 43
discipline, academic, x, xiv–xviii, 1,
    9, 11–15, 17, 21, 23, 57, 71,
    79, 85, 94, 97, 107, 116, 120,
    141–45, 156
discontinuity, 19, 51, 132
    see also continuity
discourse, 5–7, 15, 56, 63–64
    see also narrative
distribution, xv, 85, 92–93, 113
diversity, vii, x, xiii–xiv, 5, 8, 25, 27–
    28, 37, 46, 48, 50, 52, 61–65,
    69–70, 72, 74, 76, 85, 89–91,
    94–95, 101–2, 107, 109, 111,
    113–14, 119, 123, 127–29,
    131, 134, 136, 138–39, 142–
    45, 148, 153, 158, 160–61
divinity, *see* theology
Donegan, Alan, 25–26
drama, 14
Durkheim, Emile, 80–82
duty, 26–27, 81, 113, 115
    see also obligation
Duverger, Timothée, 20–21
dynamic, the, ii, vii, x, xiii, 28, 48, 52,
    54, 61, 64–65, 70, 72–75, 84,
    89–92, 94–95, 109, 113–15,
    123, 128, 140, 143, 145,
    152–53, 157
    organizational, 130–34, 140

economic growth, *see* growth,
    economic
economic rights, *see* rights, economic
economics, xv, 21, 27, 30, 56, 75, 78–
    90, 93–95, 102, 107, 112, 116,
    123, 126, 132, 143, 154–55
    behavioral, 79, 103–6
    classical, 86, 88–89, 94–95, 105,
    143
    see also history, economic
economy, xv, 17–18, 28, 56, 79, 84,
    90, 92–95, 103–4, 107, 109,
    112, 116–17, 133, 135, 140,
    143
    political, xv–xvi
education, 19, 103–4, 110, 112–13,
    116, 120, 122
efficiency, 18, 124, 126, 128–29
Einstein, Albert, 49, 53, 73–76
electricity, 49
electromagnetism, 50, 69, 75–76
electron, 22, 43, 74, 151
emotion, 37, 97, 102, 128, 151
employment, 18, 27, 83, 86, 88–89,
    93–94, 97, 100–101, 104,
    109–10, 112, 115, 120–21,
    125, 127, 135–36, 138
    see also job; unemployment; work
endowment effect, 105
energy, 49, 53, 59, 66, 73, 76, 99, 142
enforcement, 14, 131
English language, 1, 12, 85
entanglement, xvi, 1, 4, 6, 8, 17, 21,
    24, 35–37, 54, 63, 76, 82, 94,
    98, 102–3, 105, 108, 119, 126,
    130, 135, 142–43, 148, 152
epistemological
    act, 48
    critique, 44
    obstacle, 48
epoch, 53, 69
equality, 27–28
    see also inequality
equation, 40–43, 46, 53, 61, 69, 92
ethics, x, xiv, xvi, xviii, 1, 23–37, 71,
    141–42, 145, 155
    Aristotelian, 23–24, 31, 33–34, 36
    deontological, 23–26, 28, 30,
    32–33, 35–36
    foundationalist, 23, 32–36
    virtue, 24, 31, 36
    see also consequentialism;
    utilitarianism
European Union, 85, 114
event, 2–6, 8, 15, 21–22, 39, 43, 47,
    49, 51, 68–69, 73, 84, 96, 108,
    140, 155

INDEX

evidence, 13, 16–17, 20, 53, 56–61, 69, 78–79, 82, 88, 92, 94, 97, 101, 104, 118, 129, 149
evolution, 18–20, 61, 65–66, 71, 73, 75, 95, 108, 114, 139–40, 143, 154
experience, viii, 11, 16, 21, 25, 28–29, 34–35, 44–47, 50, 54, 57, 60–65, 68–70, 73–74, 78, 80, 86–88, 98, 100–101, 103, 113, 117, 129–30, 137, 139–40, 154, 157–58, 160
experiment, 18, 20, 48–51, 56–65, 69, 72–73, 76, 78–79, 96, 100, 105, 126, 131, 143

factor, xiii, 3, 5, 18, 29–30, 37, 82, 84, 88–89, 97, 105, 118, 120–21, 124, 127–28, 134
factory, 125–26, 131
fairness, 23, 28
falsifiability, 57, 66, 144
Family Allowance, 19, 118
family, 18, 29, 81, 83, 97, 100, 103, 111, 116, 120–21, 150–51
 resemblance, 3, 6–9, 16, 39–41, 43, 57, 65, 70, 80, 102, 110, 118, 125, 155
feedback loop, 74
fixation, 7, 15, 44, 56
 see also crystallization
Form, Platonic, 45, 48
form of life, 2–4
Foucault, Michel, 55, 63–65
foundationalist ethics, *see* ethics, foundationalist
framing, 104, 118
France, 20–21
free will, *see* will, free
friend, 147, 150–51, 159–61
future, the, 21, 30, 53–54, 65, 69, 73, 100–101, 118, 134, 159–61

Galileo, 73
game, 2–3, 42–43, 90–91
 see also language game, 2–4, 8, 42, 70–71

geography, 20–21, 57, 84
geology, 55–56
geometry, xv, 38, 49–50, 69
Germany, 16, 19, 82
gift, *see* given, the
Gilbreth, Lilian
given, the, ii, xiv, 32, 34, 44, 46–48, 52, 54, 60–61, 67, 148
globalization, 84–85, 112, 115–16
goal, 99, 101, 105, 109, 133, 135
 displacement, 131
God, 32, 71, 81, 137–38, 152, 159–61
Goffman, Erving, 82
good, the, 23–24, 28, 30–31, 150, 158–61
 see also life, good
goodness, 28, 156
goods, 31, 79, 84, 86, 89–95, 124, 143
 fundamental/primary, 25–27
 see also resources
government, xv, 18–19, 84, 92, 99, 104, 107, 113, 116–17, 122, 124–25
grace, 32–33, 156–61
grammar, xv, 1, 12, 70
graph, 43, 86–88, 95
grief, 161
Gross Domestic Product (GDP), 92
group, 1, 9, 13, 30, 82, 96, 103, 109, 111–12, 116, 126, 128, 130–31, 133, 152
 informal, 131
 norms, 128, 131
 task, 131
 think, 131
growth, economic, 93, 112

happiness, 24, 28–33, 36–37, 157
Hawthorne Electrical Works, 131
health, 27, 29, 62–63, 110, 112–13, 116, 120
 mental, 97–99
 physical, 98–99
 policy, xv
 social, 97–98, 105
 see also pathology

189

INDEX

healthcare, 19, 33, 104, 110, 112–13, 118
Herodotus, 15
heuristic, 29, 69, 144
hierarchy, 61, 81, 132, 136–39
historian, 1, 15–17, 20
history, xiii, xvi, 1, 13–23, 54, 57, 63–64, 107, 109, 138, 142, 154–55
   economic, 17, 21
   social, 17, 21
housing, 97, 100, 110, 116, 120, 138
human action, *see* action, human
human being, *see* being, human
human relations management theory, 131
humanities, x, xiv, xviii, 13–22, 57, 141–42, 145, 155
Husserl, Edmund, xiv, 44–47, 60
hypothesis, 56, 60–61, 78, 144

idea, 13, 20–21, 32, 34, 42, 58–60, 66, 89, 108–9, 128, 134, 136, 158–60
ideal, 29, 44–48, 60, 63
ideology, 35–36, 81, 108–9, 117
imagination, 14, 16, 46, 51, 58
imperative, categorical, *see* categorical imperative
income, 18–19, 27, 81, 86–89, 93, 97, 110–13, 115–16, 120–21, 130
   unconditional, *see* Basic Income
incommensurability, 27–28, 33–34, 37, 89, 110, 153
indifference curve, 86–89
individual, ix, xi, xvii, 5, 8, 10–11, 20–24, 26, 28–34, 36, 45, 60–63, 73, 79, 82–83, 86, 88–89, 91, 93–94, 96–98, 101, 105, 107–8, 111–12, 115, 117–18, 120–21, 124, 126–27, 130, 133–34, 136–40, 143–44
inequality, 27–28, 93, 98, 112–13, 116
   see also equality
information, 8, 74, 136
infrastructure, 124
insecurity, 97–100

institution, 11, 20, 24, 29, 31, 69–70, 82, 95, 98, 102, 104, 107–9, 112, 115, 117–18, 121–23, 144, 148, 160
interaction, 74, 82–85, 97, 132
intuition, 47, 50, 52
irregularity, 61
iteration, 16–17

Jesus Christ, 32, 157
   see also Christian Faith
job, 88, 98, 112, 132, 157
   see also employment; unemployment; work
journal, vii, 16
journalist, 110
justice, 23, 28, 101, 161
justification, 4, 26, 30, 32, 35, 61, 128

Kant, Immanuel, 16, 24–26, 47, 50
knowledge, ix, xv, 3, 15, 23, 28, 33, 37, 48–49, 51–52, 55, 58–61, 64, 71, 85
Kuhn, Thomas, 51, 57, 59–60, 72

labor, 18, 93–94, 112, 125
   market, 18, 80, 112, 115, 125
   paid, *see* employment
   voluntary, 115
   see also income
Labour Party, 109
laminar flow, 67–68
language, x, xiv, xvi, xviii, 1–14, 17, 39, 43, 51, 57, 65, 70–71, 85, 107–8, 129, 141, 145, 148, 150–52, 156
   game, 2–4, 8, 42, 70–71
law, xv, 13–14, 61–62, 67, 69, 81, 122, 138
   economic, 90
   mathematical, 44, 52–54, 142
   natural/scientific, 41, 50, 52–53, 67–73, 153
   universal, 24–26, 34–35, 81
   see also contingency
Leibniz, Gottfried, 67

INDEX

leisure, 86–88, 126
Levinas, Emmanuel, xiv, 33
liberalism, 19, 108–9
liberty, 27–28
lie, 10, 24–25, 34
life, 7, 21, 37, 62–63, 65–66, 97, 111, 114, 116, 157–58, 161
  good, 31–36
  see also form of life; way of life
lifestyle, 81
light, 142, 156
  speed of, 53, 76
likeness, *see* family resemblance
limit, 20, 43, 45, 49
linguistics, 1, 3–6, 10–12, 141–42, 155
Lister, Ruth, 112
literature, xvi, 1, 12–14, 21, 57, 155
locality, x, 18–19, 41, 50, 52–54, 62–63, 73, 84–85, 92, 94, 103, 123, 142, 144
logic, xv, 44–46, 48, 53–54
London, vii–xi, 18
London School of Economics, ix, xv, 116, 120
loneliness, 97
love, 147–48, 150–53, 156–58, 161
Lucretius, 67
Lyotard, Jean-François, 70

management, ix, 122, 127–29, 132, 138
  theory, 122–23, 127, 131, 134
  see also human relations management theory
manufacture, 115, 124–25
market, 109, 116, 124–25, 127–28, 135, 137
  see also labor market
Mark's Gospel, ix, xiv
Marion, Jean-Luc, xiv, 32, 46–48
marriage, 123, 157–58
  same sex, 84, 102–3
Marx, Karl, 80, 82, 154
mass, 51, 53, 73, 76, 142
mathematics, x, xiv, xvi, xviii, 38–55, 58, 60–61, 69, 95, 141–45, 155

  see also community, mathematical
matter, 59, 65–66, 153
  within of, 66
maxim, 24–26, 28, 34–35
Maxwell, James Clark, 61, 71
McHenry, Leemon, 53, 69
Mead, George Herbert, 80, 82
meaning, xv, 2–3, 5–9, 11, 15, 27, 39, 42, 44–45, 56, 62, 81, 83, 97–98, 107–11, 148, 150, 158
means-testing, 10, 19, 88, 111, 113, 119–21, 130
medicine, xv, 62
metanarrative, 70–71
  see also narrative
metaphor, 5–6, 127, 139
metaphysics, vii–x, xiv, xvi, xviii, 58, 66, 141, 144
method, x, xv, xvii, 9–10, 30, 38, 42, 44, 51, 65, 71, 79, 82, 85, 97, 104, 111, 145, 155
  scientific, 48, 52, 56, 59, 61–62
  see also experiment
microstressor, 99
Mill, John Stuart, 28
Miller, James, 54, 74
mind, 7–8, 10–11, 14, 16, 24, 33, 36, 40, 44–48, 65–66, 69, 79–80, 96, 98, 102–6, 112, 129, 133, 143, 149, 151, 154, 156, 158, 160
molecule, 71
model, viii, 5, 17, 52–53, 69, 71, 76–78, 85–89, 105, 140, 144
  see also paradigm
momentum, 76, 143
money, 79–80, 87, 90–95, 104, 121, 123, 143, 154
  creation of, 80, 85, 91–94
  velocity of, 92–95
motivation, 33, 97, 99–105, 131, 133, 140, 143
movement, vii, x, xiii, 69, 145, 149, 151–57
multidisciplinary, xv, xviii
music, xv, 13–14, 22, 156
myth, 68

191

INDEX

narrative, 70, 76, 95, 117, 143
   see also discourse; metanarrative
National Health Service, 33, 104, 118
natural contract, see contract, natural
natural sciences, x, xiv, xviii, 11, 55–77, 79, 141–43, 145, 155
nature, 67–73,
   see also law, natural/scientific
needs, 24, 33, 36, 89, 97–98, 100, 107, 109, 111, 113, 116, 131, 134, 157
neoliberalism, 108–9
network, 4, 8, 56, 64, 85, 95, 118–19, 126–27, 132, 135, 137–39, 144, 149
Newton, Isaac, 53, 59, 73
Niebuhr, Reinhold, 30
noosphere, 65–66
norm, 16, 62–63, 90, 128, 131, 143
   group, see group norms
   social, 63, 102–3, 105, 111
   see also role; socialization
noumenon, 49–51
noun, 26, 148
nucleosynthesis, 72
nudge, 104–5
number, 38–47
   imaginary, 41

object, 3, 8, 15–16, 43, 46–48, 56, 76, 91–92, 94–95, 124–25, 153
   see also quasi-object
objectification, 15, 56
objectivity, 28, 45–46, 111
obligation, 23, 32, 80–81, 102
   see also duty
office, 27–28, 138
omega point, 53, 65–66
ontology, xiii, 4, 35, 45, 50, 68–69, 73–76, 83, 125, 129–30, 134, 142–43, 145
opinion, 102–3
order, 38, 46, 60–62, 68, 73–74, 108, 114, 122
organization, 3, 10–11, 32, 61, 81, 104, 108, 117, 122–40, 144–45

faith-based, ix, 123, 137–39
   private, 135, 137–39
   public, 135, 137–39
   religious, ix, 123, 137–39
   voluntary, 135, 137–39
   see also self-organizing
organizational
   behavior, see behavior, organizational
   culture, see culture, organizational

π, 42–43
painting, 22, 147, 156
paradigm, 5, 51–52, 59–60, 72–73, 78, 118
   see also model
paradox, 47, 52
Participation Income, 120–21
particle, 48, 67, 69, 72, 74, 76, 142, 153–54
past, the, 7, 15–16, 21–22, 64, 73, 156, 159
path dependency, 118, 144
pathology, 62
   see also health
patterns of action, see action, in patterns/changing patterns
pension, 18–19, 104, 116
perception, 46, 60, 97, 102, 124
performative utterance, 4
   see also utterance
personality, 36, 89, 97, 103, 151
phenomenology, 44–47, 51, 60–61, 68
phenomenon, xvi, 39, 46–48, 60, 64, 70, 74, 96
   saturated, 46–48
philosophy, viii, x, xiv, xvi–xviii, 13–14, 16, 21–22, 32, 38, 55, 57–58, 141–42, 144, 155
   continental, ix, xi, xiv, 44–52, 60–67
   western, vii, ix, xiii
phrase, 1, 3, 5, 8–9
physics, xvi, 49–50, 55–56, 62, 67–69, 71
Platonic Form, see Form, Platonic
poetry, 14

INDEX

policy, *see* health policy; social policy
political economy, xv–xvi
politics, xi, xiv, xviii, 14, 16, 21, 30, 56, 75, 78–79, 81, 84–85, 94, 105, 107–22, 141, 143–45, 155
polygon, 42–43
Poor Law, the, 18–19
Popper, Karl, 57–61, 66
positions, *see* office
poverty, 18–19, 98, 107, 110–13, 116
power, 27, 30, 61, 64, 67, 109, 112, 131–32
practice, 11, 21, 31, 64, 116, 120, 133
prediction, 29, 41, 53, 61, 69, 73, 78–79, 85, 88–89, 118, 139, 144, 151, 153–54, 157, 159
preference, 28, 89
present, the, 5, 15–16, 156, 159, 161
presupposition, 25, 72, 89
price, 81, 92
process, 7, 9–11, 15–17, 21, 35–37, 43, 48–49, 51–52, 60–61, 65–66, 68, 71, 73–75, 81–84, 99, 101, 111–19, 122, 125–26, 130–33, 135–36, 139, 141, 144, 155
production, xv, 6, 13, 80, 85, 92–95, 109, 112, 115, 124, 126–28, 131, 160
promise, 4, 24–25, 81, 158, 160
proof, 13, 42, 56–57, 60, 112, 144
property, 28, 58, 61, 71, 75, 109
Protestantism, 81–82
prototype, 9–11, 39–41
psychology, xi, xiv, xviii, 56, 60–61, 75, 79, 94, 96–107, 141, 143, 145
    social, 56, 96, 107
public policy, *see* social policy
Puritanism, 81
Pythagoras's Theorem, 42

quantum theory, 59, 73–74
quasi-object, 91

Rawls, John, 27–28

reader/reading, 1, 6–8, 11, 14, 22, 36, 40, 108, 142, 147, 156
realism, 49, 59–60, 70
reality, ix–x, xiii–xvi, 1, 3–4, 7–8, 11, 14, 28, 34, 40–42, 45, 48–50, 52, 54–56, 58–61, 68–70, 72–76, 79–80, 83, 85, 90, 126, 130, 141–45, 148, 150, 152–53, 155, 158, 161
reason, 25–26, 33, 38, 50, 56, 66–67, 97
reciprocity, 67, 102
rectification, 49
regularity, 62, 72
regulations, xv, 19, 26, 109, 121, 130, 138
regulative principle, 29, 63
relation/relationship, xv–xvi, 5, 7–11, 21, 24, 26–29, 32–35, 40–43, 48, 50, 52, 54, 58, 62, 64, 66–67, 69–70, 73–74, 76, 78, 80–83, 87–92, 94–97, 100, 108, 112, 114, 117, 124, 128, 130–33, 136, 139, 141–45, 152–54, 156–57, 159
relativism, 29
relativity, 59, 73, 75
    general, 49, 75–76
    special, 76
reliabilism, 61
religion, ix, 32–36, 80–82, 123, 137–39, 160
replication, 62
research, viii–x, 10–11, 17, 38, 70–71, 75, 81, 83, 96–97, 100–101, 110, 112, 121–22, 131, 136, 141, 145
resemblance, *see* family resemblance
resources, xiv–xv, 27, 92, 98, 102, 109, 111, 115, 128
    see also goods, fundamental/primary
rest, vii, xiii
rhythm, 72
Ricoeur, Paul, 5–7, 15, 56
rights, 27
    citizenship, 113–15

193

rights (*continued*)
  civil, 114
  economic, 115
  human, 32
  political, 114
  social, 114–15
  welfare, 114
risk, 93, 98–99, 119, 124, 136, 144, 158–59, 161
role, 74, 102, 126, 131, 138
  see also norm; socialization
Rowntree, Seebohm, 18
rules, 2–3, 26, 29–31, 42, 81–82, 108–9, 112, 114, 131
Russell, Bertrand, 38, 40, 44

satisficing, 119, 134
Schelling, Friedrich, 55–56
science, 11–13, 15–17, 38, 40, 46, 48–52, 96–97, 103–4, 107, 113, 116, 123, 141–43, 145, 154–55
  natural, *see* natural sciences
  social, *see* social sciences
scientific community, *see* community, scientific
scientific method, *see* method, scientific
security, 97–98, 114, 116
self-organization, 73–75, 95, 119, 143
sensation, 97
sentence, 3, 8, 81
Serres, Michel, 55, 61, 66–68, 72, 90–91
services, 79, 91–95, 113–16, 120, 124–25, 138
skills, 112, 115, 124–25, 135
similarity, *see* family resemblance
singularity, 22, 62
Smolin, Lee, 51, 72
social
  administration, 116, 120–21
  behavior, *see* behavior, social
  care, 116
  construction, xvi, 13, 27, 80, 90, 94, 101, 111–12, 117, 133, 143
  contract, *see* contract, social

exclusion, 111
fact, 80–82
health, *see* health, social
history, *see* history, social
insurance, 19, 119
media, 84, 119
norm, *see* norm, social
policy, xv, 14, 17, 23, 32, 56, 79, 84, 90, 94–95, 97, 107–21, 123, 143–44
  see also policy community
problem, 117–18
psychology, *see* psychology, social
rights, *see* rights, social
sciences, x, xiv–xv, xviii, 13, 55–56, 78–95, 123, 141, 143, 145, 155
security, 17–19, 116, 120
  see also structure
socialism, 108–9, 154
socialization, 110, 126
  see also norm; role
society, 13, 18, 21, 23–24, 26–34, 36, 56, 63, 69, 78–84, 94, 97–99, 102–3, 105, 107–12, 114, 116, 118, 122, 124, 128, 140, 143
sociology, 6, 56, 78–85, 94–95, 107, 123, 143
space, 9, 15, 22, 27, 38, 44, 48, 53–54, 59, 68, 73, 76, 142, 154
Speenhamland, 18–19
stability, xiii, 51–53, 61, 63, 65, 68–69, 135, 143, 150–54, 157
stakeholders, 135–36
state, the, 31, 33, 107, 109, 113
static, the, vii, xiii, 14, 22, 26, 34, 36, 61, 74, 82, 84, 95, 111, 133–34, 143, 148, 152, 155, 157
stigma, 82
story, 5, 7, 16, 20, 129, 147
strategy, 9, 65, 99, 117, 134–37
stress, 97–99, 105, 143
string theory
structure, 3, 7, 11–12, 16, 20–21, 49–50, 58, 64, 79–81, 83, 112–13, 116–17, 120, 126–30, 134, 136–39

INDEX

see also conceptual framework/structure
subject, 7, 91, 113
substance, 48–49, 148, 152, 154
suicide, 80
superstructure, 41, 80
supervision, 128
supply, 27, 92, 95
   chain, 84
   river, 124–25
symbol, 38, 40–45, 53, 84, 128
symbolic interaction, 82
system, vii, 3, 5, 18–19, 26, 48, 51, 54, 57, 73, 75, 78, 88, 91, 95, 102, 104, 118–19, 121–22, 132, 140, 143

tax, 17, 92–94, 112, 115, 119–20
   carbon, 93
technology, 81, 94, 112, 127, 132, 136
Teilhard de Chardin, Pierre, 61, 65–66
temporality, 5, 45, 59
   see also time
text, x, xiv, xvii, 1, 6–8, 12, 14–16, 20–22, 40, 45–46, 108, 137, 142, 156
theology, vii–viii, x, xiv–xv, xvii–xviii, 16, 57, 65–66, 141, 144, 155
theory, 11, 13, 23–28, 31–37, 42, 45–46, 48–52, 54, 57–66, 72–76, 78–79, 88–90, 92, 94–95, 104, 118, 122–23, 127, 131, 134, 136, 139–40, 142–44
Theory X, Theory Y, 133
thinktank, 110, 117–18, 120
time, xvi, 5, 9, 11–12, 15, 17, 22, 27, 34–37, 44, 47–48, 50, 53–54, 58–59, 61–62, 64–65, 68, 71–74, 76, 80–81, 89, 97, 99, 114, 117, 123–24, 126–27, 130, 132, 134–35, 142, 148, 154, 161
   see also temporality
Titmuss, Richard, 32
trades unions, 109, 117

tradition, vii, ix, xiv, 5, 7, 14, 32–36, 58–59, 69–70, 80–81, 83, 85
transaction, 15, 56, 90–91, 93–94, 124–25, 129
transience, 45
translation, 11
transport, 84, 110
triangle, 42
trust, 10, 81, 84, 97–98, 104, 128–30, 133
truth, 14, 34, 58, 62–64, 129, 150, 155–56
turbulence, 59, 67–68, 125

unchanging, the, vii, xiii, 41, 52, 61, 64, 69, 74, 80, 143, 152–53
unconditionality, 32–34, 55, 90, 157
   see also Basic Income; conditions
unemployment, 18–19, 93, 116
   see also employment; job; work
unitary, the, vii, xiii, 52, 61, 69, 74, 143
United Kingdom, 17, 102
United States of America, 20, 81, 126
universality, 18–19, 24–28, 34–35, 41–46, 48, 50, 52, 57, 59, 64, 80–82
universe, 22, 46, 51, 53–54, 59, 67–70, 72–75, 77, 152–54, 157–59
   see also cosmos
university, xv–xvi, 13–17, 83
unpatterned action, *see* action, unpatterned
usage, 9–11, 39
utilitarianism, 28–33, 36–37
   see also consequentialism
utility, 34, 86–90, 105, 143
utterance, *see* performative utterance

value, 3, 37, 42–43, 80, 85, 89–90, 92, 97, 105, 108, 119, 128
veil of ignorance, 27
verb, 26, 117, 148
virtue ethics, *see* ethics, Aristotelian; ethics, virtue
vocabulary, 1, 3, 9, 12

INDEX

voluntary organization, *see* organization, voluntary
volunteer, 121, 135, 138
vortex, 2, 3, 68

wage, 18, 87–88, 100–101, 125–26
wave, 14, 20–21, 50, 61, 74, 76
way of life, 13, 128–29
wealth, xv, 27–28, 85, 93, 112
Weber, Max, 80–82
wellbeing, 24, 32, 36–37, 83, 97, 116
Whitehead, Alfred North, 38, 40, 44, 69
will, free, 75
Wittgenstein, Ludwig, 2–4, 39, 44, 70

word, 2–11, 23, 26, 34, 39–40, 42, 50–51, 57, 70, 81, 108, 141, 148–52, 155–56 158–59
work/worker, 10, 18–19, 33, 71, 80, 83, 89–90, 100–101, 104–5, 109, 115–16, 121, 125–33, 135, 148, 160
  see also employment; job; unemployment
workhouse, 17–18
World Health Organization, 98
Writing, 6–7, 15–17, 21–22, 42, 56, 147

Zimbardo prison study, 102
Zoology, 56

www.ingramcontent.com/pod-product-compliance
Lightning Source LLC
Chambersburg PA
CBHW070740160426
43192CB00009B/1519